# *Mountain Magic Cuisine*

# Mountain Magic Cuisine
## *Secret Recipes of the Dude & Guest Ranches of Colorado*

Compiled and Edited by
David J. Richardson and Javana M. Richardson

For information, contact:

StarsEnd Creations
8547 East Arapahoe Road, #J224
Greenwood Village, Colorado 80112

PRINTING HISTORY
First Edition, 1998
ISBN 1-889120-11-1

Library of Congress Catalog Card Number 98-65071

Published by
**Pantry Press**
**8547 East Arapahoe Road, #J224**
**Greenwood Village, Colorado 80112**

Printed and bound in the United States of America
10 9 8 7 6 5 4 3 2 1

# Acknowledgments

Unlike most books, a cookbook is almost always a collaborative effort. There are any number of individuals who develop the recipes and then there are those whose task, enviable or not, is to taste test those same recipes. There are also those who gather the recipes, selecting the best tasting, then converting the various formats into one standard to be used in the cookbook. Then there is the process of editing and verifying each recipe for accuracy. By the end quite a few people have had their hand in the creation of any cookbook. This one is no different.

First we would like to thank the chefs and owners of the participating ranches that make up the Colorado Dude & Guest Ranch Association. Not only did they have to come up with the recipes in the first place, but also had to endure the process of converting literally dozens of formats into a standardized form, thus insuring that all the information required to produce a dish was included with the recipe. We appreciate their patience, for without them there would be no cookbook.

Next, we would like to thank Harry Graham, Director of Marketing for the association. Harry was, as always, tireless in his efforts to get the ranches to meet the editorial deadlines for the book. Harry acted as our liaison with the ranches and has proven once again to have a real feel for the process of putting out a cookbook.

We also want to thank the directors of the Colorado Dude & Guest Ranch Association for sponsoring the initiative that led to this cookbook. Their faith is greatly appreciated.

To all who helped to bring this project to life, we say a heartfelt thank you.

# TABLE OF CONTENTS

Introduction                                                    7
Northern Mountains                                              9
    Cherokee Park Ranch                     11
    Laramie River Ranch                     19
    Old Glendevey Ranch                     35
    Rawah Ranch                             43
    Sky Corral Ranch                        55
    Sylvan Dale Guest Ranch                 61
    Women of the West - Augusta Tabor       73
North Central Mountains                                        75
    Aspen Canyon Ranch                      77
    Aspen Lodge Ranch Resort                89
    Bar Lazy J Guest Ranch                  95
    C Lazy U Ranch                          109
    Drowsy Water Ranch                      123
    King Mountain Ranch                     133
    Latigo Ranch                            145
    Lazy H Guest Ranch                      159
    Lost Valley Ranch                       163
    North Fork Ranch                        173
    Women of the West - Margaret Tobin Brown   185
South Central Mountains                                        187
    Coulter Lake Guest Ranch                189
    Deer Valley Ranch                       201
    Elk Mountain Ranch                      213
    Powderhorn Guest Ranch                  225
    Tarryall River Ranch                    235
    Waunita Hot Springs Ranch               251
    Whistling Acres Guest Ranch             273
    Women of the West - Ann Bassett         285
    Women of the West - Susan Anderson, M.D.   286

# TABLE OF CONTENTS

| | |
|---|---|
| **Southern Mountains** | **287** |
| Colorado Trails Ranch | 289 |
| The Historic Pines Ranch | 303 |
| Lake Mancos Ranch | 317 |
| Rainbow Trout Ranch | 333 |
| San Juan Guest Ranch | 343 |
| Skyline Guest Ranch | 357 |
| Wilderness Trails Ranch | 367 |
| Women of the West - Emily Griffith | 385 |
| Women of the West - Carrie Chapman Catt | 386 |
| Women of the West - Pat Schroeder | 387 |
| **Locator Map** | **388** |
| **Index** | **391** |
| **Cooking Tips** | **402** |
| **Spices and Herbs** | **403** |
| **Cooking Terms** | **405** |

# INTRODUCTION

It was a tradition among the ranches of the Old West that any stranger who happened by was welcome to a meal and a place to lay their head for the night. These early pioneers simply believed in the notion of hospitality toward all. Although much has changed over the past century, there are still a few places in the west where the tradition of hospitality toward strangers is honored. Many can be found in the Colorado Dude & Guest Ranch Association.

Set amidst the stunning majesty of Colorado's Rocky Mountains, these ranches keep alive many of the traditions of the Old West. The people who live on the ranches call it Mountain Magic. Here you will find yourself surrounded not only by the beauty of the mountains, but also some of the most extraordinarily friendly people found anywhere. Hospitality is the watchword for these folks and it is what they specialize in. They will make you feel welcome from the moment of arrival and, by the end of your stay, you will feel like a member of their ranch family.

Each of the member ranches offers comfortable accommodations, fun family oriented activities and a chance to experience a part of the west that has long since vanished for the most part from everyday life. Since each ranch and location is different, you have the difficult task of making the choice of which you want to visit. All offer a wide variety of activities, including horseback riding, fishing and hiking, but you may also have the choice of white water rafting, boating, jeeping, swimming, gold panning, hay rides, campfires and cookouts, square-dancing, shopping, well the list just goes on.

The ranches also treat their guests to some of the most delicious food anyone has ever eaten. Besides meals served family style in their comfortable lodges, many offer the chance to eat out on the trail or beside a campfire. Barbecues are plentiful and usually accompanied by sing-a-longs or fireside stories. Whatever the location, you can be assured that your meal will be expertly prepared from recipes developed by the gourmet chefs who work on these ranches. It is just some of those recipes that are presented here.

As you try these recipes, it's hoped that you will share a little of the life they live here on these ranches. You may also find yourself wanting to come on out for a visit. If you do, remember that the gate is always open and your bunk is waiting.

Colorado Dude & Guest Ranch Association
www.coloradoranch.com

# Northern Mountains

# Cherokee Park Ranch

**Cherokee Park Ranch**
**PO Box 97**
**Livermore, CO 80536**
**(800) 628-0949**
**(970) 493-6522**
**Dick & Christine Prince**
**Elevation 7,200 feet**

Cherokee Park Ranch has a fascinating history. Believed to be one of the first guest ranches in Colorado, it was a colorful stagecoach stop between Fort Collins, Colorado and Laramie, Wyoming during the late 1880's. The journey could be hazardous, but the rates at that time were only $8 per week.

While the old buildings have been modernized, the owners and staff of Cherokee Park Ranch have done everything possible to maintain the historical integrity. Much of the furnishings in the lodge and the cabins are from the early days of the ranch. Guests will also see the old wagons, buggies, sleighs and implements that were in everyday use in those distant days. The ranch also boasts all the conveniences you could wish for with a heated swimming pool, spa, volleyball, basketball, horseshoes, a pool table in the main lodge and a separate recreation hall with bumper pool, Ping-Pong and other games.

Guests enjoy home cooked meals in the spacious dining room located in the main lodge. The huge stone fireplace adds warmth as well as charm to the family style dining experience. Many feel as if they are back at grandma's house.

While the ranch offers horseback riding, they also feature a variety of non-riding activities from which to choose. Guests may enjoy river rafting, fishing, hiking, sightseeing trips, trap shooting or an old time black powder shoot. Evenings are filled with hayrides, square dances and sing-a-longs. There is quite a lot going on at Cherokee Park Ranch, so there are always several activities to choose from. Nothing is required, so you may do as much or as little as you like.

# Cherokee Hot Fruit

Cooking time: 1 hour
Yield: 18 servings
Temperature: 350 degrees
Can be stored overnight
  in the refrigerator

1 - 29 ounce can pear
  halves
1 - 20 ounce can peach
  halves
1 - 20 ounce can
  pineapple slices
1 cup sugar
2 tablespoons flour
$1/2$ teaspoon nutmeg
$1/2$ teaspoon cinnamon
$1/4$ cup cooking sherry

Topping:
$1/2$ cup rolled oats
$1/2$ cup flour
Pinch of salt
$1/2$ stick of butter,
  melted

Preheat oven to 350 degrees. Drain all of the fruit and slice the pieces in half. In a shallow bowl or pan mix the sugar, flour and spices together. Roll the individual fruit pieces in this mixture and place in a buttered glass baking dish. Pour the sherry over the top of the rolled fruit.

Combine the topping ingredients and spread over the fruit mixture. Cover and bake for 1 hour.

# Hash Brown Casserole

Preheat the oven to 350 degrees. Sauté the onion in butter. Combine the sour cream, soups and onion in a large bowl. Blend in the hash brown potatoes. Blend the shredded Cheddar cheese into the mixture. Spoon the mixture into baking pans, covering each with foil. Bake for 1 hour. Just before serving, add the topping. This is great for big groups and hungry people!

Cooking time: 1 hour
Yield: 60 servings
Temperature: 350 degrees

3 packages of frozen
    hash browns
1 large can cream of
    mushroom soup
1 large can cream of
    chicken soup
5 cups sour cream
1 $1/2$ sticks of butter,
    melted
1 large onion, sautéed
6 cups shredded
    Cheddar cheese

Topping:
6 cups crushed
    cornflakes mixed with
    melted butter

# Maka's Sweet Yams

Cooking time: 45 minutes
Yield: 10 to 15 servings
Temperature: 350 degrees

4 to 6 sweet potatoes,
   enough to make 6 cups
1 stick of margarine
1/2 teaspoon cinnamon
1 tablespoon vanilla
3 eggs, beaten
3/4 cup milk

Topping:
1 stick of margarine
3/4 cup dark brown
   sugar
1/2 cup water
3/4 cup chopped nuts
3 tablespoons flour

Preheat the oven to 350 degrees. Peel the sweet potatoes and cook in water until tender. Place the cooked sweet potatoes in a blender or food processor. Add the margarine, cinnamon, vanilla, eggs and milk to the potatoes. Blend until smooth and all the lumps have disappeared. Pour the mixture into a large, glass baking dish.

Mix the topping ingredients together and spread over the top of the sweet potato mixture. Place in the oven and bake for 45 minutes.

# Emily's Pumpkin Bread

Preheat the oven to 350 degrees. In a large bowl, beat the nutmeg, cinnamon, sugar, oil, eggs and salt together. Add and mix in order, the pumpkin, water, vanilla, baking soda and flour. Grease the loaf pans well. Pour the mixture into the loaf pans and bake for 1 hour or until a cake tester comes out clean. Enjoy!

Cooking time: 1 hour
Yield: 2 to 3 loaves
Temperature: 350 degrees
Can be stored overnight
  in the refrigerator

1 teaspoon nutmeg
1 teaspoon cinnamon
2 $3/4$ cups sugar
1 cup of cooking oil
4 eggs
$1/2$ teaspoon salt
$1/3$ cup canned pumpkin
$2/3$ cup water
2 teaspoons baking soda
3 cups flour
1 teaspoon vanilla

# Poppy Seed Bread

Cooking time: 1 hour
Yield: 2 loaves
Temperature: 350 degrees

3 eggs
1 1/2 cups milk
1 1/8 cups oil
2 1/4 cups sugar
3 cups flour
1 1/2 teaspoons salt
1 1/2 teaspoons baking
  powder
1 1/2 tablespoons poppy
  seeds
1 1/2 teaspoons vanilla

Preheat oven to 350 degrees. Grease and flour the loaf pans. Mix the eggs, milk, oil and sugar together in a mixing bowl. Add the flour, salt and baking powder. Blend with a mixer until smooth. Pour the mixture into the prepared loaf pans. Add the poppy seeds and vanilla, mixing until well blended. Bake for 1 hour or until a cake tester comes out clean.

# Garlic Steak Marinade

Mix all the ingredients together and store in an air-tight container. To use, marinate the meat for at least 3 hours.

This is one of our most requested recipes, since it makes any meat taste great! This is especially tasty when doing pork tenderloin.

Yield: enough for 10 steaks

Can be stored for 3 days in the refrigerator

6 cups oil
3 cups lemon juice
3 cups soy sauce
3 cups chopped green onion
4 tablespoons garlic powder
$1/2$ cup pepper
$1/2$ cup celery seed

# Laramie River Ranch

**Laramie River Ranch**
**25777 County Road 103**
**Jelm, WY  82063**
**(800) 551-5731**
**(970) 435-5716**
**www.LRRanch.com**
**ranchvacation@LRRanch.com**
**Bill and Krista Burleigh**
**Elevation 7,900 feet**

The Laramie River Ranch dates back to the 1890's and it is this heritage that is reflected in the lodge and five log cabins. While all the accommodations have been renovated to provide the comfort of modern amenities, they maintain the flavor and charm of the old west.

Still a small working ranch, the Laramie River Ranch has a total capacity of twenty-five guests. This small size allows the staff to give each guest their personal attention. While horseback riding is the principal activity at the ranch, they also offer fly-fishing on the Laramie River and in the surrounding streams and lakes.

With a large string of horses from which to choose, the wranglers can select a horse to match the ability and personality of each guest. Wranglers take out small groups of riders for morning, afternoon and all-day rides. The guest learns the basics of riding, while maneuvering their horse over sage covered hills and up and down the mountains. The Laramie River Ranch has an abundance of open terrain suitable for loping. Each guest is welcome to help groom and saddle their own horse.

Other activities include hiking, tubing down the river, bird watching, hunting for wild flowers, exploring the beaver dams, learning to swing a rope, orienteering, volleyball and horseshoes. In the evenings guests can enjoy guitar music, cowboy poetry, or late night strolls to gaze at the stars, while learning about the mythology of the constellations from the ranch naturalist.

Outdoor activities and fresh mountain air create healthy appetites. Whether it is on the trail or back at the ranch, meals are an event at the Laramie River Ranch. Warm homemade breads and desserts, fresh salads, fruits and vegetables, as well as delicious entrés keep guests coming back for more. In keeping with informal western tradition, meals are served family style.

The Laramie River Ranch prides itself on providing outstanding vacations for its guests. Come experience their hospitality and the great Rocky Mountains.

# Cinnamon Bun French Toast

Warm the cinnamon buns in their plastic and foil wrapper for about 30 minutes in a preheated 300 degree oven. Cut each bun horizontally into 2 pieces. Dip each piece into the whisked egg, coating the cut side generously. Coat only that side. Cook on a 350 degree griddle, until the egg is completely cooked.

The cinnamon buns are so sweet already that syrup is too much. Try them plain, but if you think they need something extra, try them with a little melted butter with jam mixed in. Raspberry is marvelous for this!

Cooking time: 30 to 35 minutes
Yield: 2 pieces of toast from each cinnamon bun
Temperature: 350 degrees

Nancy's Cinnamon Buns
Whisked Egg

*"I am sure everybody loved the rides, but I have to say that they weren't just nice, they were spectacular. The rides varied so much and the scenery was outstanding. We rode over mountains, through the woods and pastures, across streams and over rolling hills. We could see snow-capped mountains, antelope, deer, coyote, jack rabbits, hummingbirds, bluebirds and such a variety of plants such as wild flowers, sage and cactus. It was the one vacation our family did not want to ever leave."*

*Tammy*
*Bloomington, Minnesota*

# Nancy's Cinnamon Buns

Cooking time: 20 to 30 minutes
Yield: 20 to 25 medium size rolls
Temperature: 350 degrees
The cold rolls can be wrapped in plastic and foil, then frozen.

3 3/4 cups milk
6 tablespoons vegetable oil or melted butter
3 tablespoons dry yeast (1 package equals 1 tablespoon)
6 tablespoons sugar
1 teaspoon salt
2 eggs, beaten
10 cups white flour
Brown sugar
Pecans, chopped
Margarine or butter
Ground cinnamon

Frosting:
1/2 pound margarine
6 cups powdered sugar
1/2 cup orange juice
1 cup evaporated milk or Half and Half

Heat the milk and oil until very warm. In a large bowl, combine 5 cups of flour with the sugar, salt and yeast, stirring well to blend. Add the warm liquid to the flour mixture and beat with a mixer. Add the eggs and beat until moist. Add the remaining flour while beating, until the dough is elastic and sticky. The dough should feel soft and light to the touch.

Place the dough in a bowl that has been sprayed with a non-stick spray and let rise in a warm place until it doubles in size. Turn out onto a lightly floured board and knead for a few minutes. Roll into a 10 x 8-inch rectangle about 1 inch thick. Spread some softened margarine or butter across the entire surface of the dough. Sprinkle lightly with ground cinnamon, brown sugar and chopped pecans. Roll up tightly like a jelly-roll, starting at the long edge. Cut the log into 2-inch thick slices using a sharp knife or kitchen string.

Preheat the oven to 350 degrees. Butter a large cake pan and sprinkle it with a thin layer of brown sugar. Place the rolls cut side up in the pan and let rise until double in size. Bake for 20 to 30 minutes in the oven, until lightly golden brown. These are best hot out of the oven.

Mix the frosting ingredients with a hand mixer, adding just enough milk to achieve the desired consistency. Drizzle over the hot rolls and serve.

# Egg Asparagus Breakfast Burritos

Preheat the oven to 375 degrees. Warm the tortillas in a microwave. Snap, scale and cook the asparagus in boiling water, until cooked, but not limp. Toss with lemon juice. Scramble the eggs with the pepper. Place 3 asparagus spears, $1/8$ of the egg and $1/8$ of the cheese in the middle of each tortilla. Roll and place in a baking dish. Cover and bake 20 minutes or until the tortillas are slightly crisp on the ends. Garnish with slices of orange.

These are a nice, light breakfast.

Cooking time: 20 minutes
Yield: 4 servings
Temperature: 375 degrees

8 - 6-inch flour tortillas
24 pieces of fresh
  asparagus
1 tablespoon lemon juice
5 eggs
Pinch of pepper
$1/3$ cup skim milk
1 tablespoon minced
  chives
$1/4$ teaspoon lemon rind
$1/2$ cup Monterey Jack
  cheese, shredded
Orange for garnish

# Barbecue Chicken Salad

Cooking time: 2 hours
Yield: 4 large servings
Temperature: 350 degrees
This can be prepared
  ahead of time and
  refrigerated or frozen.

3 pounds chicken thighs
  and/or breasts, skin
  removed
1/2 cup barbecue sauce,
  your choice
1/4 cup liquid smoke
  flavor
1/2 teaspoon Cajun Jerk
  or Blackened seasoning
1/4 cup chopped onion
1/4 cup chopped celery
1/4 cup mayonnaise
1/4 cup salad dressing
1/2 teaspoon Dijon
  mustard

Mix the barbecue sauce, liquid smoke flavor and Cajun seasoning. Place the chicken in a 9 x 13-inch pan and pour the sauce over the top. Let the chicken marinate overnight in the refrigerator or at least 1 hour.

Start the grill and add hickory chips to the coals just before putting on the chicken. Grill the chicken until it is no longer pink in the middle. Cooking times will vary depending upon the heat of the fire. Grilling adds the most flavor, but if you want to do the chicken in the oven you can. Bake the chicken in a preheated 350 degree oven, covered, for about 1 hour. Uncover for the last 10 minutes.

Let the chicken cool, then take the meat off the bone and cut into bite sized pieces. Add the onion, celery, mayonnaise, salad dressing and mustard. Mix well.

This makes excellent sandwiches with a little outdoor flavor, especially when using Italian bread. Garnish with lettuce, tomato or pickle. You can also serve it on a bed of mixed greens, garnished with tomato and yellow bell pepper. Sprinkle with a little paprika for a finishing touch of color. Either way, this salad is a great way to use up leftovers from the grill.

# Fried Tomatoes

Slice the tomatoes to a thickness of $1/4$ to $1/2$-inch. Place the whisked egg in a shallow dish. Mix the flour, Parmesan, salt and pepper in a second shallow dish. Dip each tomato slice in the egg, then into the dry ingredients, coating well. Fry in a skillet with the butter and olive oil until lightly browned. Flip and cook the other side.

This makes a great appetizer. They also go well as a side dish for a hearty steak meal. Serve with ketchup or salsa.

*"I must mention the food, it was Great! You will not walk away from your table hungry at the Laramie River Ranch, I guarantee it! The Ranch along with an excellent staff made for a memorable summer vacation for our family and we will be back!!"*

*Kathy*
*Owatonna, Minnesota*

Cooking time: 30 to 45 minutes
Yield: 2 servings per tomato

Green or very firm tomatoes
Whisked egg
$1/4$ cup flour
$1/4$ cup Parmesan cheese
Dash of salt
Dash of pepper
1 tablespoon butter
1 tablespoon olive oil

# Ranch Ribs

Cooking time: 2 hours
Yield: 4 servings
Temperature: 350 degrees

3 pounds pork ribs
16 ounces barbecue
    sauce, your choice

The secret to tender ribs is to boil them before they are baked or barbecued. Boil the ribs in a large covered pot for 1 hour. Allow to cool, then drain off the liquid. Transfer the ribs to a bowl filled with the barbecue sauce a few at a time. Cover with sauce completely, then place the ribs in a baking pan lined with foil. You can either bake the ribs in a preheated 350 degree oven for 30 minutes or grill them for 15 minutes.

Serve with baked beans, fresh bread and a tossed salad. Have plenty of sauce and napkins ready!

# Harvest Winter Soup

Place the water, potatoes, carrots and celery in a soup pot and bring to a boil. Reduce the heat and simmer until the vegetables are tender. Add the remaining ingredients and cook on low until cheese is melted and soup is hot.

Serve with homemade bread or rolls and a green salad for a complete and hearty meal.

Cooking time: 2 hours
Yield: 8 to 10 servings
Refrigerate after cooling
  to store

3 cups water
2 cups diced potatoes
2 cups carrot slices
2 cups celery slices
1 pound Velveeta or 2
  cans Campbell's
  Cheddar Cheese soup
2 cups ham, cubed
2 cups chicken broth
Salt and pepper to taste
Sprinkle of parsley
Touch of garlic and
  onion powders

# Spicy Chicken Salad with Raspberry Balsamic Vinaigrette

Cooking time: 15 minutes
Yield: 4 servings
Temperature: medium-
high
This can be prepared
ahead of time and
refrigerated.

12 ounces chicken
breast, boneless and
skinless
1 tablespoon olive oil
2 cloves of garlic,
crushed
1/2 teaspoon Cajun jerk
or blackened seasoning
1/4 cup seedless
raspberry jam
1/4 cup olive oil
1/4 cup balsamic vinegar
6 cups baby summer
lettuce
2 cups fresh raspberries
1/4 cup sliced almonds

Place the olive oil and crushed garlic cloves in a large skillet over medium-high heat. Cut the chicken into strips. When the oil gets hot and the garlic starts to sizzle add the chicken. Stir to coat the chicken with oil. Sprinkle the Cajun seasoning over the chicken and stir again to mix well. Let the chicken cook for about 10 to 15 minutes, stirring occasionally, until cooked all the way through and well browned on the outside.

To make the dressing, mix the jam, olive oil and vinegar in a jar and shake well. Toss the cooked chicken with the dressing.

Place the lettuce in a bowl and top with the chicken. Sprinkle the top with the fresh raspberries and almonds. Serve with a warm loaf of French bread for a great light lunch.

*"Warren and I would like to express again to you our thorough enjoyment of the time spent with you at Laramie River Ranch. The incredible scenery, the horses, the accommodations, the food, the program and the hospitality combined to make this, for us, 'the vacation of a lifetime'."*

*Warren & Estie*
*Binghamton, New York*

# Buttermilk Corn Bread

Preheat the oven to 450 degrees. Mix the cornmeal, flour, baking soda and salt together in a large bowl. In a separate bowl, whisk the buttermilk, eggs and butter. Stir the buttermilk mixture into the dry ingredients, mixing well. Pour the batter into a 9 x 9 x 2-inch pan that has been buttered and floured. Bake for 25 minutes or until a toothpick inserted into the center comes out clean.

Serve warm with honey and softened or whipped butter.

Cooking time: 25 minutes
Yield: 12 servings
Temperature: 450 degrees
To store, wrap in plastic
   and tinfoil, then place in
   the refrigerator

2 cups white cornmeal
1 cup all-purpose flour
2 teaspoons baking soda
1 teaspoon salt
2 $1/2$ cups buttermilk
2 large eggs
$1/4$ cup butter, softened

# Banana Chocolate Chip Muffins

Cooking time: 18 to 25
  minutes
Yield: 12 to 18 servings
Temperature: 350 degrees
Store in plastic bag at
  room temperature,
  refrigerate or freeze

$1/2$ cup butter
1 cup sugar
2 eggs
3 ripe bananas
1 teaspoon vanilla
1 $1/2$ cups flour
1 teaspoon baking soda
1 teaspoon salt
$1/4$ cup milk chocolate
  chips
$1/4$ cup semi-sweet chips
$1/4$ cup butterscotch
  chips

Preheat oven to 350 degrees. In a large bowl, cream the sugar and butter with a mixer. Add the bananas, eggs and vanilla. Stir in the flour, baking soda and salt. Fold in the chips. Place paper bake cups in a muffin pan. Spoon the mixture into the cups, filling $1/2$ to $3/4$ full. Bake for 18 to 25 minutes or until they are golden brown. Let cool for 5 to 10 minutes then remove from the pan.

These are best served warm for breakfast or as dessert.

*"We were served delicious family style meals and everyone especially enjoyed the treat of fresh 'home baked' breads, rolls and desserts each day!"*

*Rita*
*Owatonna, Minnesota*

# Chocolate Sheet Cake with Raspberry Sauce

To make the cake, combine the flour, sugar and cinnamon in a large mixing bowl. In a heavy pan combine the butter, shortening, water and cocoa. Stir and heat to boiling. Pour the boiling mixture over the dry ingredients in the mixing bowl. Add the buttermilk, eggs, baking soda and vanilla. Mix well using a wooden spoon or electric mixer set on high. Pour into a well-buttered 17 1/2 x 11-inch sheet pan. Preheat the oven to 375 degrees. Bake for 15 to 20 minutes or until a cake tester inserted into the middle comes out clean.

To start the frosting, combine the butter, cocoa and milk in a saucepan. Heat to a boil, stirring continuously. Remove from heat and mix in the powdered sugar and vanilla, stirring until the frosting is smooth. Pour the warm frosting over the cake as soon as it comes out of the oven. Cool and cut into small pieces.

Place a small piece of the cake on a plate and top with a small scoop of vanilla ice cream. Spoon the raspberry sauce (recipe follows) over the ice cream and cake.

Cooking time: 1 hour
Yield: 30 servings
Temperature: 375 degrees

2 cups all-purpose flour
2 cups granulated sugar
1/2 cup butter
1/2 cup shortening
1 cup water
1/4 cup unsweetened
  cocoa
1/2 cup buttermilk
2 eggs
1 teaspoon baking soda
1 teaspoon vanilla
1 teaspoon cinnamon

Frosting:
1/2 cup butter
2 tablespoons cocoa
1/4 cup milk
3 1/2 cups powdered
  sugar
1 teaspoon vanilla

# Raspberry Sauce

Cooking time: 10 minutes

2 cups frozen,
   unsweetened
   raspberries, thawed
1 cup sugar
4 tablespoons cornstarch
1 cup water

Blend the sugar and cornstarch in a saucepan. Add the water to the mixture, stirring constantly until blended. Cook over medium heat until the glaze thickens and becomes clear. Cook until it reaches the desired consistency. It will set up as it cools. Add the thawed berries and stir. Cool, then refrigerate until ready to use.

*We have never requested recipes at other vacation spots, yet we left Laramie River with three of Nancy Parkison's desserts. It goes without saying, the food was superb."*

*Chip & Sande*
*Baltimore, Maryland*

# Coconut Barbecue Sauce

Combine all of the ingredients in a mixing bowl and blend until smooth. Transfer the sauce to a pan and heat over medium heat for 15 minutes. Do not boil.

Cooking time: 15 minutes
Yield: 4 servings
Temperature: medium
Refrigerate to store

1 cup unsweetened
   coconut milk
$1/2$ cup fresh cilantro,
   chopped
$1/2$ cup brown sugar
$1/3$ cup green onions
$1/4$ cup soy sauce
4 tablespoons garlic,
   minced
2 tablespoons fresh
   ginger, minced
$1/2$ teaspoon salt

# Old Glendevey Ranch

**Old Glendevey Ranch**
**Glendevey Colorado Route**
**3219 County Road 190**
**Jelm, WY 82063**
**(800) 807-1444**
**(970) 435-5701**
**Winter: 3605 Terry Point Dr.**
**Fort Collins, CO 80524**
**(970) 490-1444**
**www.duderanch.org/glendevey**
**glendevey@aol.com**
**Garth and Olivia Peterson**
**Elevation 8,500 feet**

Cradled gently by the Upper Laramie River Valley, surrounded by the Roosevelt National Forest and resting against the Rawah Wilderness, Old Glendevey Ranch waits to transport you back to a simpler world, one much closer to nature. Located near the Colorado-Wyoming border at an elevation of 8,500 feet, Glendevey Lodge was built in the 1920's and run as a guest ranch for many years.

The lodge contains a large dining room, a lounging area with fireplace, game room complete with pool table and a well-stocked library. There are three porches where guests can just put their feet up and relax. Upstairs are the seven guest rooms. Guests will find any number of home-style dishes awaiting them in the dining room. In addition to the family style meals indoors, there are many outdoor barbecues. There's always something to tempt your pallet at Old Glendevey Ranch.

In addition to their facilities at the Lodge, Old Glendevey Ranch offers Gourmet Pack Trips. Guests ride up to the base camp in the Rawah Wilderness on horseback where they will spend four days and three nights. The camp consists of guest tents, equipped with padded cots and wood burning stoves, a large cook tent, tack tents, staff tents, bathroom and shower tent. During their stay guests can participate in fishing, horseback riding and photography or they can just relax and enjoy the scenery.

Old Glendevey Ranch offers the freedom of mountain wilderness combined with all the comforts of home. Snow covered peaks, ice cold streams and the smell of pine and spruce await their guests. For pure relaxation there is just nothing like a turquoise lake and the silence of a clear mountain night. It is their privilege and pleasure to offer all of this to their guests.

# Crab Spread Appetizer

Place the cream cheese, Worcestershire sauce, lemon juice, grated onion and garlic powder in a blender and mix well. Pour into a serving dish, such as a 9-inch pottery pie plate. Spread 1/2 bottle of chili sauce over the layer in the serving dish. Drain the crabmeat well, then flake and spread evenly over the chili sauce layer. Sprinkle the fresh parsley over the top. Let sit overnight in the refrigerator. Serve with crackers on the side.

12 ounces cream cheese
2 tablespoons
  Worcestershire sauce
1 tablespoon lemon juice
1 very small onion,
  grated fine
Dash of garlic powder
Chili sauce
Fresh parsley
8 ounces frozen, cooked
  crabmeat

# Taco Salad

**Yield: 8 to 10 servings**

2 pounds ground beef
12 ounces nacho chips
1 medium head of
  lettuce, chopped
2 tomatoes, chopped
1 green pepper, chopped
1 medium onion,
  chopped
1 can sliced black olives
1 medium can kidney
  beans
1 tablespoon butter
10 ounces enchilada
  sauce
15 ounces tomato sauce
$1/8$ teaspoon sugar
2 to 3 cups grated cheese

Mix the enchilada and tomato sauces with the sugar in a saucepan over medium heat. In a separate pan, mix the kidney beans and butter together over medium heat. In a fry pan, brown the ground beef.

In an 11 x 13-inch pan, layer in the ingredients in the following order: Nacho chips, browned ground beef, $1/2$ the cheese, bean/butter mixture, chopped vegetables and olives. Just before serving pour the hot sauce mixture over the top. Sprinkle the remaining cheese over the top.

# Cream Cheese Pound Cake

In a large mixing bowl, cream together the margarine, butter and cream cheese. Add the sugar. Beat until light and fluffy. Add the eggs to the mixture, one at a time. Stir in the vanilla. Add the flour and mix well.

Preheat the oven to 350 degrees. Grease a 10-inch tube pan and pour in the batter. Place in the oven and bake for 70 minutes or until a cake tester inserted into the middle comes out clean.

Cooking time: 70 minutes
Yield: 1 cake
Temperature: 350 degrees

8 ounces cream cheese, softened
1 cup margarine, softened
$1/2$ cup butter, softened
3 cups sugar
6 eggs
3 cups flour
2 tablespoons vanilla

# Oatmeal Pie

Cooking time: 1 hour
Yield: 1 pie
Temperature: 325 to 350
   degrees

$2/3$ cup white sugar
$2/3$ cup brown Karo
   syrup
1 stick butter or
   margarine
$1/4$ teaspoon salt
$2/3$ cup oatmeal
2 eggs, beaten
1 teaspoon vanilla
1 - 9 inch pie shell
Slivered almonds

Preheat oven to 350 degrees. Mix all the ingredients together, beating until well mixed. Pour into the pie shell. Top with the slivered almonds. Bake at 350 degrees for 30 minutes. Reduce heat to 325 degrees and continue baking for an additional 30 minutes.

# Rhubarb Cake

Preheat oven to 350 degrees. Cream together the sugar and margarine in a large mixing bowl. Add the eggs and beat well. Add the vanilla and buttermilk. In a separate bowl, mix together the baking soda, flour, salt and chopped walnuts. Slowly add the dry mixture to the wet, while mixing constantly. Blend well. Add the rhubarb, mixing just until combined.

Pour the batter into a greased and floured 9 x 13-inch cake pan. Place in oven and bake for 45 minutes or until a tester inserted into the middle comes out clean. Remove from the oven and sprinkle the top with a little cinnamon and white sugar.

Cooking time: 45 minutes
Yield: 1 cake
Temperature: 350 degrees

2 cups brown sugar
$1/2$ cup margarine
2 eggs
1 teaspoon vanilla
1 teaspoon baking soda
1 cup buttermilk
2 cups flour
$1/2$ teaspoon salt
2 cups chopped rhubarb
1 cup walnuts, chopped

# Mustard Sauce

Yield: 2 cups
Temperature: medium

1 1/4 cups sugar
1/2 cup white vinegar
2 tablespoons dry
   mustard
2 eggs, well beaten
2 tablespoons butter

Mix all the ingredients together, making sure to combine completely. Cook in a saucepan over medium heat, until it thickens somewhat. Serve over ham or chicken.

# Rawah Ranch

**Rawah Ranch**
**Glendevey, Colorado Route C**
**11447 N. County Road 103**
**Jelm, WY  82063**
**(800) 820-3152**
**(970) 435-5715**
**Winter: 1612 Adriel Circle**
**Fort Collins, CO  80524**
**rawah@compuserve.com**
**Kunz and Zirzow Families**
**Elevation 8,400 feet**

Named for the 76,000-acre Rawah Wilderness that surrounds it and the snowcaps above, northern Colorado's Rawah Ranch is located in one of the west's most scenic mountain valleys. Enjoy the creak of well-worn saddles, the pounding of hooves across sage-covered meadows, the crackle of a roaring fire in the middle of July, the lazy rocking of a porch swing and good country cooking served up in cowboy-sized portions.

Guests enjoy cozy log cabins warmed by fireplaces or welcoming rooms in the ranch's beautiful log Lodge. Each is immaculate and has its own private bath. From the porch of each cabin you can watch for the many deer and moose that share the valley. Even in the guest cabins you are never far from the ranch's Lodge, corrals, arena or recreation room.

Mornings begin with coffee delivered to the guests, followed by a hearty ranch breakfast beside the crackling fires in the Lodge's stone fireplaces. Most guests then head out for a day of riding, fishing or hiking, each offering almost limitless opportunity. Together they form the core of the kind of ranch experience Rawah Ranch provides.

As the day winds down, the hot tub welcomes. Evenings include rousing western entertainment, a campfire, talk with a geologist or curling up near the fire with a good book. The ranch's recreation room offers Ping-Pong, pool and table shuffleboard, as well as a weekly evening western dance that has everyone kicking up their heels.

Meals are served family style in the Lodge dining room. Steaks and chicken grilled over Aspen coals, plenty of fresh vegetables and fruit, home-baked breads and homemade mouthwatering desserts are just part of the wonderful country cooking they serve up at Rawah Ranch. Guests complain that the food is too good…and there's always something set out for between-meal snacks.

Rawah Ranch invites you to join their family for a western experience you will never forget.

# Corn Meal Flapjacks

Combine the cornmeal, salt and honey. Slowly add the boiling water to the mixture. Cover and let stand for 10 minutes. Beat together the eggs, milk and butter. Add to the cornmeal mixture.

Sift the flour before measuring. After measuring, re-sift the flour with the baking powder. Swiftly stir the dry ingredients into the cornmeal batter. Drop spoonfuls of the batter onto a hot griddle and fry until golden brown.

Garnish with orange or strawberry slices. Top with a quality syrup and a side of favorite breakfast meat.

Yield: 12 4-inch cakes
Can be stored overnight

- 1 cup yellow cornmeal
- 1 teaspoon salt
- 1 to 2 tablespoons honey or sugar
- 1 cup boiling water
- 1 egg
- 1/2 cup milk
- 2 tablespoons melted butter
- 1/2 cup all-purpose flour, sifted
- 2 teaspoons baking powder

# Biscuits and Sausage Gravy

Cooking time: 25 minutes
Yield: 24 servings
Temperature: 400 degrees

Biscuits:
4 cups flour, sifted
4 1/2 teaspoons baking
  powder
1 teaspoon salt
1/2 cup vegetable oil
1 1/2 cups milk
1 tablespoon sugar

Sausage Gravy:
4 to 5 pounds bulk
  breakfast sausage
Flour
1/2 gallon milk
Salt & pepper to taste
Tabasco sauce

To make the biscuits, first sift together the dry ingredients. Then mix with the wet ingredients, making sure that everything is moist, but not over mixed. Roll out to 1 1/2-inch thickness on a floured surface. Cut into biscuit rounds using a cutter or knife. Place in a pan and bake in a preheated oven at 400 degrees until the tops and edges are well browned.

For the gravy, start by breaking the sausage into small bits and frying until brown in a large cast iron skillet. Sprinkle on enough flour to absorb the grease and stir. Add the milk, stirring over medium heat. Bring to a boil and let cook for 3 minutes. Add the salt, pepper and Tabasco. Add more milk to bring the gravy to the desired consistency.

Split the biscuits and top with gravy.

# Polla Alla Diavola
# (Devil's Chicken and Wine Rice)

Place the chicken in a deep dish. Pour the lemon juice over the chicken. Add the pepper and olive oil. Let marinate for 2 to 6 hours, stirring the chicken once every hour.

Remove the chicken from the marinade. Sprinkle with salt. Place on a grill, skin side down and cook, using the marinade to baste the chicken.

To prepare the wine rice, slowly sauté the onion in butter, until it is soft, not browned. Blend in the uncooked rice. Stir constantly over moderate heat, until the mixture takes on a milky appearance (it will first turn translucent).

Combine the chicken stock, white wine and water in a pot and bring to a boil. Pour the boiling liquid mixture over the rice mixture. Add in the remaining ingredients. Place the entire mixture into a casserole. Simmer until all the liquid is absorbed.

Serve the chicken and rice with au natural steamed sugar snap peas.

Yield: 6 servings

**Devil's Chicken:**
6 - 6 ounce skin on
   chicken breasts
$1/2$ cup lemon juice
1 tablespoon coarsely
   ground black pepper
3 tablespoons olive oil
2 teaspoons salt

**Wine Rice:**
$3/4$ cup finely minced
   onion
12 tablespoons butter
4 $1/2$ cups rice
3 cups chicken stock
3 cups dry white wine
3 cups water
3 parsley sprigs
1 bay leaf
$1/2$ teaspoon thyme
Ground black pepper
   and salt to taste

# Orzo with Thyme and Lemon Zest

Yield: 8 servings

2 cups orzo pasta
1 cup chicken stock
1 tablespoon lemon zest
2 teaspoons dried thyme
2 tablespoons butter
1/2 cup Parmesan cheese
7 teaspoons salt
1/2 teaspoon ground
  pepper

Set a large pan of salted water to boiling. Add the Orzo pasta and cook until al dente (approximately 8 to 10 minutes). Drain the pasta and rinse with hot water. Combine the orzo with the chicken stock, lemon zest, thyme, salt and pepper. Cook it over moderate heat, until most of the liquid is absorbed. Stir in the butter and Parmesan just prior to serving.

*"Everything here starts with 'too'—too beautiful, too friendly, too delicious, too bountiful, too many choices, too little time."*

*Donna*
*Hawaii*

# Honey Baked Beans

Pick over and wash the beans. Place the beans in a pot and cover with cold water. Let them soak overnight.

The next day, cook the beans in the same water used to soak them. Cook until the skins burst, approximately 1 hour. Drain the beans, discarding the liquid.

Preheat the oven to 300 degrees. Place 1/2 of the bacon and onion in the bottom of a 2 1/2-quart casserole. Add the beans and top with the remaining onion and bacon. Combine the rest of the ingredients with 1 3/4 cups of water. Pour over the beans and cover. Bake for 3 1/2 hours. Uncover and bake an additional hour or until the beans are of the desired consistency, stirring occasionally.

Cooking time: 4 to 5 hours
Yield: 6 servings
Temperature: 300 degrees
Can be stored for 2 to 3 days

1 pound dried pinto beans
8 slices bacon, diced
1 medium onion, sliced
1 cup honey
1 teaspoon salt
1 teaspoon ground ginger
1 teaspoon dry mustard

# Pink Beans with Herbs

Cooking time: 2 $^{1}/_{2}$ hours
Yield: 6 servings

2 cups dry beans, pinto
  or pink
$^{1}/_{2}$ cup olive oil
$^{1}/_{2}$ cup butter
2 tablespoons fresh
  lemon juice
$^{1}/_{2}$ cup chopped chives
1 teaspoon oregano
1 teaspoon rosemary,
  crushed
1 teaspoon salt

Soak the beans overnight in enough water to just cover them. The next day, add salt to the soaking water and simmer the beans for about 2 hours. In a separate pan, combine the remaining ingredients and simmer for an additional 10 minutes. Drain the beans, then add the sauce. Serve at once.

Excellent with any robust meat or chicken dish or just with burgers/hot dogs.

# Cole Slaw

Melt together all of the ingredients, save the mayonnaise and cabbage. Whisk the mayonnaise into the mixture. Place in the refrigerator and let chill. Just prior to serving, combine the dressing with the cabbage.

Cooking time: 10 minutes
Yield: 6 to 8 servings
Can be stored for 24
  hours

2 tablespoons butter,
  melted
$1/3$ cup sugar
$1/3$ cup vinegar
$1/2$ teaspoon salt
1 teaspoon dry mustard
1 cup mayonnaise
2 tablespoons milk or
  cream
1 large head of cabbage,
  shredded

*"It was wonderful to let my nine year old have the freedom to be on his own during the day and not worry about him. I knew it had been a great vacation when he cried when we left. (OK, I did too!)"*

*Ann*
*Tennessee*

# Apple Crisp

Cooking time: 30 to 40
  minutes
Yield: 6 to 8 servings
Temperature: 350 degrees
Can be stored overnight

5 to 6 cups tart apples
  (approximately 4
  apples)
1 cup melted butter
Cinnamon

Topping:
1 cup flour
$3/4$ cup sugar
1 teaspoon baking
  powder
$3/4$ teaspoon salt
1 egg

Preheat the oven to 350 degrees. Peel and slice the apples. Pour $1/2$ the melted butter over the apples; mix. Place the apples into a 6 x 9-inch pan. Mix the topping ingredients and spread evenly over the apples. Drizzle the remaining $1/2$ cup melted butter over the topping. Sprinkle the cinnamon over the top. Bake for 30 to 40 minutes or until the topping crisps up.

Serve warm topped with vanilla ice cream

# Blueberry Tart

In a medium saucepan, combine the blueberries, sugar and cinnamon. Cover and bring to a simmer over moderate heat. Uncover and cook, stirring occasionally, until the mixture has thickened slightly, about 20 minutes. Set aside in the refrigerator.

In a large bowl, toss the flour with the cornmeal, baking powder, salt and the rest of the granulated sugar. Cut the cold butter into the mixture, until it resembles coarse crumbs. Stir in the lemon zest. Using a fork, lightly stir the beaten eggs into the flour mixture, until incorporated.

Scatter about 2/3 of the crumb mixture in a 9-inch round tart pan with a removable bottom. Pat the crumbs evenly over the bottom and up the sides of the pan, forming a shell. Spoon the chilled blueberry mixture into the shell.

Preheat the oven to 350 degrees. On a lightly floured surface, pat the remaining crumb mixture into a square. Cut into 9 even strips. Roll each strip into a 1/2-inch thick rope and place onto the surface of the blueberry mixture, approximately 1 inch apart, crisscrossing the ropes to form a latticework. Press the rope ends against the inside rim of the shell.

Bake for 45 to 50 minutes or until golden brown. Let cool on a wire rack for 10 minutes before removing from pan. Dust with confectioner's sugar. Serve with slightly sweetened whipped cream on the top and side.

Cooking time: 90 minutes
Yield: 8 servings
Temperature: 350 degrees

Filling:
3 cups blueberries, fresh
  or frozen
1/2 cup granulated
  sugar
1/8 teaspoon cinnamon

Dough:
3 cups all-purpose flour
1/2 cup sugar
1/3 cup yellow cornmeal
1 teaspoon baking
  powder
1/2 teaspoon salt
6 ounces cold unsalted
  butter, cut into bits
2 teaspoons finely grated
  lemon peel
1 egg, plus 1 egg yolk,
  lightly beaten
Confectioner's sugar
Whipped cream

# Santa Fe Green Chili with Pork

Yield: 20 cups

Can be stored for 3 or 4 days

$1/2$ cup olive oil

3 cups finely chopped onion

6 cloves garlic, minced

1 $1/2$ cups flour

7 cups chicken stock

6 pounds ground pork or 10 cups shredded pork roast

1 $1/4$ teaspoons ground cumin

1 $1/4$ teaspoons black pepper

1 $1/4$ teaspoons oregano

1 tablespoon salt

4 $1/2$ cups diced green chiles

4 to 6 diced tomatoes

Sauté the pork, until brown. Drain off the grease and discard. Set the pork aside. Sauté the onions and garlic in the olive oil until tender. Gradually whisk the flour into the onion/garlic mixture. Cook for 3 to 4 minutes over moderate heat, stirring constantly. The flour will ball up in the whisk. Whisk in the hot chicken stock, until the mixture thickens. Add the seasonings and the green chiles. Add in the pork and let the mixture simmer for 30 to 45 minutes. Thicken with flour and water if necessary, until it naps a spoon heavily. Add chopped tomatoes and serve with steamed flour tortillas.

# Sky Corral Guest Ranch

**Sky Corral Guest Ranch**
**8233 Old Flowers Road**
**Bellvue, CO  80512**
**(970) 484-1362**
**(888) 323-2531**
**www.coloradovacation.com/duderanch/**
**   skyranch/**
**jocon72553@aol.com**
**The O'Connor Family**
**Elevation 7,800 feet**

Located in the Roosevelt National Forest, the Sky Corral Guest Ranch is set on 452 acres and offers a friendly, family oriented atmosphere. The ranch's small capacity allows for a more intimate and relaxing environment in which guests spend more time getting to know one another.

The focus of the ranch is, of course, horseback riding. The riding trails lead to scenic overlooks of the Continental Divide. Other vantage points offer guests views of both Colorado and Wyoming. Many trails wind their way through groves of Aspen and open meadows dotted with wildflowers.

The ranch also offers excellent fishing in their stocked lake. The friendly chefs are more than happy to cook whatever you might catch. Other activities include tennis, swimming, volleyball and basketball. Evenings are usually filled with square dancing, hay rides, sing-a-longs around the campfire or just sitting back and visiting with new friends. There's even a sauna and a jacuzzi available to relax in.

For those with a taste for a little more excitement, there's white water rafting on the Cache la Poudre river. This, combined with an overnight campout, can help to make your visit to Sky Corral Guest Ranch a vacation to remember.

# Chile Egg Puff

Cooking time: 30 to 35
  minutes
Yield: 8 to 10 servings
Temperature: 350 degrees

10 large or 12 medium
  eggs, slightly beaten
1 teaspoon baking
  powder
$1/2$ teaspoon salt
2 - 4 ounce cans of mild
  or medium diced green
  chiles
16 ounces cottage cheese
1 pound grated
  Monterey Jack cheese
$1/2$ cup melted butter or
  margarine

Preheat oven to 350 degrees. Mix all ingredients together in big bowl and pour into a greased 9 x 13-inch pan. Bake for 30 to 35 minutes.

Can be mixed the night before and stored in the refrigerator until ready to bake.

*"Thanks for your warm hospitality—down home food, the ride up the mountain—and the whole experience of being on the ranch—it was a great 1st time experience riding the horses. I hope to be back! Good luck! Regards,"*

*Carmen*

# Cowboy Chicken

Preheat the oven to 375 degrees. Wrap a piece of bacon around each chicken breast. Spread the chopped beef on the bottom of a casserole dish. Place the chicken over the beef. Mix the soup and sour cream. Pour over the chicken and bake for 1 hour or until brown.

Cooking time: 1 hour
Yield: 8 servings
Temperature: 375 degrees
Can be stored for 2 days

- 8 chicken breasts, boned and skinned
- 8 slices of bacon
- 4 ounce package of chipped beef (pressed beef)
- 1 can mushroom soup
- 1/2 pint sour cream

*"Thanks again for making this annual meeting one of our best! Your & your staff's efforts, dedication, and hard work were very much appreciated by our group. I am confident that Sky Corral will become one of the most successful Guest Ranches in Colorado, both for family style vacations and especially for corporate meetings. Very dedicated & professional! Kind regards,"*

*Cees Bosselaar,*
*Director of North America,*
*Holland, Netherlands Board of Tourism*

# Out of the Saddle Enchiladas

Cooking time: 30 minutes
Yield: 8 servings
Temperature: 325 degrees

1 pound beef or chicken
2 cans (10 ounces) cream
  of chicken soup
1 pint sour cream
2 teaspoons chili powder
Salt and pepper to taste
1 large green pepper,
  chopped
1 large yellow onion,
  chopped
1 pound Cheddar
cheese,
  grated
Flour tortillas

Preheat the oven to 350 degrees. Brown the meat in a skillet; drain the grease. Remove the pan from heat and stir in the soup, sour cream, chili powder, salt and pepper.

Grease a 9 x 13-inch pan. Place 2 tablespoons of the filling on each warm tortilla. Roll and lay seam down, in the pan. Top each with a sprinkle of onions, green peppers and cheese. Cover with the remaining filling, green peppers, onions and cheese. Bake for 30 minutes. Serve with chips and salsa.

*"What an amazing piece of heaven you have here! Thank you for sharing it with us! Good luck with your new venture & we hope to be back soon."*

*Tahnee*

# Lasso Lasagna

Preheat the oven to 350 degrees. Brown the ground beef. Add the chili powder and chopped onion. Add the soup and enchilada sauce, mixing well. In a 2-quart casserole dish, layer half the beef mixture, chips and cheese. Create a second layer with the remaining half of the ingredients in the same order as the first. Bake for 40 minutes.

Cooking time: 40 minutes
Yield: 5 servings
Temperature: 350 degrees

2 pounds ground beef
1 tablespoon chili powder
1 large yellow onion, chopped
2 cans cream of chicken soup
1 can enchilada sauce
1 - 10 ounce bag tortilla chips
1 - 10 ounce bag of grated Cheddar cheese

*"Thank you for arranging the most magical and incredible experience for me and my kids. Riding through your peaceful, snow-covered woods will stay with me forever. Congratulations on your new home & new lifestyle. Fondly,"*

*Beverly, Peter & David*

# Best Dude Dip in The West

Cooking time: 35 minutes
Yield: 8 servings
Temperature: 350 degrees

1 can artichoke hearts
1 cup of Parmesan
  cheese
1 cup mayonnaise
1/2 cup of grated Swiss
  cheese

Preheat the oven to 350 degrees. Chop up the artichoke hearts. Mix all the ingredients together in a large bowl. Pour into a 9 x 13-inch pan sprayed with vegetable oil spray. Bake for 35 minutes or until brown and bubbly. Serve with crackers.

*"The entire trip was a Kodak Moment! Thanks for the Great hospitality and the memories. I will be back!"*

*Kelly*

# Sylvan Dale Guest Ranch

**Sylvan Dale Guest Ranch**
**2939 N. County Road 31D**
**Loveland, CO 80538**
**(970) 667-3915**
**www.sylvandale.com**
**The Jessup Family**
**Elevation 5,280 feet**

In the Old West, working ranches were the stopping-off points for weary travelers. Here they could count on the warmth of an honest welcome, a place at the family table and a bunk for the night. This distinctive style of western hospitality took root at Sylvan Dale Ranch in the early 1920's. Located in the foothills of the Colorado Rockies, the small cattle ranch owned by Mr. and Mrs. Frend Neville carried on the tradition.

Maurice Jessup arrived at Sylvan Dale in 1934. A Kansas college kid working his way through school, he was caught with a vision of what the little ranch on the Big Thompson could really be. Eleven years later, Maurice and his wife Tillie bought Sylvan Dale. Since that time, the Jessups have increased the 125-acre ranch into a 5,000-acre complex that offers their guests the best in comfort and outdoor recreation.

Capable wranglers and quality riding stock add up to the right horse and the right riding activity for each guest. Beginners can get off to a good start with western riding instruction, while more experienced riders can take part in the annual 4th of July cattle drive to Cedar Park. The ranch has escorted trail rides daily and weekly overnight pack-trips into the backcountry. On the trail early in the morning means a fresh air breakfast of bacon, eggs and real cowboy coffee.

Sylvan Dale is also ideally located for easy access to and from the surrounding towns. Loveland and Fort Collins offer shopping, golf and white water rafting. Sightseeing drives into Rocky Mountain National Park are an easy day trip. For those who wish to simply go on a hiking expedition into the foothills, the staff will pack a great lunch and help in planning your day.

Individual and family housing in riverside cabins provides peaceful privacy and homey comfort for a good night's rest. The Wagon Wheel Barn is ideal for larger gatherings. Its carpeted lounge with fireplace and small kitchen is an added plus.

Sylvan Dale Ranch provides an ideal place for people to come together, year round. For groups large or small, strictly for business or purely for pleasure, the ranch offers the right kind of space for your particular needs. Please call or write for specific information to fit your needs.

# Oven Baked Eggs

Preheat the oven to 350 degrees. Place the bread in the bottom of a greased 9 x 13-inch pan. Beat together the eggs, milk, mustard and salt. Stir in the onions and cheese. Pour the mix over the top of the bread. Place in oven and bake for 1 hour or until golden brown. Garnish with cheese and parsley.

Serve with sausage links, hash browns and homemade cinnamon rolls for a hearty ranch breakfast.

*"My wife Sandy joined me for this trip and we were equally impressed by the level of service and overall quality of the operation. I was impressed by the quality of the Mother Lake fishery. During one 6 hour period, I was delighted to land 21 fish between 2 and 5 pounds!"*

*Tom*
*Salt Lake City, Utah*

Cooking time: 1 hour
Yield: 7 to 8 servings
Temperature: 350 degrees

4 slices of bread, cubed, crust removed
1 cup milk
5 eggs, well beaten
$1/2$ teaspoon dry mustard
$1/2$ teaspoon salt
1 cup shredded Cheddar cheese
1 $1/2$ tablespoons finely diced onion

# Oven Baked Chicken

Cooking time: 1 hour
Yield: 12 servings
Temperature: 350 degrees

2 cups flour
2 cups cornmeal
1 teaspoon salt
2 tablespoons paprika
1 tablespoon onion
  powder
1 tablespoon garlic
  powder
1 tablespoon white
  pepper
18 pieces cut up chicken
Margarine or butter,
  melted

Mix the flour, cornmeal, salt, paprika, onion powder, garlic powder and white pepper together in a mixing bowl. Roll the chicken pieces in the coating mix and place on baking sheets or in baking pans. Dab a little of the melted butter or margarine on each piece. Place in the oven and bake for 1 hour. Garnish with fresh parsley.

Serve with mashed potatoes and gravy made from the drippings, along with peas and carrots. Also delightful served with scalloped potatoes.

*"I found the food and service here are quite good, and the fishing prospect even better. There is a real chance to take a trophy fish, and the River holds wild rainbow and browns that fight as well as any trout I've caught."*

*Scott Roederer*
*The Angling Report, January 1992.*

# Sylvan Dale Corn Casserole

Preheat oven to 350 degrees. Place the corn, peppers, chiles and onions in a mixing bowl. In a saucepan, add the butter, sugar, salt and pepper, and milk. Heat to a slow rolling boil. Add the flour to thicken.

Pour the sauce over the corn mixture. Mix thoroughly. Place in a 2-quart casserole dish. Sprinkle the breadcrumbs or crushed crackers over the top. Pat with butter. Place in the oven and bake for 60 to 90 minutes, or until golden brown.

Serve at a barbecue or fish fry.

Cooking time: 60 to 90 minutes
Yield: 10 servings
Temperature: 350 degrees

1 pound fresh corn, removed from the cob
$1/4$ cup red peppers
$1/4$ cup green chiles
$1/2$ onion, diced
5 tablespoons butter
$3/4$ cup sugar
Salt and pepper to taste
2 $2/3$ cups milk
$1/4$ cup flour
Bread crumbs or crushed saltines
Pat of butter

# Spinach Salad and Dressing

Yield: 12 servings

1 pound fresh spinach
   leaves, washed
1/4 cup sliced fresh
   mushrooms
1 apple, diced
1/4 cup celery, diced
1/4 cup red onion, diced
1 cup shredded Cheddar
   cheese

Dressing:
1 cup sour cream
1 cup mayonnaise
1/4 cup milk

Combine the dressing ingredients and set aside. Mix all the salad ingredients together in a salad bowl. Just prior to serving, pour the dressing over the top of the salad and toss. Garnish with tomato slices and shredded cheese.

Serve with prime rib, twice baked potatoes and fresh vegetables.

# Heart J Dressing

Mix the onion, sugar and vinegar in a blender, until the mixture is clear. Add the remaining ingredients, with the exception of the poppy seeds, and blend for 5 minutes. Add the poppy seeds and blend until well mixed. Serve on a tossed green salad, garnished with fresh vegetables.

*"I am happy to report that the response from every single person who attended was that your ranch was the best possible choice we could have made."*

*Ron and Cathy*

Yield: 6 cups

1 medium onion,
  quartered
2 cups sugar
1 cup white vinegar
1 1/2 tablespoons
  ground mustard
1 tablespoon salt
3 cups salad oil
1 tablespoon poppy seed

# Corn Bread

Cooking time: 35 minutes
Yield: 50 servings
Temperature: 350 degrees

2 pounds plus 3 ounces
  yellow cornmeal
2 pounds plus 5 ounces
  all-purpose flour
3 1/2 ounces baking
  powder
2 1/2 tablespoons salt
10 ounces granulated
  sugar
9 eggs, beaten
1 3/4 quarts milk
10 ounces shortening,
  melted and cooled
8 ounces red peppers
8 ounces green chile
Whole kernel corn
  (optional)

Preheat the oven to 350 degrees. Combine the dry ingredients in a large mixing bowl. Blend on low speed using a flat beater. In a separate bowl, combine the eggs, milk and shortening. Add this to the bowl of dry ingredients. Mix on low speed, only until the dry ingredients are moistened. Divide the batter into 2 greased 12 x 18 x 2-inch baking pans. Place in the oven and bake at 350 degrees for 35 minutes or until a cake tester inserted into the middle comes out clean.

Serve with plenty of butter and honey.

# Fresh Apple Cake with Caramel Frosting

Preheat the oven to 375 degrees. Cream the shortening with the sugar and add the well-beaten eggs. Sift the dry ingredients together and add alternately with the apples, raisins and nuts. Bake in a greased and floured pan for 35 to 45 minutes or until a cake tester inserted into the middle comes out clean.

Combine all ingredients for the frosting in a saucepan and bring to a boil. Add the milk and cook for 3 minutes. Let stand. Add powdered sugar until it's thick enough to spread on the cake.

Cooking time: 35 to 45 minutes
Yield: 1 cake
Temperature: 375 degrees

1/2 cup shortening
1 teaspoon cinnamon
1 cup sugar
3/4 teaspoon allspice
2 eggs, well beaten
1/2 cup cold coffee
1 1/2 cups sifted flour
2 cups finely chopped apples
1 teaspoon baking soda
1 cup raisins
3/4 teaspoon salt
1/2 cup chopped nuts

Caramel Frosting:
1 cup brown sugar
1 tablespoon butter
1 cup powdered sugar
3 tablespoons vegetable shortening

# Sour Cream Pecan Tea Ring

Cooking time: 25 minutes
Yield: 2 tea rings
Temperature: 375 degrees

$1/2$ cup margarine,
  melted
1 cup dairy sour cream
$1/2$ cup sugar
1 $1/2$ teaspoons salt
2 packages dry yeast
$3/4$ cup warm water
1 egg, at room
  temperature
5 $1/2$ to 6 $1/2$ cups flour
$1/4$ cup melted
  margarine
1 cup chopped pecans
$1/2$ cup firmly packed
  light brown sugar
$1/2$ teaspoon cinnamon

Powdered Sugar
Frosting:
3 cups powdered sugar
2 tablespoons butter
$1/2$ cup hot water
1 teaspoon vanilla
Pinch of salt

Preheat the oven to 375 degrees. Combine the margarine, sour cream, salt and sugar. Dissolve the yeast in warm water. Add the sour cream mixture, egg and 3 cups flour and beat until smooth. Add more flour to make stiff dough. Knead the dough for 8 to 10 minutes on a floured board. Place in a greased bowl; grease the top of the dough. Cover and let rest for 15 minutes. Roll into two 9 x 16-inch rectangles. Brush with melted margarine. Combine the pecans, sugar and cinnamon and sprinkle over the dough. Roll up, seal the seams and place in circles on greased baking pans. Seal the ends. Cut slits $2/3$ of the way through the rings at even intervals. Turn the sections on their sides. Cover and let rise until doubled, about 1 hour. Bake for about 25 minutes.

Make the powdered sugar frosting by combining all the ingredients together in a bowl, mixing well. If necessary, add more hot water to thin to a medium consistency. Frost the rings while warm.

# Swedish Kringlor

Preheat the oven to 350 degrees. Mix together the margarine, 1 cup of the flour and 1 tablespoon of water. Pat the dough out thinly in 2 long rows on a cookie sheet. Bring the 1 cup of water and 1 stick of margarine to a boil. Remove from the heat and stir in the remaining flour. Add the eggs, one at a time, beating well after each. Paint the mixture onto the dough on the cookie sheet. Bake for 1 hour at 350 degrees. Frost with Powdered Sugar Frosting. Add nuts and cherries, if desired.

Cooking time: 1 hour
Yield: 2 pastries
Temperature: 350 degrees

$1/2$ cup margarine
1 cup water
1 $3/4$ cups flour
1 stick margarine
1 tablespoon water
3 eggs
Powdered Sugar
  Frosting
Nuts & cherries, if
  desired

# Women of the West

Most of our documented history does not contain information about the great women who were a part of the migration of pioneers to the western United States in the 19th and 20th centuries. We may have come a long way baby, but I am appalled at the lack of information in both print and electronic encyclopedias on the women of Colorado that we include in this book. Colorado was a crossroads for many people migrating from east to west, many of them women who worked for the betterment of life, blazed new trails through the frontier and contributed to bring about change for all.

Many of the women of the west, particularly in Colorado, greatly influenced other parts of the country. They were doctors, lawyers, ranchers, business people, members of Congress, mothers, writers/journalists, war veterans, teachers, the list goes on and on. We want to include here not only famous and infamous women of the west, but also those who quietly helped this country become the greatest nation on earth.

*Javana M. Richardson*
*Publisher, Pantry Press*

## Augusta Tabor
## 1837 - 1895

The woman who would one day be embroiled in the bitter scandal of Baby Doe and Horace Tabor was born in Augusta, Maine in 1837. The daughter of a quarry owner named Pierce, she grew up in a comfortable home where domestic servants took care of most chores. In 1857 she met a hard-drinking, fist-fighting young stone cutter by the name of Horace Tabor who had come to work for her father. She quickly set out to reform the man with an eye toward turning him into an acceptable husband.

After their marriage, Horace and Augusta set out to homestead in Kansas, using the $300 wedding present from her family as working capital. They arrived in the midst of the border war between pro- and anti-slavery forces, settling on a farm abandoned by Southern sympathizers. After a couple of years, Horace decided to try his luck in the newly discovered gold fields of Colorado. Despite having just given birth to their son, Nathaniel Maxcy, Augusta decided to go along with Horace, out of loyalty to her husband.

They arrived in the gold camp of Clear Creek in 1859. Horace immediately set out prospecting with the other men, while Augusta sewed and set up a 7 by 9-foot tent to shelter herself and the baby from the elements. They spent that season moving from camp to camp, before ending up in Idaho Springs. While Horace prospected, Augusta set up a bakery for the miners. She made enough that season to pay for the farm back in Kansas and provide the family with a room back in Denver for the harsh winter months. This was to be the pattern for the next twenty years, Horace chasing gold and Augusta supporting the family through one business enterprise after another.

By 1878 the Tabors were living in Leadville, Colorado, where Augusta had set up a general store and hotel. It was while he was working in the store one day that Horace invested $64.75 in grubstaking two German miners in exchange for an interest in what became the Little Pittsburgh mine. Later that year he sold out his interest for more than $1 million. Later mining ventures left the Tabors with an amazing income of $100,000 per month.

Augusta couldn't bring herself to approve the change that came over Horace with sudden wealth. She shook her head at the notion of a man who couldn't even tote up a column of numbers being president of his own bank. It was this sort of thing that drove a wedge between Horace and the woman who had been his helpmate in the lean years.

Augusta first learned of the affair between Horace and Baby Doe shortly before the opening of his grand opera house in Denver. They were soon engaged in a bitter property dispute, with Augusta requesting half of the couple's assets. Unwilling to consider an equitable split with his wife, Horace bribed a judge in Durango into granting a divorce without Augusta's approval. She finally settled for the house in Denver and $250,000 in cash.

Ironically, it was Horace who died penniless, laboring in the mines he had once owned. His second wife, Baby Doe, froze to death in a shack on the site of the abandoned Matchless Mine, source of so much of his former wealth. Augusta, displaying the business savvy that had benefited Horace for so many years, turned her divorce settlement into a considerable fortune, which she left to her son and her seven siblings upon her death.

# North Central Mountains

# Aspen Canyon Ranch

**Aspen Canyon Ranch**
**13206 County Road #3, Star Route**
**Parshall, CO 80468**
**(800) 321-1357**
**(970) 725-3600**
**Roderick**
**Elevation 8,400 feet**

Aspen Canyon Ranch is located in the Williams Fork River Valley, ninety miles west of Denver and north of Silverthorne in Grand County, Colorado. The country is mountainous and heavily forested with Aspen and various species of pine. The ranch also borders on the Arapaho National Forest, allowing for nearly endless recreational opportunities. Guests can trail ride, hike or hunt on the nearly 3,000 acres that the ranch encompasses.

The ranch sits at an elevation of 8,400 feet, providing for warm, sunny days and cool nights. The guest cabins are constructed of native Lodge Pole Pine and sit near the banks of the rushing river. They are rustically decorated with handmade log furniture and all have decks that overlook the river. Each cabin features carpeting, private baths, refrigerators, coffee makers and fireplaces. Upon arrival guests will find welcoming cookies and soft drinks.

Nearly a mile of both the Williams Fork River and Lost Creek run through the Aspen Canyon Ranch. This means that guests of the ranch have ample opportunity to try out their fishing skills on such native trout species as the Brook, Brown and Rainbow. For a bigger challenge, Williams Fork Reservoir is just minutes away, offering Northern Pike and Kokanee Salmon.

The food at the ranch is definitely something to look forward to. The menu includes homemade soups, breads, pies, cakes and a variety of main courses. Many of the meals are actually cookouts or picnics, including an early morning breakfast ride. Snacks are always available throughout the day from the refrigerator.

The most important aspect of a vacation at the Aspen Canyon Ranch is the relaxation. The ranch is a dramatic change of pace from home. The beauty of the rugged country helps guests to enjoy the days, while the roar of the white water in the river serves to lull them to sleep at night.

Come see them once and you'll come back again.

# Barbecue Pork Ribs

Lay the racks of ribs into flat baking pans. Sprinkle with white pepper, garlic and brown sugar; rub into the meat with your hands. Turn the racks over and repeat.

Preheat the oven to 300 degrees. Pour enough pineapple juice over the ribs to cover the bottom of the pan to a depth of 1 inch. Cover the pans with foil and seal tightly. Bake for 3 1/2 to 4 hours. The ribs will be well done, almost falling apart when ready to remove from the oven.

Remove the ribs from the baking pans and discard the juice. Cut the ribs into serving sized pieces. Mix the sauce ingredients, making sure to blend thoroughly. Dip the rib portions into the sauce and place them onto an open grill. Cook until the sauce is caramelized, approximately 5 to 7 minutes per side.

*"Melt in your mouth."*

Cooking time: 4 hours
Yield: 30 servings
Temperature: 300 degrees

10 racks of pork ribs
3 to 4 cups brown sugar
Pineapple juice
White pepper
Fresh chopped garlic

Sauce:
1 gallon barbecue sauce
2 cups brown sugar
2 cups molasses
1/4 cup Worcestershire
  sauce

# Ranch Chili

Cooking time: 2 hours
Yield: 15 to 20 servings
Temperature: medium
Can be frozen and stored
for up to 4 weeks

5 pounds stew meat, cut
into bite sized pieces
1 #10 can diced
tomatoes
1 #10 can kidney beans
2 small cans tomato
paste
1/2 cup beef base
1 onion, chopped
2 tablespoons oil
1/4 cup cumin
4 tablespoons garlic
powder
1/2 cup chili powder or
to taste

In a large pot, brown the stew meat with the oil and onion. Add the diced tomatoes, tomato paste, beef base and spices. Simmer for 1 hour. Add the kidney beans and simmer for an additional hour.

Serve with grated Cheddar cheese and sour cream. Add a baked potato and salad for a hearty winter lunch.

# Creamy Potato Soup

Cook the bacon and onion in a large pan, stirring often, until the bacon is brown and the onions soft. Add enough flour to the bacon and onion mixture to make a thick paste. Add the milk, potatoes and chicken base to the pan. Salt and pepper to taste. Cook over low heat until thickened.

Cooking time: 30 minutes
Yield: 15 servings
Temperature: low

$1/2$ pound bacon, sliced
  into small pieces
1 medium onion,
  chopped
$3/4$ cup flour
$1/2$ gallon milk
4 pounds frozen
  shredded potatoes
2 tablespoons chicken
  base
Salt and pepper to taste

*"I have got to have that recipe!"*

# Cowboy Beans

Cooking time: 1 hour
Yield: 60 servings
Temperature: medium
Can be stored for up to a
  month in the freezer

1 #10 can red kidney
  beans
1 #10 can black beans
1 #10 can white
  northern beans
1 large onion, chopped
2 cups barbecue sauce
1 cup brown sugar
1 cup molasses
2 tablespoons
  Worcestershire sauce
Dash of hot sauce
3 to 4 tablespoons dried
  basil
3 to 4 tablespoons dried
  parsley
1 tablespoon crushed
  thyme
1 tablespoon crushed
  rosemary

**Combine all the ingredients into a large pot. Simmer over medium heat for 1 hour. Serve over corn bread.**

*"I don't normally enjoy beans, but these are the best beans I've ever had."*

# Crunchy Cabbage Salad

Combine all the dressing ingredients into a jar with a lid. Shake well to mix and refrigerate.

Shred the cabbage with a food processor. Place in a large bowl and refrigerate.

In a skillet over medium heat, melt the butter. Sauté the almonds, sesame seeds and crushed Ramen noodles, until golden brown, stirring frequently. Allow to cool completely.

Place the chilled cabbage in a large salad bowl. Pour the dressing over the top. Add the sautéed nut mixture and toss well. Serve immediately in a bowl lined with red and green cabbage leaves.

*"The flavor of the dressing and the combination of the almonds really make this salad wonderful."*

Cooking time: 5 minutes
Yield: 15 servings
Temperature: medium

1 medium head of green
  cabbage, shredded
$1/2$ small head of red
  cabbage, shredded
2 tablespoons butter
1 cup sliced almonds
$1/4$ cup sesame seeds
1 package of Ramen
  noodles, crushed

Dressing:
$1/3$ cup rice vinegar
$1/4$ cup sesame or
  vegetable oil
$1/3$ cup sugar or honey
3 tablespoons soy sauce

# Braided Onion and Chive Bread

Cooking time: 40 minutes
Yield: 5 braided loaves
Temperature: 375 degrees

5 tablespoons yeast
1/2 cup sugar
5 cups warm water
10 tablespoons olive oil
5 teaspoons salt
15 cups flour
1/4 cup onion powder
1/2 cup dried chopped
   chives or 1 cup fresh
   green onions, chopped
1 egg

Dissolve the yeast in the warm water. Add to a large mixer equipped with a dough hook and mix with the sugar. Let stand for 2 to 3 minutes or until the mixture becomes bubbly. Add the oil, salt, flour, onion powder and chopped chives. Mix and knead for 5 minutes or until the dough forms a ball. Place the dough in a large oiled bowl. Cover and set in a warm place to let it rise to twice its original size. Turn out and punch the dough down. Replace in the bowl and set aside to let rise a second time. Turn out and punch down again. Let the dough rest for 2 minutes.

Divide the dough into 5 equal parts. Take each part and further divide into 3 equal pieces. Roll each piece into ropes that are 12 to 14 inches long. Place the 3 ropes side by side and pinch 1 end together. Braid into a tight braid and pinch the other end together. Tuck the ends under.

Preheat the oven to 375 degrees. Place the braided loaves onto parchment covered baking sheets. Beat the egg together with a small amount of water and brush the mixture over the tops of the loaves. Cover and let the loaves rise to double their size. Bake for 40 minutes.

Leftovers from these make great salad croutons.

# Cinnamon Bread

Dissolve the yeast in the warm water. In a large mixer equipped with a dough hook, mix the dissolved yeast solution and the 5 teaspoons of sugar. Let the mixture sit for 2 to 3 minutes or until it becomes bubbly. Add the rest of the sugar, salt, oil and enough flour to make stiff dough. Mix and knead in the mixer for about 5 minutes or until the dough forms into a ball.

Place the dough into a large oiled bowl. Cover and set in a warm place to let rise. When dough has doubled in size, turn it out and punch down. Replace in the bowl and let it rise a second time. Turn out and punch down. Let the dough rest for 2 minutes. Preheat the oven to 375 degrees.

Divide the dough into 5 equal parts. Roll out each piece into a rectangle about $1/4$ inch in thickness. Spread the melted butter over each rectangle and sprinkle with the brown sugar and cinnamon. Roll up each rectangle, starting with the short edge. Pinch the edges together and tuck the ends under. Place into a greased 9 x 5-inch loaf pan. Cover and let rise to twice its original size. Bake for 50 minutes.

The leftovers are great for French toast!

Cooking time: 50 minutes
Yield: 5 loaves
Temperature: 375 degrees

5 tablespoons yeast
5 teaspoons sugar
5 cups warm water
7 $1/2$ tablespoons sugar
5 teaspoons salt
10 tablespoons oil
15 cups flour
1 cup melted butter
1 $1/2$ to 2 cups brown
 sugar
3 tablespoons cinnamon

# Aspen Canyon Ranch Cookies

Cooking time: 12 minutes
Yield: 30 large cookies
Temperature: 350 degrees
The dough can be stored
 in an airtight container
 for up to 3 weeks in the
 refrigerator.

1 cup shortening
1 cup brown sugar
$1/2$ cup sugar
2 eggs
1 teaspoon vanilla
2 $1/4$ cups flour
1 teaspoon baking soda
1 teaspoon salt
1 $1/2$ cups chocolate
 chips
$1/2$ cup white chocolate
 chips
$3/4$ cup chopped pecans

Preheat the oven to 350 degrees. Cream the shortening, brown sugar and sugar together in a large bowl. Add the eggs and vanilla, mixing well. Sift the dry ingredients together and add to the creamed mixture. Mix until well blended. Add the chocolate chips and pecans to the mixture. Form into large, golf ball sized balls. Place onto an ungreased, parchment lined cookie sheet, spaced about 1 inch apart. Bake for 10 to 12 minutes or until the tops are slightly brown.

*"These are better than Mrs. Fields."*

# White Chocolate Raspberry Bars

Preheat oven to 325 degrees. Grease and flour a 9 x 13-inch pan. Melt the butter in a medium saucepan. Remove from heat and add the white chocolate chips. Let stand, but do not stir.

Beat the eggs in a large bowl. Add the sugar, continuing to beat. Stir in the melted white chocolate chips. Add the flour, salt and almond extract. Stir just until mixed. Spread $1/2$ of the batter in the bottom of the pan. Bake for 15 minutes until light brown.

While the batter is baking in the oven, melt the raspberry jam in a small pan over low heat. Remove the baked bottom from the oven and spread the melted jam over the top. Spoon the remaining batter over the top of the jam. Sprinkle with sliced almonds. Return the pan to the oven and bake an additional 20 to 25 minutes or until golden brown. Let cool completely. Cut into bars prior to serving.

*"White chocolate and raspberries together are wonderful."*

Cooking time: 45 minutes
Yield: 24 bars
Temperature: 325 degrees

1 cup butter
4 cups white chocolate
  chips
5 eggs
1 cup sugar
2 $1/4$ cups flour
1 teaspoon salt
1 tablespoon almond
  extract
1 $1/4$ cups raspberry
  jam
$3/4$ cup sliced almonds

# Aspen Lodge Ranch Resort

**Aspen Lodge Ranch Resort**
**6120 Highway 7**
**Estes Park, CO 80517**
**(800) 332-6867**
**(970) 586-8133**
**www.aspenlodge.com**
**Steve McFarland**
**Elevation 9,100 feet**

Come celebrate life in this exhilarating mountain paradise. Select superb accommodations within the majesty of Colorado's largest log lodge or in the cozy comfort of cabins framed by Aspen. Located just ten minutes from downtown Estes Park and ninety minutes from Denver, they're easy to reach any time.

Guests awaken to stunning views of Long's Peak, the highest peak in the Rocky Mountains and surrounded by forests of evergreen framing shimmering mountain lakes. This is set against skies so blue that they don't seem to be real.

Come to Aspen Lodge Ranch Resort to relax or explore. Ride adjoining horse trails into Rocky Mountain National Park or go for open country rides on 33,000 acres of countryside. Novices through experts can benefit from their excellent instructional riding program.

Open all year long, they offer an abundance of activities with year-round horseback riding, hiking, mountain biking, tennis, racquetball and much more. The Sports Center offers a weight room, sauna, hot tub and outdoor heated seasonal swimming pool. Winter offers extensive activities including cross-country skiing, snowshoeing, romantic sleigh rides and snowmobiling.

Aspen Lodge guests never have to compromise on food either. They offer meals ranging from traditional Western fare to gourmet continental, served in their casual dining room without the restriction of rigid meal times. A varied menu, prepared with imagination, rounds out the dining experience.

The dedicated staff of Aspen Lodge will help make your vacation dream come true.

# Cajun Crevettes

Cooking time: 10 minutes
Yield: 1 serving
Temperature: high

3 - 26/30 count size
  shrimp
Flour
3 ounces Kielbasa
3 ounces mushrooms
2 ounces cherry
  tomatoes
$1/4$ ounce scallions,
  chopped
4 ounces heavy cream
3 ounces Asiago cheese
4 ounces Penne pasta,
  cooked
1 ounce blended
  vegetable oil
1 teaspoon blackened
  seasoning

Coat each shrimp with flour. Place oil in a medium sauté pan on high heat. Add the mushrooms and sauté for 1 minute. Add the shrimp and brown both sides. Add the Kielbasa and heavy cream. Cook to reduce by half. Add the blackened seasoning. Remove from heat and add the Asiago cheese. Add the cooked pasta and stir until well mixed.

Serve immediately in a large pasta bowl. Garnish with the chopped scallions and half-moon cut cherry tomatoes.

# Elk Maison

Pound each piece of elk with a meat tenderizer hammer until thin. Heat the oil in a medium sauté pan over high heat. Add the elk pieces and sauté for 1 minute on each side. Remove and set aside.

Add the mushrooms to the same pan and sauté until tender. Add the Madeira wine, heavy cream and butter. Cook to reduce to desired consistency.

Place the Elk on a dinner plate. Pour the sauce and mushrooms over the top.

Cooking time: 10 minutes
Yield: 1 serving
Temperature: high

3 - 2 ounce pieces of elk
1/4 ounce shallots
2 ounces mushrooms
2 ounces Madeira wine
4 ounces heavy cream
1 ounce butter
1 ounce vegetable oil

# Farm House Chicken

Cooking time: 15 to 20
  minutes
Yield: 1 serving
Temperature: 450 degrees

6 ounce chicken breast
1 ounce smoked ham
1 ounce Monterey Jack
  cheese
1 ounce Asiago cheese

Marsala Sauce:
2 ounces mushrooms
1 ounce Marsala wine
2 ounces demi glace
1/4 ounce shallots
2 ounces vegetable oil

Divide the chicken breast into two equal portions. Place the ham and Jack cheese atop one portion. Place the second portion 3/4 of the way over the top of the first. Sprinkle the coarse grated Asiago over the top of the 2 breasts. Place in a baking dish and bake in a pre-heated oven at 450 degrees for approximately 15 to 20 minutes.

To make the Marsala sauce, sauté the mushrooms and shallots in a sauté pan until tender. Add the Marsala wine and demi glace. Reduce to the desired consistency.

Place the chicken breast on a dinner plate. Pour the Marsala sauce over the top.

# Rainbow Trout Almondine

Heat the oil in a medium sauté pan over high heat. Place the trout into the oil and sauté each side for 3 minutes. Set aside.

Add almonds, Amaretto and butter in the same pan. Turn off the heat and swirl the ingredients around in the pan until thickened.

Place the trout on a plate. Pour the sauce over the top and garnish with parsley.

Cooking time: 10 minutes
Yield: 1 serving
Temperature: high

1 trout, cleaned and
  butterflied
1 ounce sliced toasted
  almonds
2 ounces Amaretto
  liqueur
1 ounce butter
1 ounce vegetable oil

# Bar Lazy J Guest Ranch

**Bar Lazy J Guest Ranch**
**Box N**
**Parshall, CO  80468**
**(800) 396-6279**
**(970) 725-3437**
**Jerry & Cheri Helmicki**
**Elevation 7,500 feet**

Opened in 1912, the Bar Lazy J is considered the oldest continuously operating guest ranch in Colorado. Owners Jerry and Cheri Amos-Helmicki believe their ranch to be ideally located, just southwest of Rocky Mountain National Park in a peaceful valley on the Colorado River. With a guest capacity of thirty-eight, they offer their guests a friendly, informal atmosphere and a true western experience.

The Bar Lazy J has twelve comfortable guest log cabins clustered along the Colorado River, all with screened porches overlooking the river. At 7,500 feet elevation the crisp, clean mountain air will stimulate your appetite for the home-style food and fresh baked goods served in their historic log lodge.

Due to this private river frontage, Bar Lazy J can offer some of the best Rainbow and German Brown trout fishing in the state. Their organized horseback rides take you on sage covered hills and majestic mountains with sapphire skies and crystal clear views. They offer horseback riding for all skill levels, as well as jeep rides, hiking, mountain biking and sightseeing trips by van. Other available options include golf, tennis and white water rafting.

Every evening the ranch offers planned activities such as hay rides, campfire sing-a-longs, rodeos, shows put on by the staff and western dancing. The guests can participate in these or just soak in the hot tub, visit with the people in the next cabin or just organize a game of cards. Sometimes it's nice to just take a walk under the stars or sit in front of your cabin and enjoy the peaceful, cool nights with the sound of the river rushing by.

Whether you are a family, a couple or traveling alone, your every vacation need is taken care of at Bar Lazy J. Relaxation is what we offer. The pace is slower or doesn't run at all; they offer many activities or you can just sit back and do nothing. The choice is yours at Bar Lazy J.

# Adobe Chicken Casserole

Preheat oven to 350 degrees. Layer the rice, black olives, tomatoes, onion, green chiles and chicken in a 9 x 13-inch pan, in that order. Top with the sour cream and sprinkle with cheese. Bake for 45 to 60 minutes in the oven, until done. Serve with tortilla chips and salsa.

This is a great way to use any leftover rice, turkey or chicken. It can also be made without the chicken to convert it to a vegetarian dish.

Cooking time: 45 to 60 minutes
Yield: 15 servings
Temperature: 350 degrees

4 cups cooked rice of any kind
1 cup black olives, chopped
2 tomatoes, chopped
1 onion
8 ounces green chiles
2 cups chicken, cooked and chopped
2 cups sour cream
Shredded cheese (your choice)

*"The food is good home cooking and the kids have wolfed it down."*

*The Asplin Family*
*High Wycombe, Buckinghamshire, England*

# Black Bean Chili Chowder

Cooking time: 8 minutes
Yield: 4 servings

1 - 19 ounce can black
  bean soup
1 - 14 $1/2$ ounce can
  diced tomatoes with
  garlic and onion
1 - 8 $3/4$ ounce can
  whole kernel corn
$1/4$ cup traditional salsa
  or picante sauce (hot)
$1/3$ cup sliced green
  onions
Sour Cream (optional)

In a large saucepan, combine the soup, tomatoes, corn, onion and salsa. Bring the mixture to a boil. Reduce the heat to medium and cook for an additional 3 minutes. Serve with a dollop of sour cream on top, if desired.

*"The food was great at every meal, my compliments to the chef!"*

*Tim & Rachel*

# Shrimp and Angel Hair Pasta

Sauté the shrimp and garlic in the oil. Add the wine, sour cream, Parmesan cheese, chicken broth, basil, rosemary and red pepper flakes. Bring to a boil and simmer to let the flavors combine. Thicken slightly with cornstarch. Garnish with tomato and parsley. Serve over angel hair pasta.

This is served during our adults only dinner in a candle-lit atmosphere. The kids have pizza with the staff out on the river porch.

Yield: 15 to 20 servings

2 to 3 pounds of shrimp
1 tablespoon minced garlic
1/4 cup cooking oil
2 to 3 cups dry white wine
2 cups sour cream
1/2 cup Parmesan cheese
3 cups chicken broth
2 teaspoons basil
2 teaspoons rosemary
1/4 teaspoon red pepper flakes
Cornstarch
2 tomatoes, chopped
1/4 cup fresh parsley, chopped
Salt and pepper to taste

# Carrot Mushroom Loaf

Cooking time: 35 minutes
Yield: 4 to 6 servings
Temperature: 350 degrees

2 cloves of garlic
1/4 cup butter
1 cup onion, chopped
1 pound mushrooms,
  chopped
4 1/2 cups carrots,
  grated
5 eggs
1 cup fresh whole-wheat
  bread crumbs
1 cup grated Cheddar
  cheese
Salt and pepper to taste
Basil
Thyme

Preheat the oven to 350 degrees. Crush the garlic and sauté in the butter. Add the onions and mushrooms and sauté until soft. Remove from the heat. Combine the eggs, carrots, 1/2 the breadcrumbs and 1/2 the cheese with the mixture in the pan. Season to taste with the salt, pepper, basil and thyme.

Spread the mixture into a buttered, oblong baking pan. Sprinkle the top with the remaining breadcrumbs and cheese. Dot with butter. Bake for 30 minutes covered. Uncover and bake an additional 5 minutes or until brown.

This dish is a great alternative for people who don't eat red meat.

# Broccoli Tomato Salad

Thaw the broccoli completely. Chop the tomatoes and red onion. Toss together the broccoli, tomatoes and onion. Mix in the mayonnaise and season to taste.

Serve as part of a luncheon buffet.

Yield: 15 to 20 servings

2 pounds frozen broccoli
2 tomatoes
$1/4$ cup red onion
Mayonnaise
Salt to taste

# Katy's Pasta Salad

Yield: 15 to 20 servings

2 pounds multi-colored
  pasta
$1/2$ cup green olives
$1/2$ cup black olives
2 tomatoes, chopped
$1/4$ cup red onion,
  chopped
$1/4$ cup celery, chopped
$1/4$ cup carrots, chopped
$1/4$ cup shredded
  Parmesan cheese
Italian dressing
Salt and pepper to taste

Cook the pasta. Toss the olives, tomatoes, onion, celery, carrots and Parmesan together with the pasta. Mix with a creamy Italian dressing. Season with salt and pepper to taste.

Makes a great side dish for lunch.

# Wild Rice Salad

Wash the rice thoroughly by placing in a strainer and running under cold water. Place the rice in a saucepan with 2 cups of water. Bring to a boil. Reduce the heat and simmer, covered, for 35 minutes or until the kernels are tender. Uncover and fluff the rice with a fork. Drain off any excess liquid.

Toss the cooked rice with apples, celery, brown sugar and lemon juice. Mix the dressing ingredients together and mix with the salad. Refrigerate at least 2 hours before serving.

Cooking time: 35 minutes
Yield: 6 to 8 servings

$2/3$ cup wild rice
2 cups water
2 tart unpeeled apples, chopped (mix red and green apples)
2 stalks of celery, sliced
2 tablespoons brown sugar
1 tablespoon lemon juice

Dressing:
$1/2$ cup low-fat yogurt
$1/2$ cup light mayonnaise

*"The chef is excellent—as we can tell by the way our clothes fit after eating here for a week—very tight!!"*

*Bill, Pam & Emily*
*New Hartford, New York*

# Hot Fudge Cake

Cooking time: 35 to 40
  minutes
Yield: 9 servings
Temperature: 350 degrees

1 cup flour
3/4 cup sugar
4 tablespoons cocoa
2 teaspoons baking
  powder
1/4 teaspoon salt
1/2 cup milk
2 tablespoons oil
1 teaspoon vanilla
1 cup brown sugar
1 3/4 cups hot water

Preheat the oven to 350 degrees. Combine the flour, sugar, baking soda, salt, milk, oil and vanilla together in a bowl. Mix the brown sugar and cocoa together and sprinkle over the mixture in the bowl. Pour the mixture into an 8 x 8-inch cake pan.

Pour the hot water over the top of the cake mix in the pan. DO NOT STIR. Bake in the oven for 35 to 40 minutes or until done

Top with whipped cream or ice cream.

*"Wonderful Food."*

*Dan*
*Chicago, Illinois*

# Pumpkin Cake

Preheat the oven to 375 degrees. Beat together the eggs, oil and sugar until well blended. Add the pumpkin and mix. In a separate bowl, mix the flour, baking powder, baking soda, salt and spices. Gradually add the dry ingredients to the wet. Mix until smooth. Pour the batter into an 11 x 17-inch jellyroll pan. Bake for 20 minutes or until a cake tester inserted into the middle comes out clean.

Top with a cream cheese frosting (see index).

Cooking time: 20 minutes
Yield: 12 servings
Temperature: 375 degrees

4 large eggs
1 cup oil
2 cups sugar
2 cups pumpkin
2 cups flour
2 teaspoons baking powder
1 teaspoon baking soda
1/2 teaspoon salt
2 1/2 teaspoons cinnamon
1 teaspoon ginger
1 teaspoon cloves
1 teaspoon nutmeg

# Frosted Oatmeal Squares

Cooking time: 5 to 6 minutes
Yield: 24 squares
Temperature: microwave

1 cup butter or margarine, melted
4 cups quick cooking rolled oats
1 cup packed brown sugar
$1/2$ cup corn syrup
1 - 6 ounce bag of chocolate chips
$3/4$ cup peanut butter

In a large bowl, combine the butter, rolled oats, brown sugar and corn syrup, mixing well. Pat the mixture into the bottom of a 9 x 13-inch glass dish. Microwave on high for 3 $1/2$ to 4 minutes. Stir the mixture one more time, then pat down again and set aside.

In a small bowl, combine the chocolate chips and peanut butter. Microwave* on high until the chocolate melts (approximately 1 $1/2$ minutes). Stir together and spread over the top of the oat mixture. Refrigerate until firm. Cut into 2-inch squares and store in the refrigerator.

*Some microwaves cook at different speeds, so adjust time according to your particular unit.

# Ice Cream Dessert

Melt the margarine and mix together with the brown sugar, flour and chopped walnuts. Spread the mixture on a cookie sheet and brown in the oven until crumbly, stirring often. Sprinkle $1/2$ of the mixture on the bottom of a 9 x 13-inch baking pan. Layer in the ice cream, then sprinkle the remaining mix on top. Place the baking pan in the freezer and let freeze solid.

We use either a peppermint or cinnamon flavored ice cream in this dessert, but any flavor will do. Cinnamon seems to be the favorite among our guests. This is a great dessert on a hot day!

**Yield: 12 to 15 servings**

8 ounces margarine
$1/2$ cup brown sugar
$1/2$ cup flour
$1/2$ cup walnuts, chopped
$1/2$ gallon ice cream

# Salmon or Swordfish Marinade

2 tablespoons lemon
   juice
2 tablespoons Dijon
   mustard
1/4 teaspoon garlic

Mix all ingredients and spread over fish steaks just prior to grilling.

This is served when we do our steak cookout, as an alternative to beef. It is extremely popular with our guests.

*"The food is terrific."*

*Barbara & Gil*
*Littleton, Colorado*

# C Lazy U Ranch

**C Lazy U Ranch**
**PO Box 379**
**Granby, CO 80446**
**(970) 887-3344**
**FAX (970) 887-3917**
**www.clazyu.com**
**ranch@CLazyU.com**
**The Clark Murray Family**
**Elevation 8,200 feet**

The C Lazy U Ranch lies in Willow Creek Valley, overlooking the Continental Divide, six miles from Granby, Colorado. The Ranch owns approximately 2,000 acres with access to an additional 3,000.

The C Lazy U Ranch has received the prestigious AAA five diamond rating continuously since its inception in 1977, and the Mobil five star rating since 1978. All guest units meet these standards, but vary in size, set-up and decor. Rooms do not have phones or televisions. Seventy-five percent of the accommodations have fireplaces. Some also have private Jacuzzis and stocked refrigerators.

Their famous meals are served family style, ten to a table. Entrés vary from Black Angus Prime Rib cooked on an open grill to Roasted Rack of Lamb with Rosemary Apricot Glaze. Dress is casual.

The 10,000 square foot indoor arena provides a comfortable option for winter horseback riders. Guests can choose between riding our beautiful trails or practicing their skills indoors.

Cross-country and telemark ski equipment as well as figure and hockey skates and equipment are available in the Nordic Nook. For touring, metal edged Karhu skis and sturdy Asolo and Merrell boots make the hills easier. Special telemark skis and boots make skiing the back country powder easier as well. They carry some Revolution short skis for fun.

Fall offers the same activities and fun as the summer, but Adults Only to create a quiet atmosphere. The weather is mild with crisp mornings and warm afternoons, and the fall colors are spectacular. Guests can practice horsemanship skills in the new 10,000 square. ft. indoor arena or on the freshly mown hay meadows.

During the Summer Season, they have a week-long minimum stay, Sunday to Sunday., with full, supervised Children's and Teen's programs. During our Baby Seasons, early June and late August, babysitters will be available for children under three years. Otherwise, nannies are required for the regular Summer Season.

The Denver Airport is a two hour drive from the ranch. Private shuttle services are available, however, it is recommended you rent a car for personal convenience. Two local airports, Granby (VFR) and Kremmling (IFR), can accommodate private jets.

# Beef Tenderloin with Maple Sage Sauce

Roast the garlic. Add to the pot with the cream and reduce. Add the maple syrup, sage and beef base to taste. Simmer and thicken with the roux.

Serve over medallions of beef tenderloin.

For variation, you can serve this with a roasted garlic and brie cream sauce instead. Reduce the cream and then, in place of the maple and sage, add brie. Add the beef base and prepare as before. Thicken with roux, if needed.

Yield: 10 servings

10 - 6 ounce beef
    tenderloin medallions,
    cooked
$1/3$ cup roasted garlic,
    sautéed until brown in
    olive oil
$2/3$ quart heavy
    whipping cream
Maple syrup and sugar
    to taste
Small bunch of sage
Beef base to taste

*"The ranch is clearly one of the most memorable family vacations we have ever taken. It probably ranks highest on our list of trips where there were so many different and varying activities and experiences."*

# Citrus Encrusted Pork Tenderloin

Cooking time: 35 to 40
  minutes
Yield: 6 servings
Temperature: 325 degrees

1 pork tenderloin
Zest of 2 lemons
Zest of 1 orange
1 tablespoon minced
  garlic
1 tablespoon cracked
  black pepper
1 tablespoon fresh
  thyme

Preheat the oven to 325 degrees. Trim the tenderloin, making sure that you take off the silver. Mix together the lemon and orange zest, garlic and pepper and spread out on a cutting board. Roll the tenderloin in the coating, making sure to cover all of the tenderloin. Place on a roasting rack in the oven for 35 to 40 minutes.

*"The fabulous food, our beautiful room and the wonderful surrounding facilities can't be beat. But more important is the feeling of being one big family."*

# Chicken Alfredo with Vegetables

Cut the peppers and onions into strips; dice the zucchini into small pieces. Cut tops off the broccoli and cut into small pieces.

In a saucepan, add the vegetables and garlic; sauté with olive oil until al dente (still crunchy). Add the cream and white wine. Simmer over low heat and reduce by half.

Grill or pan fry the chicken, then cut into small $1/4$-inch thick strips. After all preparation is complete, add the chicken strips to the sauce. Thicken the sauce with cornstarch mixed with cold water. After the sauce thickens, season to taste with salt and white pepper.

*"The wait staff took such good care of us and made each meal an event. The meals were superb, as always...delicious with a fine presentation, family style!"*

Yield: 6 to 8 servings

$1/4$ gallon heavy cream
$9 \, 2/3$ ounces mushrooms
$3/4$ onion
$3/4$ zucchini
$2/3$ bunch broccoli
$1/3$ green bell pepper
$1/3$ yellow bell pepper
$1/3$ red bell pepper
$1/3$ tablespoon minced garlic
$1/8$ cup white wine
Salt to taste
White pepper to taste
$1 \, 1/4$ pounds chicken breast halves
Corn starch to thicken, about $1/2$ cup

# Sesame Ginger Chicken

**Yield: 4 servings**

2 tablespoons soy sauce
2 tablespoons honey
1 tablespoon sesame
seeds, toasted
$1/2$ teaspoon ground
ginger
4 boneless chicken
breasts (1 pound)

Mix the soy sauce, honey, sesame seed and ginger together in a small bowl; set aside. Flatten the chicken to approximately $1/4$-inch in thickness. Add the chicken to the sauce and let sit for about 30 minutes. Grill over a hot fire.

*"What a wonderful job your staff did to make our stay memorable. The setting and facility at C Lazy U are special, but service is what always separates the good from the great!"*

# Tarragon Chicken

In a skillet, heat the butter and oil. Add the chicken and cook until golden on both sides. Remove from the pan and drain on paper towels. Coarsely chop 1 leek. Add leek to the pan and cook until slightly softened. Add the vinegar and boil rapidly until the quantity is reduced by half. Add the wine and stock. Return the chicken to the pan, cover and simmer 25 minutes. Cut the remaining leeks and carrots into matchstick strips. Cook 4 to 5 minutes in separate pans of boiling, salted water. Drain; rinse under cold water. Drain again.

Remove the chicken from the skillet. Arrange on a warm serving dish. Strain the cooking liquid. Bring to a boil. In a bowl, whisk together the créme fraiche, cornstarch, mustard and 2 tablespoons pan juices. Return the mixture to the pan. Add the carrots, leeks and tarragon. Cook over low heat until the sauce thickens. Season with salt and pepper.

Spoon the sauce over chicken pieces and garnish with tarragon sprigs.

Yield: 10 servings

5 tablespoons butter or
  margarine
2 $1/2$ tablespoons
  vegetable oil
25 large chicken breast
  halves, skinned
5 large leeks
5 tablespoons tarragon
  vinegar
1 $2/3$ cups white wine
2 $1/2$ cups chicken stock
2 $1/2$ large carrots
1 $2/3$ cups créme fraiche
  or whipping cream
2 $1/2$ teaspoons
  cornstarch
5 teaspoons fresh
  tarragon, chopped
Salt
Pepper
Tarragon sprig, to
  garnish

# Broccoli Pasta Soufflé

Cooking time: 35 to 40
  minutes
Yield: 10 servings
Temperature: 400 degrees

1 1/4 pounds broccoli
7 1/2 tablespoons butter
7 1/2 tablespoons
  all-purpose flour
3 1/8 cups milk
2 cups shredded
  Cheddar cheese
Salt
Pepper
Nutmeg
10 egg whites
7 1/2 egg yolks
5 cups pasta shells,
  cooked

Divide broccoli into small flowerets. Cook in a medium-sized saucepan in a small amount of boiling salted water until crisp-tender. Drain.

Preheat oven to 400 degrees. In a large saucepan, melt the butter; stir in the flour. Cook for 2 minutes, stirring constantly, over low heat. Gradually stir in the milk. Cook, stirring constantly, until the sauce thickens. Simmer gently for 5 minutes. Stir in the cheese. Season to taste with salt, pepper and nutmeg. Let cool slightly.

In a large bowl, whisk the egg whites until stiff, but not dry. Stir the egg yolks into the cheese sauce, then stir in the broccoli and pasta. Stir 1 tablespoon of egg whites into the mixture; gently fold in remaining egg whites.

Grease a 2-quart soufflé dish (7 3/4 x 3 3/4-inch). Pour in the mixture, then bake for approximately 30 minutes or until the soufflé is well risen, golden brown and just set in the middle. Serve at once.

This recipe may also be baked in individual soufflé dishes, reducing the baking time to 20 minutes.

# Tomato Chowder

Sauté the carrots, celery, onions and potatoes in olive oil with garlic and thyme. Add tomatoes and tomato juice. Cook for 15 minutes. Add the chicken stock and bay leaf. Cook for another 45 minutes. Thicken soup with roux and season to taste.

Cooking time: 1 hour
Yield: 10 servings

$3/4$ cup diced onion
$3/4$ cup diced celery
$3/4$ cup diced carrots
$3/4$ cup peeled diced
  potatoes
1 cup fresh diced
  tomatoes
$1/4$ gallon chicken stock
$1/8$ gallon tomato juice
$1/4$ tablespoon minced
  garlic
Salt to taste
White pepper to taste
$1/4$ bay leaf
$1/8$ tablespoon dry
  thyme

*"Once again you have distinguished yourselves by providing outstanding quality and service. In addition to the excellent food, accommodations and recreation options, we believe that your positive and friendly attitudes create the 5 Star/5 Diamond awards which bring your guests (and ourselves) back year after year."*

# Tortellini Soup

Cooking time: 2 to 3
  hours
Yield: 10 servings

12 $^3/_4$ ounces Italian
  sausage
$^3/_4$ clove chopped garlic
$^1/_3$ medium onion,
  chopped
2 $^1/_3$ cups beef broth
$^1/_3$ cup water
1 $^2/_3$ cups fresh
  tomatoes, chopped and
  peeled
1 $^1/_3$ cups tomato sauce
1 large carrot, peeled
  and chopped
$^3/_4$ tablespoon oregano
$^3/_4$ teaspoon basil, dried
$^3/_4$ tablespoon parsley,
  dried
$^2/_3$ bay leaf
$^1/_3$ zucchini, chopped
3 or 4 - 10 ounce
  packages fresh or
  frozen tortellini, cheese
  filled only
1 package of spinach
  pasta for color

Brown the sausage, keeping it in large chunks. Remove the browned meat from the pan, reserving 8 tablespoons of the oil. Sauté the onion and garlic in the reserved drippings. In a large soup pot, mix all the ingredients, with the exception of the zucchini and tortellini. Add the sausage. Bring to a boil and then lower the heat. Simmer the soup for 2 to 3 hours. Approximately 45 minutes before serving, add the tortellini and zucchini; simmer until the tortellini are done.

Garnish with fresh grated Parmesan cheese.

# Green Chili

Sauté the carrots, onions, and celery in oil for 5 minutes. Add the pork and brown it off. Once the pork is browned, add the garlic, cumin, chili powder and diced tomatoes. Cook for another 10 minutes. After 10 minutes reduce the heat, add the chicken stock and cook for 1 hour. Use roux to thicken the mixture and season to taste with salt, pepper, chili powder and garlic. Garnish with cilantro.

Cooking time: 85 to 90 minutes
Yield: 10 servings

$1/2$ cup diced carrots
$1/2$ cup diced celery
$1/2$ cup diced onion
8 $1/8$ ounces diced pork
$1/8$ gallon chicken stock
$1/2$ tablespoon cumin
$1/2$ tablespoon granulated garlic
$1/4$ tablespoon chili powder
$1/3$ tablespoon cilantro
$1/8$ gallon diced tomatoes
Salt and pepper to taste

# Roasted Garlic Maple Sauce

**Yield: 10 servings**

1/8 cup diced garlic
1/8 cup olive oil
1/3 quart heavy
   whipping cream
1/3 cup maple syrup
1/4 bunch whole fresh
   sage
Beef bouillon to taste

Roast the garlic in olive oil, until golden brown in color. In a saucepan add the roasted garlic and olive oil to the heavy cream and reduce by a third. When reduced, add the maple syrup, sage, and beef bouillon to taste. Thicken with roux if needed.

Roux is equal parts of butter and flour (1 cup of butter to 1 cup of flour).

# Wild Mushroom Sauce

In a saucepan, reduce the mushrooms and bourbon, until the alcohol has evaporated. Add the cream and reduce by half. Once the cream has reduced, add the blue cheese and beef bouillon to taste. Add more or less blue cheese depending on how much you like blue cheese.

*"The Murray family and staff should be proud of the consistent and genuine service and comforts C Lazy U provides. Every person I met was truly friendly and service oriented...a comfortable and gracious resort."*

Yield: 10 servings

1 $1/2$ cups assorted
   mushrooms (Shitake,
   Portabello, oyster and
   domestic)
$1/4$ cup bourbon
$1/4$ quart heavy
   whipping cream
$1/3$ cup blue cheese
$1/4$ tablespoon beef
   bouillon

# Drowsy Water Ranch

**Drowsy Water Ranch**
**PO Box 147A**
**Granby, CO  80446**
**(800) 845-2292**
**(970) 725-3456**
**dwrken@aol.com**
**Ken and Randy Sue Fosha**
**Elevation 8,200 feet**

Drowsy Water Ranch is a genuine western ranch located on 640 acres in Colorado's beautiful Rocky Mountains. The ranch borders thousands of acres of backcountry and the Arapaho National Forest. They are close to Rocky Mountain National Park, the Colorado River and the famous ranch country of Middle Park. It is only a short drive to Granby, Shadow Mountain and Grand Lake.

At an elevation of over 8,000 feet, the days are warm and filled with sunshine, while the nights are cool enough to warrant sleeping under a blanket even in the middle of July. Accommodations are first class and carefully maintained by the staff every day. Western decor adds to the true ranch experience.

The ranch offers a complete program of horseback riding, swimming, horseshoes, steak cookouts, trout fishing, square dancing, jeep trips, song fests, campfires, well the list just goes on and on. Guests are free to choose whatever they want, based on how much or how little they want to do with their vacation time. There are also two challenging 18-hole mountain golf courses nearby, as well as boating and lake fishing. Guests are also invited to try their luck at fishing in Drowsy Water Creek, where brook and rainbow trout abound.

For the hunting enthusiast, the ranch boasts some of Colorado's finest mule deer and elk. The adjacent Elk Mountain and Cabin Creek areas also offer abundant game. The ranch operates a big game hunting camp beginning in mid-October and running through early November each year.

Most of the meals on the ranch are served family style in the dining room, but outdoor meals are the highlights of a visit. Be prepared to eat breakfast on a mountaintop or experience an open hearth barbecue. Chuckwagon lunches are also served or the visitor might find themselves eating lunch on the trail. Whatever the venue, there is always plenty to eat, lovingly prepared from recipes handed down for generations. Sometimes the guests eat gourmet cuisine, while other times it is simple western fare, but it is always delicious.

# Egg - Cheese Casserole

Beat the eggs and milk in a mixing bowl. Add the bread, mustard and sausage. Gently mix in the cheese. Pour into a greased 9 x 13-inch pan. Refrigerate overnight.

Preheat the oven to 350 degrees. Bake for 55 minutes or until done.

For variety, you can add cooked spinach, bacon bits or mushrooms.

Cooking time: 55 minutes
Yield: 6 servings
Temperature: 350 degrees

6 eggs
2 cups milk
6 slices cubed crustless bread
1/4 teaspoon dry mustard
1 pound pork sausage, cooked
1 cup Velveeta cheese
1 cup longhorn/Cheddar cheese

*"There's an old fashioned goodness to this ranch that brings to mind another century. When the world was less hurried and neighbors cared about neighbors."*

*J.H.*
*Los Angeles, California*

# Beef Vegetable Casserole

Cooking time: 1 hour

1 pound ground beef
1 cup water
1 can gravy
$1/2$ teaspoon salt
$1/4$ teaspoon pepper
$1/2$ teaspoon poultry
   seasoning
1 onion, sliced
1 to 2 carrots, sliced
Salt
4 potatoes, sliced
$1/3$ cup shredded sharp
   Cheddar cheese
Paprika

In a Dutch oven, cook the meat until it loses its red color. Add 1 cup of water and bring to a boil. Stir in the gravy; mix until thickened. Stir in the salt, pepper and poultry seasoning. Top with a layer of onions and carrots. Season with salt. Top with potatoes and season with salt. Cover and let simmer for 1 hour. Sprinkle with cheese and paprika, heat until cheese melts.

*"Each day one of my kids asks me how many days until we can go back to the Ranch? And I tell them 287 more days kids. Yep we're going back next summer!"*

*J.T.*
*West Palm Beach, Florida*

# Spaghetti Pie

Preheat the oven to 350 degrees. Cook the spaghetti; drain. Stir in the butter, eggs and Parmesan cheese. Form the mixture into a pie pan. In a skillet, cook the beef, pork, onion and green pepper until tender; drain. Stir in the tomatoes, tomato paste, sugar, garlic and oregano and continue heating. Spread the cottage cheese over the spaghetti mixture. Fill the pie with the tomato mixture. Bake uncovered for 20 minutes. Sprinkle mozzarella on top. Bake an additional 5 minutes.

Cooking time: 25 minutes
Yield: 6 servings
Temperature: 350 degrees

6 ounces spaghetti
2 tablespoons butter
2 beaten eggs
$1/3$ cup Parmesan cheese
1 pound ground beef
1 pound pork sausage
$1/2$ cup chopped onion
$1/4$ cup chopped green
   pepper
8 ounces canned
   tomatoes, cut up
6 ounces tomato paste
1 teaspoon sugar
1 teaspoon oregano
$1/2$ teaspoon garlic
1 cup cottage cheese
$1/2$ cup shredded
   mozzarella

# Cheesy Potato Soup

2 cups cubed potatoes
1 cup chopped carrots
$^1/_2$ cup chopped celery
$^1/_2$ cup chopped onion
$^1/_2$ cup hot water
1 chicken bouillon cube
$^1/_4$ teaspoon salt
$^1/_8$ teaspoon pepper
1 $^1/_2$ cups milk
1 cup shredded Cheddar
  cheese
1 tablespoon fresh
  parsley, chopped

In a 2-quart saucepan, combine the potatoes, carrots, celery, onion, water, bouillon, salt and pepper. Cover and cook until the vegetables are tender. Blend in a food processor until coarsely pureed. Return to the saucepan. Blend in the milk and cheese. Cover and cook until the cheese melts. Garnish with fresh, chopped parsley.

# Carrot Cake

Preheat the oven to 350 degrees. Mix the flour, sugar, baking soda, cinnamon and salt in a bowl. Add the carrots, oil, eggs and vanilla. Beat well. Stir in the pineapple, coconut, and walnuts. Pour into a 13 x 18-inch pan. Bake for 40 minutes. Test with a toothpick. Let cool before frosting.

To make the frosting, blend the cream cheese, butter, and vanilla until smooth. Add the sugar and beat until smooth.

*"Thank you for such a fun and memorable vacation. You have such a beautiful ranch and Colorado is so AWE inspiring!"*

*R.M.*
*Taylor Ridge, IL*

Cooking time: 40 minutes
Yield : 40 servings
Temperature: 350 degrees

4 cups flour
2 $1/2$ cups sugar
3 teaspoons baking soda
3 teaspoons cinnamon
$1/2$ teaspoon salt
2 $1/2$ cups cooked carrots
1 $1/3$ cups oil
4 eggs
1 teaspoon vanilla
2 cups crushed
   pineapple, drained
1 $1/3$ cups coconut
1 cup chopped walnuts

Cream Cheese Frosting:
2 - 3 ounce packages
   cream cheese, softened
$1/2$ cup butter or
   margarine, softened
1 teaspoon vanilla
4 cups confectioners
   sugar

# Peanut Butter Pie

Cooking time: 8 minutes
Yield: 1 pie
Temperature: 350 degrees

2 - 3 ounce packages
  cream cheese, softened
3/4 cup powdered sugar
1/2 cup crunchy peanut
  butter
2 tablespoons milk
2 envelopes (1 1/2 ounces
  each) whipped topping
  mix
1 cup cold milk, divided
1 teaspoon vanilla,
  divided
3 tablespoons chopped
  roasted peanuts
1 tablespoon grated
  sweet chocolate

Peanut-Graham
Cracker Crust:
1 1/4 cups Graham
  cracker crumbs
1 tablespoon brown
  sugar
2 tablespoons ground
  peanuts
1/4 cup butter, melted

Prepare the crust first. Combine the graham cracker crumbs, brown sugar, and peanuts. Stir in the butter; mix well. Press the mixture firmly and evenly into a 9-inch pie plate. Bake at 350 degrees for 8 minutes.

Combine the cream cheese and powdered sugar in a large mixing bowl; beat until light and fluffy. Add the peanut butter and 2 tablespoons milk; beat well. Add 2 tablespoons of the chopped roasted peanuts. Prepare 1 envelope of the whipped topping mix according to package directions, using 1/2 the milk and 1/2 teaspoon vanilla. Fold into the peanut butter mixture, and spoon into the baked crust.

Prepare the remaining envelope of whipped topping mix according to package directions, using the remaining milk and vanilla. Spread evenly over the peanut butter mixture. Garnish with peanuts and grated sweet chocolate. Chill at least 5 hours before serving.

# Chocolate Peanut Butter Brownies

Preheat the oven to 350 degrees. In a small saucepan, melt the chocolate and butter over low heat; set aside. In a mixing bowl, beat the eggs and sugar until light and pale in color. Add the flour and melted chocolate; stir well. Pour into a greased 9-inch square baking pan. Bake for 25 minutes or until the brownies test done. Cool.

For the filling, beat the sugar, peanut butter and butter in a mixing bowl. Stir in the cream or milk until the mixture reaches the desired spreading consistency. Spread over the cooled brownies; cover and chill until firm.

For the glaze, melt the chocolate and butter in a saucepan, stirring until smooth. Drizzle over the filling. Chill before cutting. Store in refrigerator.

Cooking time: 25 minutes
Yield: 5 dozen
Temperature: 350 degrees

Brownies:
2 squares (1 ounce each)
    unsweetened chocolate
$1/2$ cup butter or
    margarine
2 eggs
1 cup sugar
$1/2$ cup all-purpose flour

Filling:
1 $1/2$ cups confectioners
    sugar
$1/2$ cup creamy peanut
    butter
$1/4$ cup butter or
    margarine, softened
2 to 3 tablespoons light
    cream or milk

Glaze:
1 square (1 ounce) semi-
    sweet baking chocolate
1 tablespoon butter or
    margarine

# Pumpkin Bars

Cooking time: 20 to 25
 minutes
Yield: 20 servings
Temperature: 350 degrees

1 cup flour
1 cup sugar
1 teaspoon nutmeg
1/2 teaspoon cloves
1/2 teaspoon cinnamon
1 teaspoon baking
 powder
1/2 teaspoon salt
1/2 teaspoon baking soda
1 cup pumpkin pie
 filling
1/3 cup salad oil
1/4 cup milk
1 teaspoon vanilla
1/2 cup raisins

Topping:
3/4 cup brown sugar
1/4 cup soft margarine
2 tablespoons milk
1/2 cup chopped nuts

Preheat the oven to 350 degrees. Combine all the ingredients, except the raisins, and mix for 1 minute. Stir in the raisins. Pour the mixture into a greased 9 x 13-inch pan. Bake for 15 to 20 minutes.

Combine topping ingredients and spoon gently over the bars. Bake an additional 3 to 5 minutes, until light brown.

*"My mood improves as we hit the trail, a dozen dudes and dudettes playing cowboy and cowgirl for a week!"*

*P.K.*
*Daytona Beach, Florida*

# King Mountain Ranch

**King Mountain Ranch**
**PO Box 497**
**Granby, CO  80446**
**(800) 476-5464**
**(970) 887-2511**
**hosts@kingranchresort.com**
**Matt and Jennai Bachus**
**Elevation 9,000 feet**

Built as a private world class retreat and conference center, this exclusive ranch resort is now open for all to experience. Perched high up in the Rocky Mountains and surrounded by the Arapaho National Forest, the King Mountain Ranch offers a unique guest ranch vacation.

Activities at the ranch include horseback riding for all skill levels, a thirty acre lake for boating and trout fishing and a first class children's program available mid-June through August. Also enjoy their mountaintop skeet and trap  shooting range, indoor heated pool, hot tub, sauna, lighted tennis courts, antique bowling alley and guided hikes. Known for its beautiful scenery and restful atmosphere, the King Mountain Ranch offers exclusive enjoyment for their guests.

The ranch boasts spectacular gourmet and western cuisine. The meals are served next to a native stone fireplace in their spacious dining room overlooking the valley and the lake. Cowboy cookouts are held weekly. For those requiring special consideration, vegetarian and diet-friendly choices are available at every meal, along with a children's menu.

For a truly unique vacation in the splendor of the Colorado Rockies, come home to King Mountain Ranch, where making memories is their pleasure.

# Prime Rib

Cooking time: 3 1/2 hours
Yield: 15 to 20 servings
Temperature: 475 then
  300 degrees

1 whole prime rib
4 carrots, chopped
1 onion, diced
1/2 bunch celery, washed
  and diced
1 part kosher salt
1 part cracked black
  pepper
1 part garlic, chopped
1/2 part rosemary,
  chopped
2 cups red wine
3 cups beef stock

Preheat oven to 475 degrees. Chop the carrots, onion and celery, then place in a roasting pan. Set aside. Trim the excess fat off the prime rib, leaving just enough for flavor and moisture. Mix together the kosher salt, cracked black pepper, chopped garlic and chopped rosemary in the proportions stated. Rub the mixture into the roast and pat gently.

Place the prime rib atop the chopped vegetables in the roasting pan and place in the oven. Bake at 475 degrees for 20 minutes to sear the outside of the prime rib and lock in the juices. Reduce the heat to 300 degrees and let the meat slow roast for 2 1/2 to 3 hours or until the internal temperature is 115 degrees. Remove from the oven and let sit for 15 minutes.

While the meat is sitting, de-glaze the pan with 2 cups of red wine and pour into a saucepan. Heat on the stove to reduce by 1/3. Add in 3 cups of beef stock and reduce once more by 1/3. Strain this juice and use as au jus.

Serve the prime rib garnished with rosemary and vegetables. Drizzle the meat with au jus and serve with a baked potato, a horseradish and sour cream mix, and your favorite vegetables. Served every Wednesday evening here at the King Mountain Ranch.

# Grilled Ribeye with Tobacco Onions

Combine the liquid smoke, Worcestershire sauce, orange juice, brown sugar, soy sauce, salad oil, jerky seasoning, black pepper, shallots and garlic cloves in a stainless steel bowl. Place the ribeye steaks in the pan and marinate for at least 24 hours. Grill the steaks.

Slice the onions and separate. Toss the onions lightly in flour and deep fry in 350 degree oil until brown. Sprinkle over the steaks and serve.

Best if served on individual plates and garnished with onions and a vegetable. A tall sprig of sage adds height and texture to the plate.

There's nothing quite like a juicy grilled steak after a long day in the saddle. The golden tobacco onions complete this hearty ranch meal.

*"Thanks again for one of the most wonderful weeks I've ever spent. I felt as if I were saying goodbye to family when I left."*

*Memphis, Tennessee*

Cooking time: 1 hour
Yield: 4 servings
Temperature: 350 degrees

4 - 10 ounce ribeye
　steaks
2 to 3 medium onions
Flour
4 cups liquid smoke
4 cups Worcestershire
　sauce
4 cups orange juice
2 cups brown sugar
4 cups soy sauce
1 cup salad oil
4 tablespoons jerky
　seasoning
6 tablespoons cracked
　black pepper
4 shallots
4 garlic cloves
**Vegetable of your choice**

# Baked Chicken Breast Stuffed With Sautéed Spinach and Mushrooms

Cooking time: 45 minutes
Yield: 4 servings
Temperature: 350 degrees

4 ounces butter
4 ounces onion, minced
48 ounces mushrooms, minced
48 ounces spinach
32 ounces bread crumbs
16 ounces heavy cream
4 boneless, skinless chicken breasts
16 ounces dry white wine
Salt and pepper to taste
Flour

Preheat the oven to 350 degrees. To prepare the stuffing, sauté the onions in the butter, then add the mushrooms and spinach. Sauté briefly. Add the wine and cook until the contents are reduced by half. Add the bread crumbs and cook for 3 minutes. Add the heavy cream and bring to a boil. Remove the mixture from the heat and reserve.

Flatten the chicken breasts with a mallet, then season with salt and pepper. Place two tablespoons of the stuffing onto the flattened chicken breasts, then roll each up tight. Dredge the rolled chicken in the flour and pan fry in clarified butter until golden brown on all sides. Finish the chicken in the oven. Garnish with fresh, colorful vegetables and serve.

Best with fresh vegetables and fresh baked bread.

When deciding on a nightly menu, Chef DeNittis likes to provide options that please everyone. This dish is familiar and comfortable, yet unexpectedly delicious and impeccably presented.

# Chicken Pot Pie

Preheat oven to 375 degrees. Heat the butter in a large saucepan and sauté the garlic, onion, carrots, celery and mushrooms. Add in the flour and incorporate the butter. This forms a roux, which will serve as a thickening agent for the sauce. Add the herbs and then de glaze with white wine. Add the chicken stock and bring to a boil. Let this mixture simmer until it is reduced by 1/4. Add the heavy cream and let simmer once again, until the sauce has a nice smooth consistency. Season with salt and pepper, then add the chicken.

Place one puff pastry sheet into a casserole pan or cassolettes if you're doing individual servings. Pour in the mixture on top of the pastry. Cover with more of the puff pastry and trim off the excess (save the excess pastry to form decorative designs later). Brush the top of the pastry with a beaten egg and place the casserole in the oven. Bake until the puff pastry rises and turns golden brown. Garnish with decorative designs cut from the excess pastry.

Serve with fresh fruit or green salad.

*"I do not believe we could have enjoyed our stay any more—anywhere!"*

*Aylesbury, Bucks, England*

Cooking time: 20 to 30 minutes
Yield: 5 servings
Temperature: 375 degrees

1 cup flour
1 cup clarified butter
4 garlic cloves, minced
1 medium onion, diced
3 carrots, peeled, diced
3 celery stalks, diced
15 small red potatoes
2 cups button mushrooms, quartered
One stem fresh rosemary, leaves removed, chopped fine
One stem fresh thyme, leaves removed, chopped fine
One stem fresh oregano, leaves removed, chopped fine
4 cups chicken stock
1 cup white wine
1 cup heavy cream
5 pounds boneless, skinless chicken breasts, grilled, cooled, diced
2 puff pastry sheets
Salt and pepper to taste

# Blackened Buffalo Quesadilla

Cooking time: 30 minutes
Yield: 4 servings
Temperature: 350 degrees

4 - 6 ounce buffalo
  medallions
Blackened seasoning to
  taste
24 ounces of feta cheese
4 flour tortillas
2 tomatoes, sliced
Sour cream
Salsa
Cilantro

Preheat the oven to 350 degrees. Season the buffalo medallions with the blackened seasoning and bake in the oven to the desired doneness. Buffalo generally tastes better cooked medium rare to medium. Remove from the oven and slice. Spread the feta cheese generously around the flour tortilla. Place buffalo slices across half of each tortilla. Fold the tortillas in half and grill to desired crispness. Garnish with salsa, cilantro and a dollop of sour cream.

A western twist on a Mexican favorite. With its low fat and cholesterol, excellent flavor and old west appeal, buffalo meat works great for King Mountain Ranch's gourmet western cuisine.

*"The Ranch: wonderfully run, amazing children's program, super staff, fantastic food, the best!!"*

*Scituate, Massachusetts*

# Baja Seafood Taco with Purple Cabbage, Chayote and Nopali Cactus Slaw

To prepare the seafood marinade, combine the garlic, citrus juices, salt and pepper in a stainless steel bowl and whisk. Add the tequila and scallions, then whisk again. Place the shrimp and scallops in a stainless steel pan and pour the marinade over them, making sure to cover entirely. Let the shrimp and scallops marinate for at least 24 hours so the acid from the citrus will "cook" the seafood.

Place the red corn tortillas in a taco shell wire basket and deep fry until crisp. You can also bake the tortillas in the oven for a heart healthy variation.

To prepare the slaw, mix the cabbage, Chayote, Nopali cactus leaves, lime juice, salad oil, salt and pepper together in a stainless steel bowl. Place in the refrigerator and let chill for at least 2 hours so that all the flavors come out.

Fill the bottom of each taco shell with the slaw. Lay out 4 scallops and 4 shrimp in each shell and serve. Garnish with half cactus leaves.

Best served with a Pinot Grigio or ice cold Mexican beer.

This isn't your regular taco. With its Southwestern Mexican and American influences and incredible creative presentation, this is a fabulous entré. With a great wine from our list the dining enthusiast will be in ranch heaven.

Cooking time: 1 hour
Yield: 8 servings

32 - 21/25 count size shrimp, peeled and deveined
32 sea scallops
2 garlic cloves, minced
Juice of 6 lemons
Juice of 2 limes
1/2 cup Tequila
1 bunch scallions, chopped fine
8 red corn tortillas
Salt and pepper to taste

Purple Cabbage, Chayote and Cactus Slaw:
1 head purple cabbage, chopped fine
1 Chayote vegetable, shredded
4 Napoli cactus leaves, heads off, slice medium and julienne finely
Juice of 3 limes
2 tablespoons salad oil
Salt and pepper to taste

139

# Grilled Raspberry Wheat Marinated Quail

Cooking time: 30 minutes
Yield: 5 servings
Temperature: 350 degrees

5 quail
16 ounces raspberry
  wheat beer
2 shallots, minced
1 clove garlic
10 juniper berries
1 cup pureed
  raspberries
1 tablespoon powdered
  sugar
1 1/2 cups vegetable oil
1 teaspoon tarragon
Salt and pepper to taste

Garnish:
1/2 pound lentils,
  cleaned
1 ear roasted corn
1 small onion
1 carrot, quartered
2 cups chicken stock

Combine the beer, shallots, garlic, juniper berries, raspberries, sugar, oil, tarragon, salt and pepper together in a stainless steel bowl. Place the quail in the mixture and marinate for 4 to 6 hours. Preheat the grill and mark the quail. Preheat the oven to 350 degrees. Finish the quail in the oven for 3 minutes. Cut the birds lengthwise and across, then place on a plate.

Trim the corn off the husk and place in reserve. Simmer the lentils, carrots and onions in the chicken stock for 20 to 25 minutes or until tender, but not mushy. Strain and stir in the reserved corn. Season with salt and pepper to taste and spoon over the quail. Garnish with juniper berries and a tall sprig of sage.

Best if served with an ice cold raspberry wheat beer. At the King Mountain Ranch we use the local Estes Park Brewery's version called Long's Peak Raspberry Wheat. This creation by Chef Mark DeNittis has become one of our guests' favorites.

# Trout a'la Meuniere

Season the fish with salt and pepper, then dredge in flour. Heat the clarified butter in a pan and add the fish. Sauté until the fish is slightly brown and remove from heat. Remove the fish from the pan and put it aside, making sure to keep it warm. Remove the excess grease from the pan, then add the whole butter and cook it to beurre noisette. Add the lemon juice and parsley. Swirl the contents of the pan to lightly emulsify it. Pour the sauce over the fish.

Serve with fresh vegetables and rice. After a day of catching and releasing the 18 to 20 inch brook trout in our lake, some of our guests work up an appetite for this Rocky Mountain treat. They get the best of both worlds, all the fun of fishing and none of the work cooking.

*"Horseback riding, fishing, skeet shooting, children's program—it was all wonderful"*

*New York, New York*

Cooking time: 30 minutes
Yield: 4 servings
Temperature: medium

4 - 8 ounce trout, pan
   dressed
Salt and pepper to taste
Flour
Clarified butter
1 tablespoon whole
   butter
Juice of 1 lemon
2 teaspoons parsley,
   chopped

# King Mountain Ranch Casserole

Cooking time: 10 to 15
  minutes
Yield: 10 servings
Temperature: 375 degrees

2 cups flour
8 ounces clarified butter
3 cloves garlic, minced
2 cups mushrooms,
  washed and quartered
1 medium onion, peeled
  and diced small
1 cup diced chiles
1 red bell pepper,
  cleaned and diced
1 cup diced tomato
4 cups chicken stock
2 cups heavy cream
3/4 cup red chili powder
Salt and pepper to taste
1 package 12-inch
  round flour tortillas
2 cups shredded cheese
3 pounds boneless,
  skinless grilled chicken
  breast, cooled and
  diced

Preheat the oven to 375 degrees. In a large pan, sauté the garlic, onions, mushrooms, bell pepper and tomato in the butter, until they are tender. Add in the chili powder and diced chicken. Add the flour slowly, mixing well. Add in the chicken stock, heavy cream and green chiles and bring to a boil. Season with salt and pepper and let simmer to thicken.

Spray a large casserole dish with non-stick vegetable spray and line the bottom with a layer of flour tortillas. Pour the mixture over them, then add another layer of flour tortillas. Cover the top of the tortillas with shredded cheese, then place in the oven. Let bake until the cheese has melted. Garnish with Nopali cactus or sour cream.

Serve with a nice salad.

# Almond Cheesecake

Make the crust by first mixing the sugar and graham cracker crumbs together. Add just enough butter to moisten. Press the crumbs into the bottom of timbales or a spring form pan. Set aside.

Preheat the oven to 275 degrees. Cream the sugar and cream cheese together, scraping down the sides continuously in the process. Mix in the cornstarch and cream. Slowly add the eggs while mixing and scraping down the sides of the bowl. Pour the mixture into the crust and place in a hot water bath. Bake in the oven for 1 3/4 hours. Remove from the oven and water bath; chill.

To make the nut melange, start by mixing the sugar into 1/2 cup water and heating it to a boil. Continue boiling until the sugar water is slightly thickened. Mix the sugar water with the remaining melange ingredients and set aside.

Remove the cheesecake from the pan. Garnish with the nut melange and peaches.

*"We felt welcomed, pampered and very comfortable."*

*Fort Collins, Colorado*

Cooking time: 1 3/4 hours
Yield: 8 servings
Temperature: 275 degrees

Crust:
1/2 cup sugar
1/2 cup graham cracker
  crumbs
1/4 cup butter, melted

Cheesecake:
2 pounds cream cheese,
  room temperature
8 ounces sugar
1 tablespoon cornstarch
2 tablespoons cream
3 eggs
Almond extract

Nut Melange:
3/4 cup sugar
1/2 cup water
1/4 cup chopped walnuts
1/4 cup chopped pecans
1/4 cup almonds,
  slivered
2 tablespoons sun-dried
  cherries
2 tablespoons brandy

1 can peach halves and
  juice

# Latigo Ranch

**Latigo Ranch
PO Box 237
Kremmling, CO  80459
(800) 227-9655
(970) 724-9008
Yost and George Families
Elevation 9,000 feet**

From the moment guests arrive they know Latigo is a special place. Many want to linger on the front porch forever, taking in the breathtaking views and breathing in great lungfuls of fresh mountain air. From this vantage point the fortunate guest can take in over one hundred miles of the Continental Divide.

The Latigo staff and accommodations are as inviting as the scenery. Skilled wranglers will instruct beginners through advanced riders in horsemanship. These same, trained personnel will take guests on a variety of trail rides, such as family rides, sunset rides, breakfast rides and loping rides across some of the most spectacular terrain in the Rockies. Over two hundred miles of mountain trails wander through lush Aspen groves and expanses of wildflowers, to remote beaver ponds or high vistas.

Every week of the summer Latigo guests can work on a cattle roundup or participate in team penning. In September, more advanced riders can join Latigo's wranglers as they help neighboring ranches move hundreds of head of cattle from the high country to winter pastures in the valley. This is not a tourist event, but the real thing, a living vestige of the Old West.

Whether you come for the horseback riding, flyfishing or just to relax. Latigo offers the ideal vacation experience. Families love Latigo and you will too.

# Spinach Balls

Cooking time: 30 minutes
Yield: 40 balls
Temperature: 350 degrees
The uncooked balls will
  freeze very well

72 ounces frozen
  spinach, thawed,
  drained and chopped
12 eggs
6 cups croutons, blended
  medium fine
2 cups diced onions
1 1/2 cups Parmesan
  cheese
1 1/2 teaspoons thyme
1 tablespoon salt
1 1/2 teaspoons pepper
1 1/2 teaspoons garlic
  powder
2 1/4 cups melted
  margarine

Preheat the oven to 350 degrees. Mix all the ingredients together in a large mixing bowl. Shape into balls 1 1/2-inch in diameter and place onto a baking sheet. Bake for 30 minutes. Normally we serve 3 balls per adult.

We often make a big batch, then bake only what we are serving that evening. The rest can be frozen and used on a later date.

*"Best vacation we have ever had. We'll tell all!"*

# Zippy Carrots

Preheat the oven to 350 degrees. Layer $1/2$ of the carrots into a baking dish, then cover with $1/2$ the cheese. Add the rest of the carrots, then the remaining cheese.

Sauté the onions in the margarine. Blend in the flour and seasonings and cook for 1 minute. Gradually add the milk, stirring until thickened. Pour the sauce over the carrot/cheese layers.

Combine the breadcrumbs, margarine and bacon. Sprinkle over the top of the carrot mixture in the baking dish. Bake for approximately 30 minutes.

This dish can be prepared ahead of time and baked later. Increase the baking time, if starting with a cold dish.

*"Horseback riding was fantastic! The rides so varied. Wranglers were very considerate of where we were in our experience, and very thorough in their instruction."*

Cooking time: 30 minutes
Yield: 16 servings
Temperature: 350 degrees

12 cups sliced carrots, blanched until tender crisp
12 slices Swiss cheese
1 cup diced onion
$1/2$ cup margarine
6 tablespoons flour
2 teaspoons salt
2 teaspoons chili powder
4 cups milk
2 cups soft breadcrumbs
$1/4$ cup melted margarine
10 slices bacon, cooked and crumbled

# Creamy Tomato Soup

Cooking time: 10 minutes
Yield: 4 servings

2 tablespoons margarine
3 tablespoons flour
2 teaspoons sugar
1/2 teaspoon salt
1/8 teaspoon pepper
1/2 teaspoon onion
   powder
Dash of garlic powder
Dash of basil
Dash of oregano
Dash of thyme
2 cups tomato juice
2 cups milk

Melt the margarine in a saucepan. Blend the flour, sugar, salt, pepper, onion powder and the spices into the margarine. Cook and stir for 1 minute. Gradually blend in the tomato juice and bring to a boil. Add the milk and heat through.

Serve with grilled cheese sandwiches. It's nearly as quick as those big name commercial soups and tastes better! True comfort food.

*"I learned more in one week about horseback riding than I thought possible. This week was truly a relaxing, yet adventurous vacation...a challenge to our abilities and definitely a learning process."*

# Southwestern Couscous

Sauté the onion, peppers, mushrooms, carrots and garlic in the olive oil for 5 minutes. Add the chicken broth, cumin, salt and pepper. Bring the mixture to a boil and cook for an additional 5 minutes. Add the couscous, stir and cover. Turn off the heat and let the mixture sit for approximately 10 minutes before serving.

This is a nice alternative to traditional starch dishes.

*"I felt comfortable after my first week of riding—look forward to many more."*

Cooking time: 20 minutes
Yield: 8 to 10 servings
Can be stored in the
　refrigerator for up to a
　week

2 tablespoons olive oil
$1/4$ cup chopped onion
$1/2$ cup chopped green
　or red pepper
$1/2$ cup chopped
　mushrooms
$1/2$ cup chopped carrots
1 clove garlic, minced
1 $3/4$ cups chicken broth
1 teaspoon cumin
1 teaspoon salt
$1/4$ teaspoon pepper
1 can garbanzo beans,
　rinsed and drained
$3/4$ cup couscous

# Korean Salad Dressing

Yield: 40 servings

Store in the refrigerator
 for up to one month

1 cup canola oil

1/2 cup white vinegar

3/4 cup sugar

1/4 cup brown sugar

1/3 cup ketchup

1 tablespoon
 Worcestershire Sauce

1 medium onion,
 chopped

Dash of salt

Combine all the ingredients together in a blender and mix until smooth.

Excellent served over a salad of spinach leaves, bean sprouts, water chestnuts, hard boiled eggs and bacon bits.

*"We'll be back! The meals were excellent—loved the variety, and the 'service with a smile' made every meal that much more enjoyable."*

# Strawberry Pretzel Jell-O Salad

Preheat the oven to 350 degrees. Mix the crushed pretzels, 3 tablespoons sugar and melted margarine together. Press into a 9 x 13-inch pan to form a crust. Bake in the oven for 10 minutes. Remove and allow to cool.

Mix the cream cheese, remaining sugar and whipped topping together and spread over the cooled crust. Chill.

Mix the strawberry Jell-O, boiling water and chopped strawberries together. When softly set, pour over the top of the cream cheese mixture in the pan. Chill until the Jell-O is set.

*"I felt spoiled at each meal."*

Cooking time: 10 minutes
Yield: 15 servings
Temperature: 350 degrees
Make 4 hours ahead of
  time

8 ounces crushed
  pretzels
3 tablespoons sugar
3/4 cup melted
  margarine
8 ounces cream cheese
1 cup sugar
Whipped topping
6 ounces strawberry
  Jell-O mix
2 cups boiling water
16 ounces chopped
  strawberries

# Raspberry Dijon Salad Dressing

Yield: 12 servings
Can be stored in the
  refrigerator for up to a
  week

1/2 cup sour cream
2 tablespoons country
  Dijon mustard
1/4 cup honey
3 tablespoons raspberry
  vinegar
1 tablespoon dried
  parsley
1 tablespoon poppy
  seeds
1 1/2 teaspoons lime
  juice

Whisk all the ingredients together and chill.

*"As my 13 year old son said, 'Hey mom, I ate lots of really good, nutritious stuff all week—and I didn't even miss junk food'."*

# Parmesan Mini Loaves

Mix the dry yeast and warm water together in a large mixing bowl. Add the gluten flour, margarine, egg, sugar, salt, onion, Italian seasoning and garlic salt. Beat on low speed for 30 seconds. Increase to medium speed and beat for an additional 2 minutes.

Stir the bread flour and Parmesan cheese into the bread dough and beat until smooth. Cover the bowl and let the dough rise. Spread into mini loaf pans that have been sprayed with a non-stick vegetable oil spray. Brush the tops with melted margarine and sprinkle with some additional Parmesan. Cover and let rise again, until doubled in size. Place in a preheated 350 degree oven and bake for 35 minutes or until done. Allow the loaves to cool for 10 minutes in the pans before removing.

Cooking time: 35 minutes
Yield: 6 loaves
Temperature: 350 degrees
Stores well frozen

1 tablespoon yeast
1 cup warm water
2 cups high gluten bread
   flour
$1/4$ cup softened
   margarine
1 egg
2 tablespoons sugar
1 teaspoon salt
1 $1/2$ teaspoons dried
   minced onion
$1/2$ teaspoon Italian
   seasoning
$1/2$ teaspoon garlic salt
1 cup bread flour
$1/3$ cup Parmesan cheese

*"I can't think of a word to describe how outstanding, how superb, how excellent every part of the food was! It was a delight to be served by your staff, and I do mean served, and it was an honor to eat!"*

# Overnight Potato Rolls

Cooking time: 10 to 15
  minutes
Yield: 30 rolls
Temperature: 400 degrees
Dough can be made up
  ahead of time and stored
  for up to 1 week in the
  refrigerator.

1 tablespoon yeast
1 teaspoon sugar
1 1/2 cups warm water
1 teaspoon salt
2/3 cup sugar
2/3 cup oil
1 cup mashed potatoes
2 eggs
7 cups flour

Dissolve the yeast and teaspoon of sugar in warm water in a large mixing bowl. Add the salt, remaining sugar, oil, mashed potatoes and eggs, stirring until well blended. Add 3 cups of the flour, stirring until smooth. Gradually add the rest of the flour. Knead for 5 minutes. Place the dough in a greased bowl and cover with plastic wrap. Refrigerate until needed, but for at least 12 hours.

Remove the dough from the refrigerator and roll out to a thickness of 3/4 of an inch. Cut out the rolls and place on a baking sheet. Spray with a non-stick vegetable spray, cover with plastic wrap and let rise in a warm place until doubled in size. Bake in a preheated 400 degree oven until lightly browned.

*"As in any business it is the people that make the difference and your staff was great; I know they work hard at remembering everyone's name and that effort is very impressive and certainly creates a friendly atmosphere."*

# Fluffy Strawberry Pie

Beat the cream cheese until fluffy. Add the condensed milk. Stir in the strawberries and lemon juice. Beat the whipping cream until peaks form. Fold into the strawberry mixture. Pour into the crusts and freeze until firm.

Serve the pie frozen. Cut and garnish with additional strawberries, if desired.

*"We appreciate having so many choices for meals. The salads, baked goods are an excellent touch."*

Yield: 3 pies
Stores frozen indefinitely

3 graham cracker pie
   crusts
3 ounces softened cream
   cheese
14 ounces sweetened
   condensed milk
1 $1/2$ cups pureed
   strawberries
3 tablespoons lemon
   juice
1 cup whipping cream

# Pumpkin Ice Cream Pie

Yield: 4 pies
Stores frozen for one
   month

8 cups crushed
   gingersnaps
2 cups pumpkin
1 1/2 cups sugar
1 teaspoon salt
1 teaspoon ginger
1 teaspoon cinnamon
1/2 teaspoon nutmeg
1 cup chopped pecans
1/2 gallon vanilla
   ice cream, softened

Press 1/2 of the crushed gingersnaps into 4 pie pans. Mix the pumpkin, sugar, salt, ginger, cinnamon, nutmeg and pecans. Combine thoroughly. Fold the pumpkin mixture into the ice cream. Pour into the pie shells. Sprinkle with the reserved crushed gingersnaps. Freeze until ready to serve.

*"The meals were excellent in all respects. Even the sack lunches were 5 star quality and quantity."*

# Incredible Latigo Dinner Muffins

Preheat oven to 350 degrees. Mix the flour, sugar and baking powder together. Cut the butter into the dry ingredients. Stir in the buttermilk and mix until just moistened through. Spoon into greased muffin tins and bake. Serve warm.

Cooking time: 35 to 45 minutes
Yield: 12 muffins
Temperature: 350 degrees

2 cups flour
3 tablespoons sugar
1 tablespoon baking powder
10 tablespoons butter
1 cup buttermilk

*"I am overwhelmed by how patient and accommodating you all are with families. When Brandon and Sue walked to the top of Kasdorf Peak so children could ride on Tuesday night, I knew you ran a ranch where families come first. I always felt as though my children were safe and everyone was looking out for them. It is wonderful to be at a place where children may have such freedom to play and learn."*

# Lazy H Guest Ranch

**Lazy H Guest Ranch**
**PO Box 248**
**Allenspark, CO  80510**
**(800) 578-3598**
**(303) 747-2532**
**Phil and Karen Olbert**
**Elevation 8,300 feet**

Join us high on a Rocky Mountain ridge for an action packed week of fun at the Lazy H Guest Ranch. Create memories of a lifetime with spectacular scenery, your personal horse, mouthwatering buffets and exciting nightly entertainment.

Our Children's Program keeps the most restless busy with riding lessons, nature hikes, animal studies and crafts. Hiking takes all ages to wonderful places such as caves and waterfalls and you'll thrill to the sight of elk, deer and bighorn sheep.

Your riding skills will improve each day as you, your wrangler and your horse take off on new trails and new adventures. In your spare time, enjoy fishing, swimming, rafting, shopping or sightseeing in Rocky Mountain National Park.

You'll never forget your week at the Lazy H! Open year round with limited winter activities.

# Paprika Chicken

Cooking time: 1 $1/2$ hours
Yield: 20 servings
Temperature: 350 degrees

20 small to medium
  chicken breasts or
  equivalent
4 cups melted butter
3 tablespoons garlic salt
$1/2$ cup paprika
Salt and pepper to taste
2 cups lemon juice
4 tablespoons brown
  sugar
$1/2$ cup leaf oregano

Preheat the oven to 350 degrees. Mix together all the ingredients. Lay out chicken on paper lined sheet pan. Brush on sauce. Turn chicken and brush on sauce onto second side. Cover with foil and bake for 1 hour. Uncover pan, baste chicken with sauce and return pan to oven for another 30 minutes.

*"We came to Colorado expecting to ride and relax for a week. We never expected the warmth and friendliness we experienced here at Lazy H. The staff was wonderful and made us feel as if it were a pleasure to serve us, and not a job. Even though we took many pictures, we know they won't capture the beauty of the state, nor the spirit of Lazy H!"*

# Scalloped Corn and Sausage

Preheat the oven to 350 degrees. Brown the sausage. Drain off the grease and set aside. Mix the corn, eggs, and milk together with a whisk. Add the crushed saltine crackers, salt and pepper and mix well, but lightly. Add the browned sausage and stir until evenly distributed. Pour into a lightly greased baking pan. Cover with foil and bake for 1 hour. Uncover and return to oven for an additional 30 minutes.

Serve with a baked potato and tossed green salad.

Cooking time: 1 1/2 hours
Yield: 20 servings
Temperature: 350 degrees

3 pounds ground
  sausage
1 #10 can cream style
  corn
10 lightly beaten eggs
1 cup milk
40 crushed saltine
  crackers
Salt and pepper to taste

*"The meals were superb. There were healthy choices at every meal. I especially appreciated the fruits and vegetables."*

# Mandarin Orange Salad

Yield: 25 servings

3 cups sliced almonds
4 large heads iceberg
  lettuce
2 cups chopped celery
1 cup chopped onion
1 cup sugar
4 bunches leaf lettuce
1/2 of #10 can mandarin
  oranges (drained)

Dressing:
2 teaspoons salt
3 tablespoons parsley
3/4 cup vinegar
2 teaspoons pepper
3/4 cup sugar
1 1/2 cups soy oil

Cook almonds and sugar in a large skillet over medium heat, stirring until the almonds and sugar are candied. Chill for 3 hours in an airtight container. Mix all the dressing ingredients and chill for at least 3 hours. Just before serving, tear lettuce into bite-sized pieces and put into a 2 x 12 x 20-inch serving pan. Add celery, onions, almonds and mandarin oranges. Toss with dressing until the lettuce is well coated.

*"As last year, we had an excellent experience again. We can't say enough about the staff. As before, everyone went out of their way to accommodate our every request. We appreciate the individual attention given to our children as well. These are the reasons we come to Lazy H!"*

# Lost Valley Ranch

**Lost Valley Ranch**
**29555 Goose Creek Road**
**Box 70**
**Sedalia, CO 80135**
**(303) 647-2311**
**www.ranchweb.com/lost**
**lostranch@aol.com**
**Bob Foster Family**
**Elevation 7,200 feet**

The tradition at Lost Valley Ranch is to create an atmosphere that makes guests feel like friends and friends feel like family. That's why every year more than half of their guests have been to the ranch before. Why do people return time after time? Walt Disney himself had the answer when he vacationed at the ranch more than thirty years ago. "People think that all they want is recreation, but what they really need is re-creation," Disney said. That's just what they do.

The land was settled over a century ago and is still a working ranch. The staff of the Lost Valley Ranch believes in old-fashioned hospitality and welcomes a few friends to share a lifestyle that is far too rare these days.

Although the ranch is located a scenic two hour drive from Denver and Colorado Springs, it is the last nine miles the arriving guest will remember forever. That is where the pavement ends and the adventure begins. Half the fun of getting to the ranch is the change in pace; leaving the concrete world behind and learning to listen to the trees. Watch for wildlife and enjoy the great outdoors, it is a different world than the one to which most are accustomed.

The best way to see the Rocky Mountains is on horseback. There are more than 26,000 acres of the Pike National Forest for guests to explore. Well-marked trails follow old logging roads, criss-cross wooded ridge tops and wind through stands of shimmering Aspen.

Guests feel at home in the saddle in no time as the wranglers custom-fit them with saddle and mount especially selected from the remuda of over one hundred ranch raised and trained quarter horses. Every age and riding ability is carefully accommodated. The staff provides instruction for new riders and personal attention for all, insuring the guests will ride with new confidence and skill.

Lost Valley Ranch offers one, two and three bedroom cabin suites that are cozy, comfortable and immaculately serviced. Guests enjoy many niceties such as a porch swing, plenty of over-sized towels, in-room refrigerator, king and queen beds, non-allergic pillows and electric coffee maker. Wood is delivered daily for the fireplace. This is ranch living at its best and with a view that is unforgettable.

Each and every meal offers food that is home cooked from scratch. Healthy, hearty and delicious, it is carefully prepared from well-loved Foster family recipes by cooks who just love to tantalize the taste buds. Most meals are served in the main dining room, but guests are delighted to discover how lunch in a meadow makes something good taste even better.

The people at Lost Valley Ranch are committed to making their guests' ranch vacation the best ever. Every member of the family has the opportunity to do what they want, even if that is doing nothing at all. Family memories are made at Lost Valley Ranch and there are plenty more to go around.

# Beef Teriyaki

Bring the cup of water to a boil. Add in the ginger and garlic. Reduce the heat and let the mixture simmer for 10 minutes. Add the soy sauce and brown sugar, mixing thoroughly. Simmer until the sugar dissolves. Add the sherry and stir. Remove from heat and let the mixture cool completely.

Marinate the sirloin in the cooled teriyaki sauce for 24 hours. Remove the beef from the marinade and grill or broil approximately 20 minutes on each side. Use a meat thermometer for best results. Thinly slice the beef against the grain before serving.

To use the teriyaki as a glaze to serve with the beef, prepare another batch as before. Just before you add the sherry, mix the sherry with some cornstarch. Add to the mixture. This should thicken the teriyaki sauce to the consistency of a glaze.

Garnish the beef with chopped parsley and the glaze. Serve with mixed vegetables and new potatoes.

Cooking time: 40 to 60 minutes
Yield: 4 to 6 servings

2 pounds top sirloin
1 cup water
$1/4$ teaspoon grated fresh ginger
1 teaspoon crushed garlic
$1/2$ cup soy sauce
$1/2$ cup brown sugar
1 tablespoon cooking sherry
1 tablespoon corn starch

# Oven Fried Chicken

Cooking time: 1 $1/2$ to 2 hours
Yield: 8 to 10 servings
Temperature: 350 degrees

2 whole fryers, cut-up
1 - 12 ounce can evaporated milk
2 cups bread crumbs
2 cups flour
1 teaspoon seasoning salt
$1/2$ teaspoon pepper
$1/2$ teaspoon paprika
$1/2$ teaspoon poultry seasoning
Melted butter

Preheat the oven to 350 degrees. Mix the breadcrumbs, flour, salt, pepper, paprika and poultry seasoning in a bowl. Put the cut-up chicken in a second bowl. Pour the milk over the chicken. Take the chicken out of the milk and roll in the crumb mixture until well coated. Place the chicken pieces on a baking sheet that has been sprayed with a vegetable spray. Drizzle the pieces very lightly with the melted butter. Place in the oven and bake for 1 $1/2$ to 2 hours or until golden brown.

Serve with mashed potatoes, gravy, peas and biscuits.

# Chile Relleno Soufflé

Preheat the oven to 300 degrees. Layer $1/3$ of the diced green chiles in the bottom of a 4-quart baking dish. Cover these with a layer of Cheddar cheese. Layer in another $1/3$ of the green chiles. Cover this with a layer of Jack cheese. Layer in the last of the green chiles.

Separate the eggs. Beat the yolks, then add the evaporated milk, flour, salt, and pepper. Mix well.

In a separate bowl, beat the egg whites until stiff. Fold the whites into the yolk mixture and pour over the layered chile/cheese mixture. Bake for 2 hours, uncovered. Pour the enchilada sauce over the top and bake for an additional 30 minutes.

Cooking time: 2 $1/2$ hours
Yield: 20 servings
Temperature: 300 degrees

- 1 - 27 ounce can diced green chiles
- 1 pound Cheddar cheese, grated
- 1 pound Monterey Jack cheese, grated
- 5 eggs
- 1 - 14 ounce can evaporated milk
- 3 tablespoons flour
- $1/2$ teaspoon salt
- $1/4$ teaspoon pepper
- 10 ounces enchilada sauce

# Tabouli

Yield: 8 to 10 servings

1 $1/4$ cups Bulgar wheat
2 cups finely chopped
 parsley
$1/2$ cup finely chopped
 onion
2 cups finely chopped
 tomato
1 teaspoon salt
$1/2$ teaspoon pepper
$1/2$ cup lemon juice,
 freshly squeezed
$3/4$ cup oil

Combine all the ingredients in a bowl. Let stand for 24 hours before serving.

# Chicken and Wild Rice Salad

Cook the rice according to directions. Cool to room temperature. In a separate bowl, combine the pepper, cayenne, garlic, sugar and mayonnaise. Mix well. Add the rice, chicken and grapes to the mixture. Cover and chill. Add the cashews or almonds just before serving.

Serve on a bed of lettuce on individual plates or in a bowl lined with lettuce leaves.

Yield: 6 servings

1 cup uncooked wild
   rice
2 cups chicken, diced
   and cooked
1 $1/4$ cups halved green
   grapes
$3/4$ cup mayonnaise
$1/2$ cup cashews or
   sliced almonds
$1/4$ teaspoon black
   pepper
$1/4$ teaspoon cayenne
$3/4$ teaspoon garlic
   powder
2 tablespoons sugar

# Dill Rolls

Cooking time: 10 to 20
  minutes
Yield: 40 rolls
Temperature: 350 degrees

3 tablespoons dry yeast
3/4 cup warm water
3 cups cottage cheese
6 tablespoons sugar
3 tablespoons onion,
  chopped fine
3 tablespoons butter or
  margarine, melted
2 tablespoons fresh dill
  weed, chopped fine
1 tablespoon salt
3/4 teaspoon baking
  soda
3 eggs, well beaten
7 to 8 cups flour

Preheat the oven to 350 degrees. Combine the yeast and water in a large mixing bowl, mixing well. Add the other ingredients with the exception of the flour. Using a mixer or food processor, start beating the mixture on low speed using a dough hook. Slowly add the flour to the mixture. Continue beating for approximately 5 minutes. When the dough pulls away from the bowl and sticks to the hook, stop beating.

Place the dough in a round, buttered stainless steel pan. Turn the dough until it is evenly coated with butter. Cover the pan and place in a warm spot. Let rise until the dough volume is doubled. Punch the dough down and turn out onto a floured surface. Cut up into rolls and place back into the pan. Let the dough rise a second time for approximately 30 to 45 minutes.

Place the rolls in the oven and bake for approximately 10 minutes or until golden brown. Remove from the oven and brush the surface with melted butter. Serve immediately or cool and store for later use.

# Strawberry Cookie Pie

Mix the ice cream, cookies and strawberries together. Pour the filling into the graham cracker pie shell. Cover tightly and place in the freezer. Remove from the freezer and let sit for 10 minutes before serving.

Serve with fresh strawberries and whipped cream.

Yield: 10 to 12 servings

Graham cracker pie
  shell
Vanilla ice cream,
  softened
2 cups fresh
  strawberries
2 cups chopped oreo
  cookies

# John Mancini
# A Real Cowboy

When the Foster family acquired the Lost Valley Ranch in 1961 they inherited a head wrangler named John Mancini. John was a real cowboy who followed his own track through life. If the fried chicken in the staff room was a bit greasy, he took it outside and washed it in the little stream beside the swimming pool. Too much mayonnaise on the sandwich? No problem; John wiped the bread on his jeans without blinking an eye. John rolled his own cigarettes and at the Wednesday night cookout he'd always sing his version of *Tyin' a Knot in the Devil's Tail.*

Each year after Labor Day, John headed south and wintered on a ranch near Wickenburg, Arizona. He loved horses, tolerated dudes and would never admit to being lonesome. Later in life he married at the little Chapel in the Pines in Buffalo. It was a winter day with logs cracking and popping in the fireplace as the foot-pump organ wheezed through the *Wedding March.* The knot tied, the entire wedding party headed up County Road 126 to Pine Junction for a reception at the Red Rooster Inn.

Like the cowboys who preceded him by a hundred years, John was mobile. He followed opportunities just as people did when the West was first being settled. Most people picture homesteaders ranching in the mountains as having been year round residents, but it was also a constantly shifting scene full of real estate speculators, cattlemen trying, failing, then moving on, and ranch families wintering in nearby towns, so their kids could attend school. Gunfights and raids by horse thieves were rare, but hard work was every day.

When John Mancini died in January, 1984 he made the national news. His friends around Lake George, Colorado got a court order halting family plans for a traditional funeral and burial in a veterans' cemetery in Denver. "John couldn't ever be at rest there," they said. John himself expressed the wish to be wrapped in an Indian blanket and dropped into a crack in a rock somewhere in the mountains. The media picked up the story of a 19th century cowboy stuck in 20th century society—a man born after his time. His casket was placed on a horse drawn sleigh for his final ride in the Rockies with a simple graveside ceremony following.

# North Fork Ranch

**North Fork Ranch**
**PO Box B**
**Shawnee, CO  80475**
**(800) 843-7895**
**(303) 838-9873**
**www.northforkranch.com**
**northforkranch@worldnet.att.net**
**Dean and Karen May**
**Elevation 8,100 feet**

North Fork Ranch is a family oriented ranch located along the historic North Fork of the South Platte River, adjoining Pike National Forest and Wilderness Areas. Despite being located in the heart of Colorado's Rocky Mountains, the ranch is a scant ninety minutes from Denver International Airport. Pickup service is available.

The North Fork's Lodge offers comfortable accommodations, each with carpeting and private baths. The Homestead Cabin and The Stonehenge offer family accommodations of two to three bedrooms, each with private bath and common living room areas with large stone fireplace. The Klondike cabin offers two, two bedroom suites, each with a fireplace, sitting area, full bath and featuring cathedral ceilings.

The ranch offers a wide variety of activities for the vacationing family. You can choose to go horseback riding, white water rafting, on overnight pack trips, hiking, trap shooting, fishing or a variety of other western activities.

Whatever you are looking for in a western vacation, the exceptional staff at North Fork Ranch will do everything possible to make sure you have the best experience possible. They will truly make you feel at home.

# Grand Marnier French Toast

Yield: 4 servings

1 - 1 pound loaf unsliced
  white bread
4 eggs
1 cup milk
2 tablespoons Grand
  Marnier liqueur
1 tablespoon sugar
1/2 teaspoon pure
  vanilla extract
1/4 teaspoon salt
1/4 teaspoon freshly
  grated orange peel
Vegetable oil
3 tablespoons butter,
  melted
Powdered sugar
1 orange, thinly sliced
  (optional)

Slice the bread into 8 slices, each 3/4-inch thick. In a medium bowl, beat the eggs with the milk, Grand Marnier, sugar, vanilla, salt and orange peel, until well blended. Dip each piece of bread into the liquid mixture until well saturated. Place in a flat baking dish. Pour the remaining liquid over the bread, Cover and refrigerate overnight.

In a skillet, heat the oil and sauté the bread until golden brown on both sides. Brush with butter and sprinkle with powdered sugar. Top with the orange slices and serve immediately with maple syrup. The delicate orange flavor gives this French toast a new twist.

*"...perfect just before our morning ride!"*

*J.P.*
*Illinois*

# Blueberry Smoothie

Combine all of the ingredients in a blender and puree until smooth.

Yield: 1 serving

1 ripe medium banana
$3/4$ cup fresh or frozen
  blueberries
$1/4$ cup nonfat vanilla
  yogurt
$3/4$ cup skim milk
Pinch of cinnamon
$1/2$ cup crushed ice

# Kiwi Crush

Yield: 1 serving

1 ripe medium banana
1 medium kiwi, peeled
   with the center core
   scooped out
$1/3$ cup fresh orange
   juice
$1/2$ cup crushed ice

**Combine all of the ingredients in a blender and puree until smooth.**

*"Few vacation spots leave one with an emotional attachment that results in a sincere sadness when it's time to leave."*

*Bill*

# Teriyaki Pork Loin

Mix all the ingredients well. Place the pork loin in a roasting pan and pour the marinade over the top. Marinate for at least 4 hours in the refrigerator.

Slowly Grill the loin over charcoal for 2 hours, turning frequently. Slice thinly and top with any remaining sauce. Garnish with fresh rosemary.

*"Definitely beats Disneyland!"*

*Nathan*

Cooking time: 2 hours
Yield: 8 to 10 servings
Temperature: grill

1 pork loin
2 tablespoons brown
  sugar
2 cloves minced garlic
2 tablespoons dry sherry
4 tablespoons minced
  onion
1 teaspoon ginger
1 cup soy sauce

# Smoked Trout

Cooking time: 2 hours

Trout
Salt
Water

Place the whole, cleaned trout in a metal pan. Cover with water and add a generous amount of salt. Cover and set in the refrigerator overnight.

The next day, remove the trout from the pan and place on the racks in a smoker. Smoke for 2 hours. Allow the trout to stand in the smoker all day or overnight. Fillet and serve.

*"This is the closest I've been to heaven."*

*Mary*

# Colorado Pine Nut Salad

Toast the pine nuts under the broiler, until golden brown. Watch them carefully! Set aside.

In a small saucepan, boil the garlic in water for 10 minutes; drain. In a large salad bowl, mash the garlic and salt to a paste. Whisk in the mustard and vinegar. Add the oil in a stream, whisking the dressing until the oil is emulsified. Add the romaine; toss well and season with the pepper. Sprinkle the Parmesan and pine nuts over the salad and serve.

For a festive salad, try garnishing with a few cranberries.

*"Your ranch is a first class operation that my family will remember forever."*

*David*

Yield: 6 servings

$1/4$ cup pine nuts
2 cloves garlic
1 cup water
$1/4$ teaspoon salt
1 teaspoon Dijon
　mustard
2 tablespoons white wine
　vinegar
$1/2$ cup virgin olive oil
1 large head romaine
　lettuce, torn into pieces
Freshly ground black
　pepper to taste
$1/4$ cup coarsely
　shredded Parmesan
　cheese

# Blueberry Streusel Cake

Cooking time: 40 minutes
Yield: 12 to 15 servings
Temperature: 350 degrees

1/3 cup margarine
3/4 cup sugar
1 cup sour cream
2 eggs
1/2 teaspoon vanilla
1 1/4 teaspoons baking powder
1/4 teaspoon salt
1/4 teaspoon baking soda
1 3/4 cups flour
1 1/2 cups canned blueberries

Topping:
1/2 cup flour
1/2 teaspoon cinnamon
1/4 cup brown sugar
1/4 cup margarine

Preheat the oven to 350 degrees. Cream the butter and sugar together. Add the wet ingredients and stir. Add the dry ingredients. Pour into a greased spring-form pan. Cover the batter with the blueberries.

Combine the topping ingredients by cutting in the margarine until the consistency of fine crumbs. Sprinkle the topping over the blueberries. Bake the cake for 40 minutes or until a cake tester inserted into the middle comes out clean.

# Apple Cider Syrup

Place all the ingredients, with the exception of the apples, in a saucepan and heat to boiling. Reduce heat and simmer, uncovered, for 20 to 25 minutes or until the mixture is the consistency of maple syrup. Just before serving, add the apple slices and heat for several minutes.

Ladle onto pancakes or waffles topped with whipped cream.

Cooking time: 30 to 35 minutes
Yield: 10 servings
The syrup can be stored for up to 2 weeks in the refrigerator

1 $1/2$ cups clear apple cider
1 cup packed light brown sugar
1 cup corn syrup
4 tablespoons butter
2 tablespoons fresh lemon juice
$1/8$ teaspoon ground cinnamon
$1/8$ teaspoon ground nutmeg
2 teaspoons freshly grated lemon peel
2 Granny Smith apples, peeled, cored and thinly sliced

# Gonzales Sauce

Cooking time: 33 to 40 minutes

Yield: 1 quart

1/4 cup vegetable oil
1/2 cup onions, finely diced
2 cloves garlic, minced
2 tablespoons flour
1 cup chicken stock
1 1/2 cups green chile peppers, roasted, peeled, seeded and diced
1 tomato, diced
1 teaspoon ground coriander
1 tablespoon fresh cilantro, chopped

Place the vegetable oil in a medium saucepan and heat it over medium high heat. Add the onions and garlic, sautéing them for 5 minutes or until the onions are tender. Add the flour and whisk it in for 3 minutes. While whisking constantly, slowly add the heated chicken stock. Continue to whisk the sauce for 5 minutes or until it thickens. Add the green chile peppers, tomatoes, coriander and cilantro. Cook the sauce for an additional 20 minutes.

Serve over grilled steaks.

*"...this is my idea of a western steak!"*

*B.L.*
*Ohio*

# Honey Pecan Butter

Blend the butter, honey and pecans in a food processor, until smooth. Serve at room temperature. A delicious spread for your favorite waffle, pancake or muffin.

Yield: $3/4$ cup
Can be stored covered for up to 1 week in the refrigerator.

$1/2$ cup well-chilled, unsalted butter, cut into 4 pieces
$1/4$ cup honey
$1/3$ cup pecans, toasted

# Women of the West

## Margaret Tobin Brown
## 1867 - 1932

Maggie Tobin (who never went by Molly) was born on July 18, 1867 in Mark Twain's hometown of Hannibal, Missouri. The daughter of poor Irish immigrants, Maggie completed school at the age of 13. She found work in a tobacco factory, then as a waitress in a hotel. During her formative years, she read books by Mark Twain and magazine articles that romanticized life in the west, in particular Colorado. Maggie Brown was 19 years old when she read of the enchantment and prospects of life in the west. Acting upon what she learned and taking the advice of Horace Greeley, Maggie moved to Leadville, Colorado.

Maggie arrived in the "City of Clouds" an excited and ambitious young hopeful. She worked at the dry goods store and lived with her sister Mary Ann. Her sister's husband Daniel, worked as a miner making $3 a day. She was bright and charming, and an excellent conversationalist, but it was the physical charms of buxom, blue-eyed, red-haired Maggie Tobin that drew the attention of the young and ambitious Jim Brown.

James Joseph Brown, originally from Wymert, Pennsylvania was Irish Catholic, like Maggie. He came to Colorado to try his hand at mining and to make a great fortune; the same thing everyone in the little mountain towns was seeking. Working for a time in Aspen and other small towns, he ultimately settled in Leadville. He was quite the lady's man; tall and blue-eyed, but was smitten by Maggie.

After a short courtship they were married in September of 1886. J.J., as he was called, was 31 years old and Maggie just 19. They lived in a typical two-room log cabin near the mines where J.J. worked. There they lived until just before their second child, Catherine Ellen (also known as Helen) was born, at which point they moved to their permanent home in Leadville. During this period, J.J. purchased stock in the Ibex Mining Company and shortly thereafter, the company's Little Johnny mine hit the largest copper and gold strike in the world. J.J. and his family were suddenly very wealthy.

They left Leadville for Denver and purchased a home in the Capitol Hill section of the city. Maggie, in her quest to become a woman of society, furnished their home in quite an array of styles, including Gothic, Oriental and Eastlake, all with the newest, most beautiful furniture, tapestries and artwork. The famous gilt lace gown, Maggie's hand-painted dress, the Venetian satin gown, decorated with embroidered chrysanthemums, gilded thistles and gold embroidered lace with black velvet ribbons were photographed and commented on frequently. Her hair styles and jewelry were well documented, and the parties she threw were famous.

Soon after becoming wealthy, Maggie took up the study of languages, literature and drama at New York's Carnegie Institute. The Browns were listed in all the society pages and Maggie became a member of the Denver Women's Club and the Denver Woman's Press Club. Although these were high times for Maggie, there were a few drawbacks that excluded her from the true elite. The fact that she was outspoken and an Irish Catholic were some of the social disadvantages that kept her off the list of the "Sacred 36".

There are many stories surrounding Maggie Brown, but the one that has immortalized her has to do with her voyage aboard the RMS *Titanic*. The transatlantic luxury liner boasted a first-class passenger list of the very wealthy including Maggie, John Jacob Astor, Benjamin Guggenheim, Isador Straus and J. Bruce Ismay, head of the White Star Line. The ship, weighing 46,000 tons and costing $10 million, hit an iceberg and sank in the freezing cold waters of the Atlantic Ocean on April 15, 1912. Of the more than 2,200 souls aboard, 1,500 died by drowning or freezing to death. Maggie survived in a lifeboat containing fewer than 20 people, earning her the name "The Unsinkable Mrs. Brown".

This episode changed her forever. She helped with rescue efforts and raised money for the destitute victims. She organized maritime reform and volunteered to serve during the First World War as a nurse and later as an entertainer for the troops.

Maggie's personal life deteriorated in later years with her marriage to J.J. ending in divorce after 23 years. Their fortune dwindled and J.J. died in September, 1922 after suffering a heart attack. Maggie was quite a remarkable woman, surviving many hardships, a true rags-to-riches-to-rags story. She continued her charitable causes, living until October 1932. In everything she did, Maggie Brown loomed larger than life as a true Woman of the West.

# South Central Mountains

# Coulter Lake Guest Ranch

**Coulter Lake Guest Ranch**
**PO Box 906**
**Rifle, CO  81650**
**(800) 858-3046**
**(970) 625-1473**
**Norm and Sue Benzinger**
**Elevation 8,100 feet**

Coulter Lake Guest Ranch came into existence around the turn of the twentieth century when its founder, O.V. Coulter homesteaded the land in 1903. His son, Claude Coulter, began operating a hunting camp in 1938. It was at the request of hunters, wanting to bring their families out to enjoy the forest, that he began offering hospitality during the summer months as well, marking the start of the slow transformation of the property into a guest ranch.

Located on the Western Slope of the Colorado Rockies, Coulter Lake Guest Ranch is in the White River National Forest at an elevation of 8,100 feet. The town of Rifle is only twenty-one miles away to the southwest.

Some of Colorado's most spectacular scenery stretches in all directions from the ranch, virtually unchanged since the coming of the early settlers. Forests of quaking Aspen and towering Spruce cover the area. During the summer, every mountain meadow is covered with a riot of colorful wildflowers.

The ranch offers guest facilities in the form of log cabins, each with private bath and capable of accommodating parties of anywhere from two to eight. There is a maximum capacity for the ranch of twenty-five to thirty guests, allowing the staff to provide the personal attention that is so important to a great vacation experience.

Mealtime at Coulter Lake is an experience as everyone gathers at the Lodge for excellent home cooking, served family style. Outdoor life is a terrific appetite booster, as are the fresh baked breads, rolls, pies and hot cakes served on a daily basis. Main entrés might feature such selections as barbecue beef, chicken, pasta, trout, turkey, juicy steaks or any one of a number of tempting fare. Vegetarian or special diets can easily be accommodated with advance notice.

Rest and fun await the guests at Coulter Lake—away from all the noise and confusion of city life. Their tradition of friendly hospitality encourages the return of many of their guests year after year.

# Yummy Oatmeal Pancakes

In a large mixing bowl, combine the dry ingredients well. Add the oil, buttermilk, egg, vanilla and maple flavoring. Mix thoroughly. Let stand at room temperature for at least 30 minutes. If the batter appears too thick, it may be thinned with buttermilk.

Cook on a hot griddle until golden brown. Garnish with syrup and fresh fruit. These are excellent served with bacon or country sausage and scrambled eggs.

*"Our week with you was so beautiful and so special. We returned totally rested and renewed."*

Yield: 7 to 8 pancakes
Temperature: medium to
  hot griddle
Batter can be stored
  overnight, but bring to
  room temperature
  before cooking

1 1/2 cups oatmeal
1 teaspoon salt
2 cups buttermilk
1 tablespoon sugar
1 egg, beaten
1/2 cup flour
1 teaspoon baking soda
1 teaspoon vanilla
3 tablespoons cooking
  oil
1/2 teaspoon maple
  flavoring

# Sloppy Joes with A Twist

Cooking time: 1 hour
Yield: 8 to 10 servings
Can be stored for several
   days or can be frozen

1 onion, chopped
2 pounds lean ground
   beef
2 teaspoons paprika
$1/2$ teaspoon garlic salt
Salt to taste
Chili powder to taste
1 quart tomato juice
Cracker meal
Cabbage, shredded
Hamburger buns
Butter or margarine

Brown the ground beef and chopped onion in a skillet, Drain off the excess fat. Add the paprika, garlic salt, chili powder, salt and tomato juice. Heat the mixture just until boiling. Add the cracker meal to thicken the consistency and let simmer.

While the mixture is simmering, finely shred the cabbage and butter the buns. When you are ready to serve, toast the buns on the griddle.

Spoon the sloppy Joe mixture on the buns. Top with the cabbage and serve immediately. This is good with potato or tortilla chips on the side with a dill pickle.

This was a favorite sandwich at a Mid-western drug store lunch counter during the early 1940's.

*"We are still filled with warmth, smiles, a few extra pounds and all the wonderful and unforgettable memories of your ranch."*

# Chicken 'n Rice

Preheat the oven to 350 degrees for metal or 325 degrees for a glass baking dish. Layer the rice into the bottom of a greased 9 x 13-inch pan or casserole dish. Salt and pepper the chicken to taste and place on top of the rice. Sprinkle the dried onion soup mix over the chicken. Pour the diluted soup mixture over the chicken. Bake for 1 hour.

Remove from oven and garnish with parsley. Serve with tossed salad and fresh baked rolls.

*"Thanks for making our vacation so special—we're really glad we chose Coulter Lake."*

Cooking time: 1 hour
Yield: 6 servings
Temperature: 325 to 350
  degrees

1 cup dry rice
1 package dried onion
  soup mix
1 - 10 $^3/_4$ ounce can
  cream of chicken,
  celery or mushroom
  soup, mixed with 1 $^1/_2$
  cans of water
1 frying chicken or
  favorite pieces
Salt and pepper to taste

# Broccoli - Cauliflower Salad

Yield: 12 servings

1 head fresh cauliflower,
  uncooked
1 bunch fresh broccoli,
  uncooked
1 small onion

Dressing:
1/4 cup sour cream
1/4 cup mayonnaise or
  salad dressing
1/2 cup sugar
1/4 cup vinegar
Dash of salt

Cut the cauliflower, broccoli and onion into small pieces and place in a large salad bowl. Mix the sour cream, mayonnaise and sugar together in a separate bowl. Add the vinegar and salt, combining well. Pour over the cut vegetables and toss.

This is good for company or pot lucks.

# Fresh Cranberry - Pineapple Salad

Drain the pineapple, reserving the syrup. Combine the Jell-O and sugar, then dissolve in the boiling water. Add the cold water, lemon juice and reserved pineapple syrup. Chill until it reaches the consistency of syrup. Add the pineapple, cranberries, orange, celery and nuts. Turn the mixture into a 2-quart Jell-O mold. Chill until set. Garnish with mayonnaise or whipped cream.

This is attractive served on a lettuce leaf on a salad plate.

Yield: 12 servings

2 1/2 cups crushed
    pineapple
6 ounces cherry
    Jell-O mix
3/4 cup sugar
2 cups boiling water
1/2 cup cold water
2 tablespoons lemon
    juice
1 1/2 cups ground, raw
    cranberries
1 orange, ground
1 cup chopped celery
1/2 cup broken walnuts

# Super Easy Beer Bread

Cooking time: 55 minutes
Yield: 1 loaf
Temperature: 350 degrees

3 cups flour
$^1/_2$ cup sugar
4 teaspoons baking
   powder
1 teaspoon salt
12 ounces beer, room
   temperature (non-alco-
   holic brands work as
   well)
Butter

Preheat the oven to 350 degrees. In a large mixing bowl, combine the flour, sugar, baking powder and salt. Add the beer and mix with a fork. Spread the dough in a 5 x 9 x 2 $^1/_2$-inch bread pan. Bake for 55 minutes. Brush the top of the loaf with butter when done.

This is particularly good served with steaks or roast beef.

*"This was one of the best vacations we've had and you all were responsible for that. We've seen beautiful country most every year, but never before such a friendly and comfortable people to be with."*

# Old Time Gingerbread

Preheat the oven to 325 degrees. Cream the shortening and sugar together in a bowl. Add the egg and mix well. Blend in the molasses and water. In a separate bowl, mix together the flour, baking soda, salt, ginger and cinnamon. Stir slowly into the liquid mixture, beating until smooth. Pour into a greased and floured 9-inch square pan. Bake for 45 to 50 minutes. Garnish with whipped cream and serve warm.

*"Fond memories of the nice rides and your good cooking. Plus of course you nice people. We send our best wishes."*

Cooking time: 45 to 50 minutes
Yield: 9 servings
Temperature: 325 degrees

$1/2$ cup shortening
2 $1/4$ cups flour
2 tablespoons sugar
1 teaspoon baking soda
1 egg
$1/2$ teaspoon salt
1 cup molasses
1 teaspoon ginger
1 cup boiling water
1 teaspoon cinnamon

# Pumpkin Cake Dessert

Cooking time: 1 hour
Yield: 15 servings
Temperature: 325 to 350
  degrees

1 - 29 ounce can
  pumpkin
1 cup evaporated milk
1 cup sugar
3 eggs, slightly beaten
$1/2$ teaspoon ginger
$1/4$ teaspoon cloves
1 teaspoon cinnamon
$1/4$ teaspoon salt
1 spice cake mix
1 $1/2$ sticks margarine
  or butter
$3/4$ cup walnuts

Preheat the oven to 325 degrees for a glass baking dish or 350 degrees if using a metal cake pan. Mix together the pumpkin, evaporated milk, sugar, eggs, ginger, cloves, cinnamon and salt. Pour the batter into a greased 9 x 13-inch pan or casserole. Sprinkle the dry spice cake mix over the top of the batter. Set the butter or margarine to heating. Sprinkle the walnuts over the top of the dry spice cake mix. Drizzle the melted butter or margarine over the top of the nuts. Bake for 1 hour or until the top is browned. Remove from the oven and let cool. Top with whipped cream.

# Mother's Apple Pie Crisp

Preheat the oven to 350 degrees. Slice the apples into a 9-inch square pan that has been sprayed with a non-stick vegetable spray. In a mixing bowl, combine the sugar, flour, salt and baking powder. Add the egg and mix in with a fork, until crumbly. Pour mixture over the sliced apples. Drizzle with butter or margarine. Sprinkle with the cinnamon. Bake for 30 to 40 minutes or until the apples are soft.

Cooking time: 30 to 40
  minutes
Yield: 9 servings
Temperature: 350 degrees
Can be stored in the
  refrigerator for several
  days

6 apples, sliced
1 cup sugar
1 cup flour
3/4 teaspoon salt
1 teaspoon baking
  powder
1 egg
1/3 cup butter or
  margarine
Cinnamon to taste

# Rhubarb Crumble

Cooking time: 45 minutes
Yield: 12 to 16 servings
Temperature: 350 degrees

1 cup quick oatmeal
1 cup brown sugar
Pinch of salt
1 cup flour
1 cup margarine

Filling:
4 cups diced rhubarb
  (about 10 stalks)
1 can cherry pie filling
1 cup water
1 cup sugar
2 tablespoons cornstarch
1/2 cup chopped
  almonds, slivered

Preheat the oven to 350 degrees. Mix the oatmeal, brown sugar, salt, flour and margarine, until crumbly. Press 1/2 the mixture into the bottom of a 9 x 13-inch pan. Layer the diced rhubarb on top of the crust. Boil together the sugar, cornstarch and water, until thick. Add the pie filling and stir. Spread over the rhubarb. Sprinkle the remaining crust mixture over the top. Sprinkle the almonds over the crust. Bake for 45 minutes. Top with whipped cream or non-dairy whipped topping of your choice.

*"Thank everyone there at Coulter Lake for one of the most enjoyable vacations we've ever had. Each time we tell someone about it, we find that it's almost impossible for us to describe the wonderful things we saw and did—but even more impossible to convey how at-home-on-the-range we felt."*

# Deer Valley Ranch

**Deer Valley Ranch**
**PO Box MM**
**Nathrop, CO  81236**
**(800) 284-1708**
**(719) 395-2353**
**deervalley@sni.net**
**John Woolmington/Harold DeWalt**
**Elevation 8,400 feet**

Deer Valley, which is located at the base of the scenic Chalk Cliffs in central Colorado, is a family owned and run business. It was started by Parker and Clara Woolmington in 1955 and is now owned and operated by Harold and Sue DeWalt (daughter) and John (son) and Carol Woolmington. Harold and Sue's eldest son, Scott, and his wife, Carolyn, are now working full-time in the business, also.

Besides being known for delicious "company cooking", guests long remember the outstanding riding, fishing and hiking programs; as well as natural hot springs pools and their excellent staff.

Chalk Creek was a roaring mining valley in the late 1800s, and many of the old roads and trails now serve as horseback and four wheel drive roads to mines and ghost towns. By the early 1950's Tony Stark and Annabelle Ward, a brother and sister living in the town of St. Elmo, became well known in the area as the last residents of the mining period and with their deaths went a fascinating link with the past.

Deer Valley Ranch was started as a Christian family guest ranch in 1955. Parker and Clara Woolmington selected the beautiful valley as the place to raise their family of four and invite guests into their home for summer activities of horseback riding, swimming in the hot springs pool, hiking and enjoying family activities.

In 1978 John Woolmington and his wife Carol, along with Harold and Sue DeWalt, bought the ranch and continued the family tradition. They added fishing trips, river rafting, tennis, golf and many specialized meals to the ranch activities. The ranch also caters to retreats and groups as well.

Sue is a very "hands-on" cook at Deer Valley, and is rarely out of the kitchen in the busy summer months. The ranch takes great pride in their food presentation and goes to great lengths to train their fine kitchen and dining room staff. Meals are still of the hearty western tradition, though special diets are accommodated as well. Cookout breakfasts, Mexican buffets, deck lunches, barbecues, steak cookout rides and a noon cookout, complete with a family softball game, give variety to the ranch meal program. Eat as much as you like. There is no fried food and they serve a great selection of fruit and vegetables.

# Mexican Cheese

Preheat the oven to 325 degrees. Line the bottom of a 2-quart casserole dish with $1/2$ can of the peppers. Grate the cheese and sprinkle over the peppers. In a blender, mix the eggs, flour and evaporated milk. Pour over the cheese and top with the remaining peppers. Bake uncovered for 1 hour.

Mexican Cheese is also good served as a side dish with ham or fried chicken. It re-warms well.

Mexican food is a favorite with most people and at Deer Valley Ranch it is no exception. Tuesday noon is Mexican Buffet time. The food is fresh, spicy (not too hot for those Easterners) and creative. One of our favorites is Mexican Cheese.

Cooking Time: 1 hour
Yield: 8 servings
Temperature: 325 degrees

1- 13 $1/2$ ounce can chopped green chile peppers
2 cups grated Monterey Jack cheese ($1/2$ pound)
2 cups grated Cheddar cheese ($1/2$ pound)
2 eggs
$1/4$ cup flour
1 large can evaporated milk
Salt and pepper to taste

# Ranch Baked Beans

Cooking time: 30 to 45
  minutes
Yield: 8 servings
Temperature: 350 degrees

1/4 pound bacon, diced
1 1/2 pounds ground
  beef or elk
2 medium onions,
  chopped
2 or 3 28-ounce cans
  pork and beans
1 #303 can tomatoes,
  diced
1/2 cup brown sugar
1/2 cup catsup
Salt and pepper

Preheat the oven to 350 degrees. Brown the bacon and drain. Add the ground meat and brown with the chopped onions, cooking until the onions are tender. Drain well. Add the remaining ingredients, including the bacon and season to taste with salt and pepper. Bake in a greased casserole dish.

Serve as a main dish with a green salad and home-made bread or at a buffet or potluck.

*"Sweet are the family times that will have a lasting impact...sweet is the thankfulness of having this mountain ranch experience."*

# Buttermilk Banana Bread

Preheat the oven to 350 degrees. Grease a 9 x 5-inch loaf pan. Beat together the sugar, oil and eggs. Add the bananas, buttermilk and vanilla. Add the flour, baking soda and salt. Mix well. Add the nuts. Pour into the prepared pan. Bake until done or until a toothpick inserted in the center comes out clean. Allow to cool for 5 minutes, then remove from the pan. Finish cooling on a baking rack.

This Banana Bread is a bit more unique than a traditional recipe, because it is made with buttermilk (or sour cream).

Cooking time: 50 to 60 minutes
Temperature: 350 degrees

1 cup sugar
$1/2$ cup oil
2 eggs
1 cup (2 medium) bananas
$1/2$ cup buttermilk
1 teaspoon vanilla
1 $1/2$ cups flour
1 teaspoon baking soda
$1/2$ teaspoon salt
$1/2$ cup or more walnuts or pecans (optional)

# Swiss Cheese Rolls or Bread

Cooking time: 20 minutes for rolls, 30 minutes for loaves
Yield: 36 rolls or 2 loaves
Temperature: 350 degrees

5 ounces processed Swiss cheese (1 1/2 cups, grated)
2 cups milk
1/2 cup sugar
4 tablespoons butter or margarine
1 tablespoon salt
2 packages active dry yeast
5 to 5 1/2 cups flour
1 egg

In a medium saucepan, melt together the cheese, milk, sugar, butter or margarine and salt until warm, but not hot, stirring constantly. In the meantime, put the yeast and 2 cups flour in a large mixing bowl. Add warm, not hot, liquid and egg; mix well. Continue adding remainder of flour until a soft dough is made.

Preheat the oven to 350 degrees. Place the dough on a floured surface and knead for 10 minutes. Put the dough in a bowl, brush with oil and let rise until doubled in bulk. Punch down and shape into two long loaves of bread or about 3 dozen rolls. Let rise again until about doubled in bulk. Put into baking pans and place in the oven. Bake for the correct time, depending on whether you are making rolls or loaves. This bread browns very quickly, so be certain it is done before removing from the oven.

Because we make almost all of our own bread at Deer Valley, we make a large variety, so that it is not duplicated during the week. One of the favorite breads, served with our steak dinner on Friday nights, is Swiss Cheese Bread or Rolls.

# Buttermilk Pie

In a bowl, combine the flour, sugar and salt. Add the butter and beaten eggs; beat some more. Stir in buttermilk; beat again. Blend in flavoring. Pour mixture into a pie shell and bake at 350 degrees for 45 to 50 minutes. This pie browns quickly. Make sure it is set in the center.

A dollop of whipped cream is a nice garnish, but not necessary.

Deer Valley is famous for its Saturday Night Buffet dinner, which includes a dessert table with about 20 offerings. The following pies can usually be found there: Buttermilk Pie, Key Lime Pie and Cowboy Cookie Pie.

Cooking time: 45 to 50 minutes
Yield: 1 pie
Temperature: 350 degrees

$1/4$ cup flour
1 $3/4$ cups sugar
$1/2$ teaspoon salt
$1/2$ cup butter, melted
3 eggs, beaten
$1/2$ cup buttermilk
1 $1/2$ teaspoons vanilla or 1 teaspoon vanilla plus 1 teaspoon lemon extract
9-inch unbaked pie shell

# Key Lime Pie

Yield: 1 pie

1 chocolate or graham
   cracker crust
1 can sweetened
   condensed milk
1 small can frozen
   limeade, thawed
16 ounces size frozen,
   whipped topping,
   thawed
Green food coloring -
   use just enough for a
   light green tint

Combine the milk and limeade. Gently fold in the whipped topping and the food coloring. Pile high in the crust and freeze overnight. Top with whipped cream.

Recipe may easily be doubled if you cannot find a small can of limeade or you may use half the can of limeade. Drink the rest!

# Cowboy Cookie Pie

Mix the sugar, flour and salt well with a fork. Add the melted butter, then the eggs and vanilla, blending well. Fold in the nuts and chocolate chips, then pour into the pie shell.

Serve in small pieces, since it's very rich. May serve with ice cream or whipped cream.

Cooking time: 40 to 45 minutes
Yield: 1 pie
Temperature: 325 degrees

1 cup sugar, white or brown
$1/2$ cup flour
1 stick butter, melted (use real butter)
2 eggs, slightly beaten
1 teaspoon vanilla
1 cup pecans, chopped
1 cup chocolate chips
1 unbaked 9-inch pie shell
Pinch of salt

*"Sue...you are the true celebrity of Deer Valley...your meals were incredibly good. Your waitresses were so accommodating, even when I informed them I was vegetarian (which I said at a whisper for fear I would have my head put on one of the walls by a hunter.) Great food would definitely be at the top of the list when recommending Deer Valley."*

# Cowboy Cookies

Cooking time: 10 to 15
  minutes
Yield: 20 large cookies
Temperature: 350 degrees

2 eggs
1 cup granulated sugar
1 cup lightly packed
  brown sugar
2 sticks (1 cup) butter or
  margarine, softened
1 teaspoon vanilla
1 teaspoon baking soda
$1/2$ teaspoon baking
  powder
$1/2$ teaspoon salt
2 cups unsifted flour
2 cups regular oats (not
  quick-cooking oats)
1 package (6 ounce)
  semisweet, mini-choco-
  late bits or regular size
  chocolate bits
Chopped pecans or
  walnuts to taste
  (optional)

Preheat the oven to 350 degrees. Beat the eggs, granulated sugar, brown sugar and butter in a large bowl until the mixture is fluffy, scraping down the sides of the bowl frequently with a rubber spatula. Mix in the vanilla.

In another bowl, stir together the baking soda, baking powder, salt, flour and oats. Add the dry ingredients to the creamed mixture; mix well. Stir in the chocolate bits and nuts. Dough will be very stiff.

Drop about $1/4$ heaping cupfuls or a small ice cream scoop of the dough onto a greased baking sheet. Put only 8 mounds of dough on each baking sheet, staggering them about 3 inches apart. Cookies will spread as they bake. Bake until golden brown, but still spongy when touched on top with fingertips. Don't over-bake cookies. They should have a chewy texture. Let cookies cool about 5 minutes before removing them from the baking sheet.

Deer Valley is famous for these delicious, chewy oatmeal chocolate chip cookies. They are served every Wednesday, in the summer, at our noon cookout lunch and at Saturday lunch in the winter. Guests and staff alike never want to leave DVR without having had yet another Cowboy Cookie.

# Jennie's Granola

Preheat oven to 250 degrees. Mix the dry ingredients together in a large bowl. In a separate bowl, blend together the liquid ingredients. Add the liquid to the dry ingredients and blend. Spread onto cookie sheets and bake for 90 minutes. Remove from the oven and add in the dates and raisins; mix well.

Named after Sue's friend and running companion of 25 years, the granola appears on our breakfast table at DVR every morning. It also makes a wonderful snack for the trail. Makes a great gift!

Cooking time: 90 minutes
Yield: 2 quarts
Temperature: 250 degrees

6 cups regular oatmeal
2 1/2 cups whole wheat flour
1/2 cup sunflower seeds
1 1/2 cups walnuts
1 cup coconut
1 tablespoon salt
1 cup powdered milk
1 cup almonds, sliced
1/2 cup honey
1 cup oil
1 cup water
1 1/2 teaspoons vanilla
1 1/2 teaspoons maple flavoring
1 cup brown sugar
1 cup chopped dates
1 cup raisins

# Coffee Mocha

Yield: 30 servings

1 $1/2$ cups dairy creamer
$1/2$ cup instant coffee
1 cup granulated sugar
$1/2$ cup cocoa powder
Dash of salt

Combine all the ingredients in mixer or food processor. Store in an airtight container. Use 2 heaping teaspoons per cup.

Makes a great gift in a festive container.

# Elk Mountain Ranch

**Elk Mountain Ranch**
**PO Box 910**
**Buena Vista, CO  81211**
**(800) 432-8812**
**(719) 539-4430**
**www.elkmtn.com**
**Tom and Sue Murphy**
**Elevation 9,435 feet**

One hundred years ago the Arkansas Valley was teeming with mining activity. The site of what is now the Elk Mountain Ranch was the original ore processing mill for the Futurity mine. The Trading post on the ranch dates from that time, a reminder of the mining heritage of the area.

Located at an altitude of 9,435 feet, the ranch is among Colorado's highest. Nestled in the remote San Isabel National Forest near Buena Vista, the ranch is surrounded by a breathtaking panorama of snow-capped peaks, Aspen and evergreen. Add in Little Bull Creek running through the property and you have a nature lover and photographer's paradise.

Elk Mountain Ranch offers log cottages and rooms in the lodge. All are carpeted, tastefully furnished and have daily housekeeping service. Activities enjoyed by the guests include horseback riding instruction and daily trail and off-trail rides into the thousands of acres of unspoiled wilderness. Other activities offered by the ranch include trap shooting, square dances, hiking, archery, horseshoes, riflery, volleyball, movies, fishing and softball. Guests can also thrill to white water rafting, visits to abandoned mining towns, day trips to Aspen or Breckenridge, or overnight camping trips high into the Rockies.

While visiting the Elk Mountain Ranch you will sample some of the most superb food to be found anywhere. Each day features full course meals meant to satisfy appetites both hearty and discerning. Other culinary experiences include trail ride cookouts, steak cookouts, nightly hors d'oeuvres and candlelight suppers. And don't forget the fabulous desserts!

If you have a taste for the high country and enjoy riding through unspoiled wilderness, come to Elk Mountain Ranch for a week that will be unsurpassed. Leave your cares at home, but be sure to bring your appetite.

# Cheese and Bacon In A Bread Boat

Preheat the oven to 350 degrees. Crisp the bacon and dice into small pieces; set aside. Beat the cream cheese and sour cream together. Add the bacon, peppers and onions. Warm the filling at 350 degrees for approximately 30 minutes. Hollow out the shepherd's bread, saving the hollowed out pieces. Fill the bread with warmed filling and return it to the oven for an additional 15 to 20 minutes. Serve it with the extra pieces of bread and a knife to cut the bowl.

Cooking time: 45 minutes
Yield: 20 servings
Temperature: 350 degrees
Filling can be prepared
  the night before

1 pound bacon, cooked
  and diced
1 loaf shepherd's bread
8 ounces softened cream
  cheese
1 cup sour cream
$1/2$ cup green peppers,
  chopped
$1/2$ cup green onions,
  thinly sliced

*"Thank you for a wonderful vacation. Everyone there went far beyond the call of duty to make our trip special! Good luck the rest of this summer and thanks again for your hospitality and many great memories!"*

*Ray, Mary & Corey*
*Rockville, Maryland*

# Beef Stroganoff

Cooking time: 30 minutes
Yield: 4 to 6 servings

2 tablespoons margarine
1 pound beef sirloin or
   round steak, cut into
   1/4-inch strips
1/2 cup onion, chopped
1 teaspoon paprika
1/4 teaspoon salt
1/8 teaspoon pepper
1/8 teaspoon garlic
   powder
1 - 10 3/4-ounce can
   condensed cream of
   mushroom soup
1 1/4 cups beef broth
2 tablespoons flour
1/2 cup sour cream
Egg noodles, cooked

Sauté the meat and onions in margarine in a 12-inch skillet over medium-high heat, until brown. Season with paprika, salt, pepper and garlic powder. Stir in the soup and one cup of beef broth (reserving 1/4 cup). Reduce the heat; cover and simmer for 20 minutes. Blend the remaining 1/4 cup beef broth with the flour. Stir into the meat mixture. Cook 5 minutes more, stirring frequently. Add the sour cream and heat through. Do not boil. Serve over egg noodles.

# Sherry's Barbeque Brisket

Preheat the oven to 325 degrees with the rack in the lower third, but not bottom, position. Sear the meat, fat side down first, in the bottom of a heavy-duty roasting pan. Turn the meat over and sear the other side. This searing can also be done on a grill. Stir together all the other ingredients and pour over the brisket. Cover and cook for 3 to 4 hours, or until tender.

Remove the meat from the pot and pour the sauce into a bowl. Discard the bay leaves. Allow the broth to cool. Slice the meat when cool. Skim the fat off the sauce, then pour back over the sliced meat. Reheat on the stove, covered, or in the oven. Meat can be refrigerated overnight and heated for a meal the next day.

Garnish with parsley sprigs.

Good with lemon carrots, mashed potatoes and rolls.

Cooking time: 4 hours
Yield: 10 servings
Temperature: 325 degrees
Can be cooked and sliced
  the night before

5 to 6 pound brisket
$1/4$ cup water
1 large onion, peeled
  and sliced
1 8-ounce bottle chili
  sauce
4 cloves garlic, peeled
  and chopped
2 bay leaves
$1/2$ cup brown sugar
$1/3$ cup Dijon mustard
$1/4$ cup red wine vinegar
3 tablespoons molasses
$1/4$ cup soy sauce

# Florentine Lasagna Rollups

Cooking time: 45 minutes
Yield: 6 servings
Temperature: 350 degrees

12 fluted lasagna
   noodles
1 package (10 ounces)
   frozen chopped
   spinach, thawed &
   drained well
1 1/2 cups mozzarella
1 cup ricotta
1 egg slightly beaten

Preheat the oven to 350 degrees. Cook the lasagna noodles as per package directions. Cool with cold water. Make the filling by combining spinach, mozzarella, ricotta and egg. You can spice it up by adding garlic powder and oregano to taste. Spread the dried noodles with 1/2 cup filling, roll and place in a greased pan. Cover with your choice of sauce (marinara or white). Sprinkle generously with parmesan cheese. Bake for 45 minutes.

*"For about a week or two after our return home our heads and hearts were still at Elk Mountain. Checked our lottery ticket as soon as we hit Florida and if we had won we would have packed up our cats and headed west. Too bad—we had to face reality."*

*Larry and Betty*
*Pompano Beach, Florida*

# White Sauce For Lasagna

Melt the butter in a saucepan. Stir in the flour, chicken base and pepper. Whisk thoroughly. Stir in the milk and cream. Bring to a boil, stirring constantly. Pour over your favorite recipe for lasagna rollups. Sprinkle generously with Parmesan cheese and garnish with parsley. Cook as directed.

Yield: 6 servings

1/4 cup butter
1/4 cup flour
1 1/2 teaspoons chicken
　base
1/8 teaspoon pepper
1 cup light cream or
　Half and Half
1 cup milk

# Lemon Nut Bread

Cooking time: 75 minutes
Yield: 1 or 2 loaves
Temperature: 325 degrees
Can be stored for a week
  or frozen

$^1/_2$ cup margarine
1 $^1/_2$ cups sugar
3 eggs
2 $^1/_4$ cups flour
$^1/_4$ teaspoon salt
$^1/_2$ teaspoon baking
  soda
$^1/_2$ cup buttermilk
Grated rind of 1 lemon
$^3/_4$ cup chopped pecans
  or walnuts (optional)
Juice of 2 lemons
$^3/_4$ cup powdered sugar

Cream together the margarine and sugar. Add 3 eggs and blend well. In a separate bowl, combine the flour, salt and baking soda. Alternately add the buttermilk and the dry ingredients to the creamed mixture, beginning and ending with the buttermilk. Stir in the grated rind of lemon. Add the pecans or walnuts (optional).

Spoon the batter into a greased and floured loaf pan ($^1/_3$ filled). Bake at 325 degrees for 75 minutes or until the bread tests done. Cool for 15 minutes and remove from the pan.

Combine the juice of 2 lemons and powdered sugar, stirring well. Punch holes in the top of warm bread with a toothpick. Pour on the glaze. Cool on a wire rack.

Great for outdoor brunches when the bread is served cold.

# Blueberry Filled Coffee Cake

Preheat the oven to 350 degrees. Cream together the butter and sugar. Add the eggs and sour cream. Stir the flour, salt, baking powder and baking soda into the creamed mixture. Add the vanilla. Pour $1/2$ the batter into a greased pan. Spread the pie filling over the top of the batter. Top with the remaining batter. Combine all of the ingredients for the topping and sprinkle over the batter. Bake for approximately 1 hour.

*"We wanted to take a moment to thank you for a wonderful vacation. We all had a wonderful time and have many great memories to look back on. The first evening we said we were at Elk Mountain for fresh air, vistas and fun. There's no question our wishes were fulfilled. What we didn't expect was how much we'd enjoy the outstanding staff & other guests. Your staff was always friendly, fun loving and welcoming. Our enjoyment felt like a priority and we're all grateful! Thanks for your great Dude Ranch hospitality & the great Food—diets for the rest of the summer."*

*The Turcot Family*
*Peoria, Illinois*

Cooking time: 1 hour
Yield: 24 servings
Temperature: 350 degrees

Cake:
1 cup butter
2 cups sugar
4 eggs
2 cups sour cream
4 cups flour
1 teaspoon salt
3 teaspoons baking
　powder
1 teaspoon baking soda
2 teaspoons vanilla
2 cans blueberry pie
　filling

Topping:
$1/2$ cup butter, softened
1 cup sugar
2 teaspoons cinnamon
1 cup flour
1 cup nuts, chopped
　(optional)

# Homemade Oreo Ice Cream

Churning time: 1 hour
Yield: 20 servings
Can be stored in the
   freezer for 3 weeks

7 cups heavy whipping
   cream
2 cups sugar
2 tablespoons vanilla
2 tablespoons lemon
   juice
2 - 13 ounce cans
   evaporated milk
Oreo Cookies, crushed

Pour the cream into a large bowl. Stir in the sugar, vanilla and lemon juice. Gradually add the evaporated milk. Refrigerate until chilled. Pour into an ice cream freezer container and churn until thick. Add the crushed Oreos and blend well. Freeze.

Fashion the ice cream into balls before serving.

*"You and your staff did an excellent job helping us have a great vacation. We will be back."*

*Rick and Karen*
*East Windsor, New Jersey*

# Pizza Dip

Preheat oven to 350 degrees. Mix the cream cheese, sour cream and chopped onion. Spread in a round glass quiche pan or 10-inch pie pan. Spread with pepperoni. Bake for 10 minutes. Top with the mozzarella cheese. Bake 5 minutes more.

Serve with thick crackers or nacho chips.

Cooking time: 15 minutes
Yield: 10 servings
Temperature: 350 degrees

8 ounces cream cheese
8 ounces sour cream
Chopped onion
1 jar spaghetti sauce
Pepperoni
8 ounces mozzarella
   cheese
Thick crackers or Nacho
   chips

# Spicy Apple Cider Sauce

Cooking time: 30 minutes
Yield: 3 cups
Can be stored for 2 weeks

1 cup sugar
3 tablespoons biscuit
  mix
1/4 teaspoon cinnamon
1/4 cup margarine
1/4 teaspoon nutmeg
2 cups apple cider
2 tablespoons lemon
  juice

Mix the sugar, biscuit mix, cinnamon and nutmeg in a saucepan. Stir in the cider and lemon juice. Heat over a medium-high burner, stirring constantly, until the mixture thickens and boils. Boil for 1 minute. Remove from the heat and stir in the margarine. Let the sauce simmer until it reaches the desired consistency.

Apple Cider Sauce is wonderful with pancakes. A great change from maple syrup with added spice.

*"What a wonderful time we had at the ranch! Never dreamed it would be so great! Yours is a 'first class' operation, and we're looking forward to a return visit with a group of 30."*

*Jim and Bobbie*
*Orange, California*

# Powderhorn Guest Ranch

**Powderhorn Guest Ranch**
**Powderhorn, CO  81243**
**(800) 786-1220**
**(970) 641-0220**
**entertain.com/wedgwood/powder.html**
**Jim and Bonnie Cook**
**Elevation 8,500 feet**

The Powderhorn Valley gets its name from its shape—narrow at the upper end, then gently curving northwest to a wide entrance at the lower end. Settlers first tried potato farming, then turned to cattle ranching more than a century ago. Cattle ranching is still the primary occupation for much of the valley's population. Electricity finally reached the valley in 1953, representing a considerable change in the lives of the sturdy ranchers.

Powderhorn Guest Ranch is a family-owned and operated resort. Surrounded by cattle ranches and public forest, there is none of the background noise, pollution or traffic city-dwellers have come to expect. Activities are geared to all ages and interests, with everything included in the package. Children are included in all activities, rather than having a separate schedule.

The Powderhorn Guest Ranch's experienced wranglers will take you to beautiful scenery and breathtaking views by way of their surefooted horses. Rides go out twice each day and include a supper ride in the Aspen and pine-scented forest. Other excursions feature lunch rides along streams and beaver ponds. The staff will assign the right horse for the week for each guest, selected according to riding ability. Riding instruction is included in the week long program.

A vacation at Powderhorn Guest Ranch is like staying with family. By the end of the week you will have made fast friends of the owners, staff and other guests.

# Sausage Balls

Cooking time: 45 minutes
Yield: 30 balls
Can be stored for several
  days or even frozen

Sausage Balls:
1 pound pork sausage
1 egg, slightly beaten
$1/3$ cup bread crumbs
$1/4$ teaspoon poultry
  seasoning
Dash of garlic salt

Sauce:
$1/4$ cup catsup
$1/4$ cup salsa
1 tablespoon soy sauce
$1/2$ cup water
1 tablespoon vinegar
2 tablespoons brown
sugar

Combine all the ingredients for the sausage balls. Shape into quarter-sized balls and brown in a skillet, making sure to cook all the way through. Pour off the excess grease.

Combine all the sauce ingredients, mixing thoroughly. Pour the sauce over the cooked sausage balls and simmer for 30 minutes.

This can be served either for breakfast or over rice.

# Hominy and Green Chile Casserole

Preheat the oven to 350 degrees. Drain the hominy. Layer half the green chiles in a 1-quart greased casserole. Add the hominy and top with the rest of the chiles.

Mix together the parsley, onion, sour cream and chile powder. Pour the mixture over the contents of the casserole dish. Top with cheese. Bake covered for 30 minutes.

Cooking time: 30 minutes
Yield: 4 servings
Temperature: 350 degrees

2 - 15 ounce cans of
   hominy
1 - 4 ounce can green
   chiles
1/4 cup parsley flakes or
   chopped parsley
1/4 cup onion, chopped
1/2 cup sour cream
1/2 teaspoon chili
   powder
3/4 cup grated Cheddar

# King Crab and Shrimp Noodles

Cooking time: 35 minutes
Yield: 8 servings
Temperature: 350 degrees

6 ounces crab meat,
  canned or frozen
12 cooked medium
  shrimp
2 cups fine noodles
  (angel hair), uncooked
1 - 10 1/2 ounce can
  cream of mushroom
  soup
1/2 cup mayonnaise
1/2 cup milk
Cheddar cheese,
  shredded

Preheat the oven to 350 degrees. Mix everything, except for the cheese, together carefully, making sure not to break up the shrimp and noodles too much. Pour into a 1 1/2-quart casserole dish. Sprinkle the Cheddar cheese on top and bake for 35 minutes.

# Barbecue Beans

Heat the chopped onion in the water, until boiling. Reduce heat to low and let simmer until the onion is tender. Remove the onion from the water and place into a saucepan. Drain the black beans and place them in the saucepan. Add the kidney beans, with their liquid, along with the frozen lima beans and the barbecue sauce. Bring the mixture to a boil. Reduce the heat to low and let simmer for 20 minutes, stirring occasionally.

*"It's been the best vacation we've ever taken and we haven't stopped talking about it!"*

Cooking time: 45 minutes
Yield: 10 servings
Can be stored for several
  days or frozen

1 large onion, chopped
2 - 16 ounce cans black
  beans
2 - 16 ounce cans red
  kidney beans
1 - 10 ounce package
  frozen lima beans
1 cup bottled barbecue
  sauce
$1/2$ cup water

# Dirty Rice

Cooking time: 1 hour
Yield: 30 servings
Temperature: 350 degrees
Can be stored for several
  days or even frozen

4 cups onion soup
  prepared from dry mix
4 cups beef broth
  prepared from either
  bouillon cubes or
  granules
4 cups regular white rice
4 sticks margarine

Preheat the oven to 350 degrees. Combine all the ingredients in a casserole dish and mix thoroughly. Cover and bake for 1 hour.

# Pea and Cauliflower Salad

Combine the peas, cauliflower, celery, onion and cashews together in a large salad bowl. Toss with the ranch dressing.

**Yield: 30 servings**

1 large bag frozen peas, thawed
2 heads cauliflower, cut into bite-sized pieces
3 or 4 stalks of celery, diced
$1/2$ large onion, chopped
1 can of cashews
Ranch salad dressing

*"It's probably the closest to Heaven I'll ever get."*

# Chinese Chews
# (Chewy Butterscotch Brownies)

Cooking time: 20 minutes
Yield: 24 servings
Temperature: 350 degrees
Can be stored for several
  days or frozen

1 stick of margarine
2 $1/3$ cups brown sugar
3 eggs
1 $1/2$ cups flour
1 teaspoon baking
  powder
$1/8$ teaspoon salt
1 tablespoon vanilla
1 cup chopped walnuts
Powdered sugar

Preheat the oven to 350 degrees. Cream the margarine, brown sugar and eggs together in a bowl. Add the flour, baking powder, salt and vanilla; mix by hand. Add the chopped nuts. Spread into a greased 9 x 13-inch pan. Bake for 20 minutes. Cool and dust with powdered sugar.

# S'more Pudding Dessert

Preheat the oven. Follow the package directions to cook the pudding along with the milk. Allow to cool for 5 minutes.

Line the bottom of a 1 $^1/_2$-quart glass baking dish with 3 of the graham crackers. Spread $^1/_2$ of the pudding over the crackers. Place 3 more crackers on top of the pudding, forming another layer. Place the candy bars atop the crackers. Spread the remaining pudding over the candy bars. Top with the remaining crackers. Sprinkle the marshmallows over the top. Broil until the marshmallows are golden brown.

This can either be served warm or chilled in the refrigerator prior to serving.

Cooking time: 10 minutes
Yield: 8 servings
Temperature: broil

9 full-sized graham
   crackers
5 ounces vanilla pudding
   and pie filling
3 - 1 $^3/_8$ ounce chocolate
   candy bars
2 cups mini-
   marshmallows
3 $^1/_4$ cups milk

# Glogg
# (Hot Spiced Wine)

Yield: 3 quarts

Can be stored for up to 2
  years

2 quarts water
4 cinnamon sticks
5 figs
10 whole cardamom
  seeds
2 tablespoons cloves
4 dried orange peels
1 cup raisins
1 cup almonds
2 quarts port wine
1 pint grain alcohol
3 cups sugar

Place the cinnamon sticks, figs, cardamom seeds, cloves and orange peels in a cloth and tie it up into a bag. Place the bag in the water and bring to a boil. Boil for 1 hour. Cover and let stand over night.

The next day, squeeze out the bag, saving all the liquid. Discard the bag and its contents. Add sugar to the liquid in the pan and heat until the sugar is dissolved. Add the raisins, almonds and wine.

Add the alcohol just prior to serving. Light the top and let the excess alcohol burn off for a minute.

This beverage can be stored in airtight bottles and reheated at any time.

# Tarryall River Ranch

**Tarryall River Ranch**
**27001.5 County Road 77**
**Lake George, CO  80827**
**(800) 408-8407**
**(719) 748-1214**
**Jimmy and Jeannine Lahrman**
**Elevation 8,600 feet**

Tarryall River Ranch is located in the central Rocky Mountains in Park County, Colorado, where it adjoins the Lost Creek Wilderness Area. Elevation at the ranch is 8,600 feet, at which there is an abundance of Aspen and Ponderosa pine, as well as wildflowers along the banks of the river that runs through the ranch. The views are spectacular, with Pikes Peak looming to the southeast. The region is famous for its plentiful wildlife, including bighorn sheep, elk, deer, bear and mountain lion.

The ranch was settled in the 1880's when gold fever was running rampant in the region. Numerous remnants of that period are still to be seen today, such as abandoned log cabins, mines and ghost towns. After the turn of the century, mining gave way to ranching as the mainstay of the area. By 1920 the region had caught the interest of wealthy citizens in Colorado Springs who were impressed by its pristine beauty and seemingly sculpted mountains. It was about that time that the Taylor family purchased the ranch as a summer retreat. The first record of it being operated as a dude ranch was after it was acquired in 1930 by prominent Colorado Springs attorney Leon Snyder. Present owners, Jim and Mary Dale Gordon, purchased the property in 1994.

The Tarryall River Ranch offers a wide variety of activities. You can choose to spend the entire week riding both morning and afternoon, enjoying the company of a good horse and extraordinary scenery. The all day rides will take you deep into the wilderness, often climbing above timberline. Overnight pack trips can be arranged. Beginners will be made to feel comfortable on the most gentle of horses and will be given special attention.

Other options available to guests include day trips to the casinos in historic Cripple Creek, tours of old gold mines or rides on authentic railroads. Also nearby is Pike's Peak, which can be ascended by either car or cog railway. Guests can also choose from other nearby attractions, including the Cave of the Winds, Florissant Fossil Bed National Monument, Manitou Cliff Dwellings and Garden of the Gods.

For those who like to fish, Tarryall River Ranch will seem like rainbow heaven. The famed Tarryall River runs right through the ranch, providing the enthusiast with miles to fish. Upstream is the Tarryall Reservoir, which provides a wide variety of fishing. Perhaps the best part of your fishing experience is that members of the ranch staff will cook up your catch for you. Whether a dyed-in-the-wool fisherman or a first-timer, you will find fishing to suit.

Each week the ranch offers several choices of river rafting, depending upon your desire for excitement. All the trips are on the Arkansas River, either through Brown's Canyon or through the Royal Gorge. This kind of activity might just prove to be the thrill of your lifetime.

Long after leaving the ranch you will be talking about the food. It is a source of pride for the crew in the kitchen to provide the very best in cuisine for their guests. No short-cuts or instant ingredients; only home baking and almost everything from scratch. The ranch is small enough to truly cater to the particular guests each week. You can count on plenty of fresh fruit and vegetables, along with wonderful steaks, chicken, turkey, fish and pastas. Virtually every day there is a cookout. Be sure to bring a pair of jeans with a little extra room!

# Banana Nut Pancakes

Combine all the ingredients in a mixing bowl. Beat well with a wire whisk until the mixture has no lumps. Add regular milk to thin, if it appears too thick. Cook on a griddle until golden brown.

For variety, you can add either blueberries, pecans or chocolate chips.

Yield: 10 to 12 pancakes

1 cup flour
2 tablespoons sugar
1 teaspoon baking powder
$1/2$ teaspoon baking soda
2 bananas, mashed
$1/2$ teaspoon salt
2 tablespoons oil
1 cup buttermilk
1 egg
1 cup walnuts, chopped
Vanilla

*"I was afraid my expectations were too high, you all have exceeded them beyond any possible imaginings! The setting, the people, the food, and the horses all mixed to make this the BEST vacation ever. I MUST DO IT AGAIN!"*

*Kris*
*California*

237

# Chicken Quesadillas

Cooking time: 30 to 45
  minutes
Yield: 12 to 15 servings
Temperature: 350 degrees

Marinade:
2 cups vegetable oil
$1/2$ cup lemon juice
$1/2$ cup soy sauce
$1/2$ cup green onions,
  chopped
1 tablespoon garlic
  powder
$1/8$ cup pepper
$1/8$ cup celery salt

24 flour tortillas
15 boneless breasts of
  chicken, marinated
1 pound refried beans
8 ounces green chiles
3 cups salsa
4 cups Cheddar cheese,
  shredded

Rinse and trim the chicken breasts. Mix all the ingredients for the marinade together in a pan. Arrange the chicken breasts in a single layer in the marinade, cover and let sit for at least 2 hours in the refrigerator.

Preheat the oven to 350 degrees. Place the marinated chicken breasts in a baking pan and bake for 20 to 30 minutes, making sure they are thoroughly cooked. Remove from the oven and slice the chicken into strips. Set aside.

Lay out 12 tortillas and spread them with refried beans, green chiles and salsa. Add the reserved chicken slices and top with Cheddar cheese. Finish with another tortilla. Put the tortillas in a lightly greased fry pan and fry for 10 to 15 minutes per side. Serve with Mexican rice, sour cream and salsa.

# Chicken Scaloppini with Linguini and Mushrooms

On a plate, mix the bread crumbs, salt, pepper and Parmesan. Fold back the small fillet of meat on the underside of each chicken breast half. Place the breasts between 2 sheets of wax paper and pound to a thickness of $1/8$ inch. Coat each breast with the crumb mixture, shaking off the excess.

In a 14 to 15-inch skillet, melt 1 tablespoon of the butter over moderately high heat. Add the chicken and cook 4 to 5 minutes on each side, until golden, adding more of the butter as needed. Transfer the cooked chicken to a dish and keep warm.

Add the bouillon and sherry to the skillet and stir briskly to release the browned bits from the bottom. Lift the skillet and swirl the frothing liquid around. Return to heat. Add the mushrooms and lemon juice, cooking for a few seconds, stirring constantly, until the sauce looks syrupy.

Quickly arrange the linguini on a platter and toss with the mushroom sauce. Arrange the chicken breasts and lemon slices on top.

Yield: 4 servings

$1/4$ cup bread crumbs
$1/4$ teaspoon salt
Pepper
2 tablespoons grated Parmesan cheese
2 chicken breasts, boned and skinless, cut in half
2 tablespoons butter
1 teaspoon chicken flavor instant bouillon, dissolved in $1/4$ cup hot water
2 tablespoons dry sherry wine
8 ounces fresh mushrooms, sliced
1 teaspoon lemon juice
6 ounces linguini, cooked and drained
Lemon slices (optional)

# Beef Stew with Shitake Mushrooms and Baby Veggies

Cooking time: 2 hours
Yield: 6 servings

All-purpose flour
Salt and pepper
6 tablespoons butter
3 pounds boneless beef
  chuck, trimmed and
  cubed (1 $1/2$-inch)
2 large onions, chopped
$1/4$ cup tomato paste
3 cups dry red wine
2 - 14 $1/2$ ounce cans beef
  broth
1 tablespoon dark
  brown sugar
1 $1/2$ pounds baby red-
  skinned potatoes,
  quartered
30 baby carrots,
  trimmed
12 - 14 ounce baby
  pattypan squash,
  halved
1 pound fresh Shitake
  mushrooms, stemmed
  and caps thickly sliced
3 tablespoons chopped
  fresh marjoram or 1
  tablespoon of the dried

Place the flour in a baking pan. Season with salt and pepper. Melt 4 tablespoons of the butter in a large heavy Dutch oven over medium-high heat. Working in batches, coat the meat with the flour and add to the pot, browning the pieces on all sides. Using a slotted spoon, transfer the browned meat to a plate.

Melt the remaining butter in the same pot over medium-high heat. Add the onions and sauté until tender, about 6 minutes. Mix in the tomato paste, then the wine. Bring to a boil, scraping up any browned bits. Add the broth and sugar. Next, add the beef and any accumulated juices from the plate. Bring the mixture to a boil again. Reduce heat, cover partially and simmer for 1 $1/2$ hours.

Add the potatoes and carrots. Simmer uncovered until the meat and vegetables are almost tender, about 25 minutes. Add the squash and simmer until almost tender, approximately 10 more minutes. Add the mushrooms and the marjoram, letting it simmer until the mushrooms are tender or about 5 minutes. Season with salt and pepper.

This dish can be made a day ahead. If you do, cool it slightly, cover and refrigerate. Before serving, cook over medium heat, stirring occasionally, until hot. Also is delicious served in a bread bowl.

# Caciucco Alla Livornese
# (Fish Stew)

Heat the oil in a large saucepan over moderate heat. Chop the onions, carrots, celery, parsley and chile pepper finely, then add to the saucepan. Cook until the onion begins to color. Cut the squid and octopus into small pieces. Add the lobster, shrimp, squid and octopus and mix well. Cook gently for 10 minutes. Pour in the wine and hot water.

Remove the lobster and shrimp from the stew. Run the tomatoes through a food mill and add to the remaining mixture; simmer for 10 minutes. Season with salt. Remove all of the remaining seafood from the stew and set aside.

Steam the mussels and clams in another large saucepan of water over moderate heat. Be sure to steam them just until the shells open. Strain the cooking liquid and add it to the stew. Slice all of the remaining fish into small pieces and add to the stew; simmer until opaque. Return the reserved seafood to the stew.

While the stew is cooking, toast the bread slices and rub them with garlic. Place the slices in the bottom of a soup tureen. Pour in the fish stew and serve while still very hot.

Note: If some of the seafood, such as the scorpion fish, shark or dogfish are difficult to obtain, locally available fish can be substituted. You may also increase the portions of the other seafood to compensate.

Yield: 6 to 8 servings
Can be stored 5 to 7 days

$1/2$ cup extra virgin olive oil
1 onion
1 carrot
1 celery stalk
$1/2$ cup parsley leaves
1 small hot red chile pepper
1 small lobster, in shell
1 pound large shrimp
1 cuttlefish or squid
10 ounces octopus
1 cup of dry, white wine
$1/2$ cup hot water
10 ounces tomatoes
Salt
1 pound fresh mussels
1 pound fresh clams
2 red mullet or snappers
1 $1/4$ pounds fillets scorpion fish or bream
10 ounces dogfish or shark, cut into pieces
8 thin slices firm course textured bread
2 garlic cloves, halved and crushed

# Coq Au Vin
# (Chicken Stew)

Cooking time: 2 hours
Yield: 4 servings
Temperature: 400 degrees

2 $1/2$ pounds broiler
　chicken, quartered
6 slices of bacon, diced
2 tablespoons butter
8 whole mushrooms
8 small white onions,
　peeled
$2/3$ cup green onion,
　sliced
1 clove garlic, crushed
2 $1/2$ tablespoons flour
1 teaspoon salt
$1/4$ teaspoon dried thyme
　leaves
$1/8$ teaspoon pepper
2 cups red wine
1 cup chicken broth
8 small new potatoes
Parsley, chopped

Wash the chicken and dry on paper towels. In a Dutch oven, sauté the bacon until crisp, then remove. Add butter to the bacon drippings and heat. Add the chicken and brown well all over before removing.

Pour off all but approximately 2 tablespoons of the fat from the Dutch oven. Add the mushrooms and white onions. Cook until browned, then remove the onions and set them aside. Add the green onion and garlic to the Dutch oven. Sauté 2 minutes, then remove from the heat. Stir in the flour, salt, thyme and pepper. Return to the heat and cook, stirring constantly, until the flour is browned, approximately 3 minutes.

Gradually add in the wine and chicken broth and bring to a boil, stirring. Remove from the heat. Stir in the bacon, chicken, onions and mushrooms. Cover the Dutch oven and refrigerate overnight.

Next day, preheat the oven to 400 degrees. Add the potatoes to the chilled chicken mixture and bake, covered, for approximately 2 hours or until the chicken and potatoes are tender. Garnish with parsley.

# Carrot Soup

Melt the butter in a saucepan. Add the carrots, potato, onions and parsnip. Sauté just to coat with butter. Add the broth, bay leaf and nutmeg. Bring to a boil, then reduce to simmer. Salt and pepper to taste. Simmer until the vegetables are soft. Remove the bay leaf, set the soup aside and allow to cool. Puree the vegetables in batches and return to the saucepan. Add the heavy cream. Reheat and serve with a dollop of sour cream.

Cooking time: 1 hour
Yield: 6 to 8 servings
Can be stored for 1 week

1 pound carrots, peeled and diced
1 large potato, peeled and diced
1 medium onion, chopped
1 small parsnip, peeled and diced
2 tablespoons butter
6 cups chicken broth
1 bay leaf
1/4 teaspoon ground nutmeg
1/2 pint heavy cream
1 pint sour cream
Salt and pepper to taste

*"My husband and I just added up all the events we did and there really wasn't any time when we weren't doing something fun. And the food...I thought I would gain ten pounds it was so good..."*

*Cindy*
*Woodland, Texas*

# Jeannine's Garlic Bread

Cooking time: 25 to 30
  minutes
Yield: 2 loaves
Temperature: 375 degrees

4 cups flour
1 tablespoon salt
1 tablespoon sugar
1 package yeast
  (2 teaspoons)
1 teaspoon garlic
  powder
1 cup butter
1 tablespoon parsley
1 tablespoon Parmesan
  cheese
2 cups warm water
Cornmeal

Combine the salt, sugar, yeast and warm water. Slowly add the flour to the mixture until it's no longer sticky. Turn the dough out onto a floured surface and knead, adding extra flour as required. Place the dough in a bowl and cover. Set in a warm place and let rise for 1 hour or until doubled.

Knead the dough a second time. Split the dough into 2 equal portions. Roll out each half into a flat round. Melt the butter, then add the parsley, Parmesan cheese and garlic powder, stirring until combined. Brush the mixture onto the rolled out dough rounds. Roll them up into 2 loaves. Place the loaves on a baking sheet that has been sprinkled with cornmeal. Let rise until doubled in size. Score the tops of the loaves 3 times each, then place into an oven that has been preheated to 375 degrees. Bake for 25 to 30 minutes or until golden brown.

# Colorado's Cheese Cake

Preheat the oven to 400 degrees. Make the crust first by combining the flour, sugar and lemon zest. Cut in the butter, until the mixture is crumbly. Add the egg yolk and vanilla, then blend. Pat 1/3 of the dough mixture into the bottom of a greased 9-inch spring form pan (sides removed).

Bake the crust in the oven for 8 minutes at 400 degrees or until golden brown. Let cool and attach the sides to the pan. Butter the pan lightly and pat the remaining dough on the sides to about 2 inches.

Let the cream cheese stand at room temperature to soften. Beat until creamy, then add the vanilla and lemon zest. Mix together the sugar, flour and salt before gradually adding to the cream cheese mixture. Add the eggs and yolks, one at a time. Gently stir in the cream.

Turn into the crust lined pan. Place in the oven and bake at 450 degrees for 12 minutes. Reduce heat to 300 degrees and continue baking for 55 minutes. Remove and let cool for 30 minutes. Remove the sides of the pan and let cool an additional 2 hours.

Refrigerate the cheese cake and serve topped with fresh berries of your choice.

Cooking time: 75 minutes
Yield: 12 servings
Temperature: 450 then
   300 degrees

Crust:
1 cup flour
1/4 cup sugar
2 tablespoons lemon zest
1/2 cup butter
1 egg yolk
1/2 teaspoon vanilla

Filling:
5 - 8 ounce packages of
   cream cheese
1/2 teaspoon vanilla
1/2 teaspoon lemon zest
1 3/4 cups sugar
3 tablespoons flour
5 whole eggs plus 2 yolks
1/2 teaspoon salt
1/4 cup heavy cream

# Scrumptious Chocolate Cake

Cooking time: 45 minutes
Yield: 12 servings
Temperature: 375 degrees

16 ounces chocolate
  chips, melted
1 cup whipping cream
1/2 cup sugar
4 eggs
1/2 cup cold, strong
  coffee (may substitute
  1/4 cup Kailua and 1/4
  cup coffee)

Preheat the oven to 375 degrees. Beat together the sugar and eggs. Slowly add the cream and coffee. Add the melted chocolate chips and mix well. Pour into a greased and floured spring form pan and bake for approximately 45 minutes or until a cake tester inserted into the middle comes out clean.

*"Not only is Tarryall a place to come on vacation, it is also a place to make friends."*

*Helen*
*England*

# Strawberry - Blueberry Fool

In a small non-reactive saucepan, combine the blueberries, strawberries, lemon juice, granulated sugar and the water. Cook over medium heat, stirring frequently, until the berries begin to burst or breakdown and the juice thickens (about 10 minutes). Remove from the heat and transfer to a small bowl. Place the bowl in a larger bowl filled with ice water and stir occasionally until cold.

In a separate bowl, combine the cream, confectioners sugar and vanilla. Beat until stiff peaks form. Fold in $1/3$ cup of the fruit mixture.

Serve in custard bowls or dessert cups with extra fruit sauce drizzled on top. It can also be served on a slice of angel food cake with extra sauce drizzled over it and a chocolate dipped strawberry on the side.

Cooking time: 10 to 15 minutes
Yield: 4 to 6 servings

$1/2$ pint fresh blueberries, washed and picked over
$1/2$ pint fresh strawberries, washed and sliced
1 teaspoon lemon juice
2 to 3 tablespoons granulated sugar (adjust to taste)
2 tablespoons water
$3/4$ cup heavy whipping cream
2 tablespoons confectioners sugar
1 teaspoon vanilla extract

# White Chocolate Macadamia Cookies

Cooking time: 9 to 11
  minutes
Yield: 5 dozen
Temperature: 350 degrees

2 1/4 cups all-purpose
  flour
2/3 cup baking cocoa
1 teaspoon baking soda
1/4 teaspoon salt
1 cup butter
3/4 cup sugar
2/3 cup packed brown
  sugar
1 teaspoon vanilla
  extract
1 teaspoon mint extract
2 whole eggs
2 cups white chocolate
  chips
1 cup macadamia nuts,
  chopped

Preheat the oven to 350 degrees. In a mixing bowl, combine the flour, baking soda, salt and cocoa. In a separate bowl, beat the butter, both sugars, vanilla and mint until creamy. Beat in the eggs and gradually beat in the flour mixture. Stir in the chips and nuts. Drop the cookie dough by well-rounded teaspoons onto an ungreased baking sheet. Bake for 9 to 11 minutes.

# Tarryall Ham Glaze

Mix all the ingredients together. Place on a baked ham during the last 30 minutes of cooking.

Yield: Covers a 10 pound ham

$1/4$ cup pure maple syrup
$1/4$ cup brown sugar
$1/4$ to $1/3$ cup honey
3 tablespoons mustard, stone ground or Dijon
$1/4$ to $1/2$ tablespoon cinnamon (optional)

*"Your ranch is so picturesque, the staff so friendly and warm, and the food—well, I had to let out my britches, it was so delicious."*

*Sally*
*California*

# Waunita Hot Springs Ranch

**Waunita Hot Springs Ranch**
**8007 County Road 887**
**PO Box 7D**
**Gunnison, CO 81230**
**(970) 641-1266**
**rpringle@csn.net**
**The Pringle Family**
**Elevation 8,946 feet**

Waunita Hot Springs Ranch, located high in the Colorado Rockies at 8,946 feet, is 10 miles west of the Continental Divide. The ranch is surrounded by Gunnison National Forest land and summer pasture. U.S. Forest permits and private leases enable them to ride on, pasture and otherwise enjoy use of thousands of acres in eastern Gunnison County.

Buildings at the ranch are a wonderful combination of new comfort and old charm, spacious and cozy. Carpeted, paneled guest rooms have private baths and most have queen beds, bunks and doubles for the kids. The deck spa and 35 x 90 foot swimming pool are fed by crystal clear hot springs. The pool is one of the largest private pools in Western Colorado. The barn complex includes a rec room/music hall.

Summers at Waunita are crisp and cool, interrupted by an occasional afternoon thundershower. Flowers and wildlife abound on and near the ranch. Winters are cold enough for snow to cover the ground from November through March.

Meals are served family and buffet style–all you can eat, with snacks of cookies, fruit, coffee and punch in between. Cookouts include breakfast, lunch and dinner at different locations on forest-land. The yard barbecue area is used a couple of times each week. Our experienced and talented kitchen staff provides wholesome, delectable meals, featuring homemade breads and desserts. Their no-alcohol policy compliments the family atmosphere.

Horseback riding is available every summer day except Sunday and you have your own horse for the week. Rides are grouped by age and ability. If they wish, families may ride together. Instructions in the arena and on the many trails are designed to give you a truly enjoyable riding experience. Featured each week are three cookout rides and a morning of arena games. One of the high points of the week is the high country ride to the snow ridged peaks of Stella and Granite Mountains overlooking the Continental Divide.

Children are included in most activities at the ranch, so your family can enjoy doing things together. However, rides and some activities are planned especially for kids. Waunita is a natural playground–and there are no poisonous snakes! When it's time to head for home, you just may have to pull your kids off the front-porch rail!

The many other activities available at the ranch include scenic 4 x4 trips, evening hay-rides, overnight camp-outs, fishing, hiking, Gunnison River raft trips, square dancing, rock-hunting, softball, movies, slide shows, ping-pong, pool, horseshoes and swimming. A full week's activities are planned for you...or you may just choose to do nothing at all.

September is a special time in the mountains. The brilliant display of fall colors is a once-a-year show. In October and November guided hunts are provided for a limited number of hunters. From December thru mid-April ranch facilities are available for downhill ski groups, church retreats, or small group meetings. Contact them for winter rates.

# Egg Rolls

Sauté the onions and celery in 2 tablespoons oil. Shred the cabbage. Mix with the onions, celery, bean sprouts, mushrooms and shrimp. Spoon about $1/3$ cup of the cabbage mixture onto each wrapper. Roll up tightly and seal with paste made of flour and water. Fry in oil until lightly brown, turning to fry evenly. Serve with sweet and sour sauce.

Yield: 6 servings

2 tablespoons vegetable oil
$1/4$ cup onions, chopped
$1/4$ cup celery, chopped
$1/2$ small head cabbage
1 $1/2$ cups bean sprouts
1 cup fresh mushrooms, sliced
1 to 1 $1/2$ cups cooked shrimp or pork
12 egg roll wrappers
Cooking oil

*"I want to thank you and your staff for an outstanding week!"*

*Wayne B.*
*Littleton, Colorado*

# Swiss Cream Steak

Cooking time: 50 minutes
Yield: 6 servings
Temperature: medium

6 tablespoons cooking
  oil
2 cups onions, sliced
2 pounds round steak
$1/2$ cup flour
1 tablespoon salt
1 teaspoon black pepper
1 teaspoon paprika
1 cup water
$1/2$ cup sour cream

In a large skillet, sauté the onions in 4 tablespoons cooking oil. Remove from the skillet and set aside. Cut the steak into $1/2$-inch thick strips and dredge in flour seasoned with salt, pepper and paprika. Add 2 tablespoons cooking oil to the skillet and brown the meat well on both sides. Mix in the sautéed onions, water and sour cream until blended. Cover and cook over medium heat, until the meat is tender, about 40 minutes. Uncover and cook until the sauce thickens, about 10 minutes.

*"Our week at Waunita was special and your personal touch made it extra special. Thanks for a great vacation!"*

*Ron & Susan Y.*
*Granada Hills, California*

# Mushroom Chicken Bake

Preheat the oven to 335 degrees. Spray a 9-inch square baking dish with cooking spray. Arrange the chicken in the dish. Mix together the sour cream, soup and mushrooms. Pour over the chicken. Sprinkle parsley flakes and paprika on top of the chicken mixture. Bake for 1 hour.

Good served with rice or noodles.

*"Thank you once again for making our summer complete. Our week at Waunita was truly a blessing. We look forward to seeing you again next summer."*

*Marge P.*
*Bartlesville, Oklahoma*

Cooking time: 1 hour
Yield: 6 servings
Temperature: 335 degrees
Can be stored overnight
  in the refrigerator.

6 chicken breasts (or
  your favorite pieces)
1 cup sour cream
2 cans cream of
  mushroom soup
1 - 4 ounce can
  mushrooms, undrained
2 tablespoons dried
  parsley flakes
1 teaspoon paprika

# Baked Spiced Pork Chops

Cooking time: 1 hour
Yield: 8 servings
Temperature: 325 degrees

8 pork chops
1/2 teaspoon cloves
1/2 teaspoon allspice
1/4 teaspoon pepper
3 tablespoons vinegar
1/3 cup brown sugar
1 tablespoon cornstarch

Brown pork chops in a skillet. Remove and place in a casserole dish. Mix the remaining ingredients in a skillet and cook for 3 minutes. Pour over the pork chops and bake 1 hour at 325 degrees.

*"Our family reunion at Waunita Hot Springs was all that we could have hoped for and more."*

*Jim & Ann N.*
*SugarLand, Texas*

# Tacoritas

Preheat the oven to 350 degrees. Combine the chicken soup, water, chili powder, onion powder, sage and cumin to create the sauce. Brown the meat and onions. Add $1/4$ of the sauce mixture to the meat. Spoon the meat mixture into tortillas, using $1/2$ cup of the mixture for each tortilla. Fold like an envelope and place the folded side down in a greased 9 x 14-inch baking dish. Pour the remaining sauce over the tortillas. Top with cheese and bake for 30 minutes. Serve warm, topped with salsa and sour cream, if desired.

*"...we had a wonderful time and can't wait to come back. Thank you for clean rooms, fresh towels, delicious meals, wonderful hospitality and that warm family feeling we had during our entire stay..."*

*Pam & Mike S.*
*Northville, Michigan*

Cooking time: 30 minutes
Yield: 10 servings
Temperature: 350 degrees
Can be stored for 2 days
  in refrigerator.

3 cans cream of chicken
  soup
2 soup cans water
2 tablespoons chili
  powder
1 teaspoon onion
  powder
1 teaspoon sage
  (optional)
1 teaspoon cumin
2 pounds lean ground
  beef
1 onion, chopped
10 large flour tortillas
  (8-inch)
1 cup cheese, grated
Salsa and sour cream
  (optional)

# Salmon Patties

**Yield: 4 servings**

1 large can salmon,
  flaked
1/4 teaspoon pepper
1 tablespoon prepared
  mustard
2 eggs, beaten
1/2 cup milk
1 tablespoon flour
Soda cracker crumbs
Corn oil
Lemon wedges

In a bowl, mix together the salmon, pepper and mustard. Mix the eggs, milk and flour in a heavy saucepan. Cook slowly, stirring constantly, until very thick. Add the salmon mixture and the crumbs of 4 crackers. Mix and let cool. Form into patties. Roll in additional cracker crumbs. Fry in corn oil in a skillet, until brown on each side. Serve with lemon wedges.

*"A big thank you for the wonderful week we just spent at the ranch. Your entire staff did everything possible to make our stay memorable. The variety of activities at Waunita and the organized way they were carried out was truly amazing. We're ready to plan our next trip to Waunita."*

*Bill & Anita N.*
*Ames, Iowa*

# Country Egg Casserole

Layer the potatoes, eggs, sausage and mushrooms in a 9 x 11-inch casserole dish. Combine the soup and milk and pour over the casserole. Salt and pepper to taste. Top with cheese and onions. Bake in preheated 350 degree oven for 25 minutes or until bubbly.

Cooking time: 25 minutes
Yield: 8 servings
Temperature: 350 degrees

3 cups frozen potatoes, diced or baked potatoes, chopped
8 hard-boiled eggs, sliced
8 cooked link sausages, quartered
1 - 4 ounce can mushrooms or $2/3$ cup fresh
1 can cream of mushroom soup
1 soup can milk
1 cup Monterey Jack cheese
3 green onions, chopped
Salt & pepper to taste

*"...all of you have a special place in my heart... thank you for a great and memorable week at Waunita. I really miss Waunita and can't wait to get back. Unfortunately, I must wait a whole year to see you all again."*

*Sarah B. (age 14)*
*Quakertown, Pennsylvania*

# Corn Chowder

Cooking time: 25 minutes
Yield: 8 to 10 servings

4 slices lean bacon
1 large onion, thinly
  sliced
2 cups raw potatoes,
  diced
2 cups water
Salt and pepper to taste
2 - 17 ounce cans
  cream-style corn
2 cups milk
1 tablespoon margarine

Fry the bacon in a large saucepan. Remove from pan and sauté onion in the bacon drippings. Add the potatoes, water, salt and pepper. Stir, cover and simmer about 20 minutes. Add the undrained corn and milk. Stir and simmer 5 minutes longer. Crumble the bacon into the chowder. Add margarine, stir and serve.

*"...it really was the best week of the year. I wanted to say bye, but we all would of cried when we said bye. See ya next year!"*

*Lisa G. (age 9)*
*Louisville, Kentucky*

# Sweet Potato Crisp

In a bowl, mix the potatoes, sugar, margarine, eggs, milk and vanilla until creamy. Combine the brown sugar and flour. Add the melted margarine and pecans. Place the sweet potato mixture in a large casserole dish. Cover with the brown sugar mixture. Bake in an oven preheated to 350 degrees for about 30 minutes or until thoroughly heated.

*"...I just wanted to say how much Clint and I enjoyed our week at the ranch for our honeymoon. Thank you for sharing your home with us."*

*Jill K.*
*Savoy, Illinois*

Cooking time: 30 minutes
Yield: 10 to 12 servings
Temperature: 350 degrees

7 cups cooked sweet
  potatoes, mashed
3/4 cup sugar
3/4 cup margarine
2 eggs
1/3 cup milk
1 teaspoon vanilla
3/4 cup margarine,
  melted
3/4 cup light brown
  sugar
1/2 cup flour
3/4 cup pecans, chopped

# Aloha Banana Bread

Cooking time: 1 hour
Yield: 1 loaf
Temperature: 350 degrees

2 cups flour
1 tablespoon baking
  soda
1/2 teaspoon salt
1/2 cup margarine
1 cup sugar
2 eggs
1 cup bananas, mashed
1 tablespoon orange
  peel, grated
1/4 cup milk
1 teaspoon vanilla
1/2 teaspoon almond
  flavoring
1 cup coconut, shredded
1/2 cup nuts, chopped

Preheat the oven to 350 degrees. Sift together the flour, baking soda and salt in a bowl. Cream the margarine and sugar together in a separate bowl. Add the eggs, bananas and orange peel; blend. Combine the milk with the vanilla and almond extract. Add alternately to the batter with sifted dry ingredients. Stir in the coconut and nuts. Turn into a greased loaf pan. Bake for 1 hour.

*"Jane and I just wanted to thank you again for a wonderful week. It was the perfect way for us to celebrate our 25th anniversary."*

*Steve J.*
*Joplin, Missouri*

# A TYPICAL SUMMER WEEK

**SUNDAY**
Afternoon .........Check-in
Evening ...........Orientation and softball

**MONDAY**
Morning............Horse assignments, instruction
               ride to Lower Springs
Afternoon .........1 hr. ride to Tomichi Dome
.........................2 hr. ride to Tomichi Dome
.........................North Star Mine Area 4x4 trip
Evening ...........Hay-ride & marshmallow
               roast

**TUESDAY**
Morning............Breakfast cookout ride
.........................Suburban trip to breakfast
               cookout
Afternoon .........Gunnison/Taylor River raft
               trips
.........................2 hr. ride to Greathouse Gulch
Evening ...........Western music show

**WEDNESDAY**
Morning............1 1/2 hr. ridge ride
.........................3 hr. Bear Valley ride
.........................Loping lessons & trail ride
.........................Fishing trip
Afternoon .........1 1/2 hr. Big Valley ride
.........................3 hr. Bear Valley ride
.........................Loping lessons & trail ride
.........................Van trip to Alpine Tunnel area
Evening ...........Square dancing and ice cream
               social

**THURSDAY**
Morning............Arena games and competitive
               cattle penning
.........................Van trip to Gunnison for
               shopping and/or museum
Afternoon .........3 hr. ride to Canyon Creek
               camp for evening cookout
.........................Vehicle trip to Canyon Creek
Evening ...........Overnight at Canyon Creek
               (optional)

**FRIDAY**
Morning............High country ride
Afternoon .........Lunch ride at ranch
.........................Van trip to Crested Butte
Evening ...........Slide show

**SATURDAY**
Morning............3 hr. ride over Little Baldy
.........................1 1/2 hr. ride to lunch cookout
.........................Vehicle trip to lunch cookout
Afternoon .........1 hr. return ride to ranch
.........................Check-out

# Toffee Banana Bread

Cooking time: 1 hour
Yield: 2 loaves
Temperature: 350 degrees

3/4 cup margarine,
  softened
1 1/2 cups sugar
4 eggs
1 1/2 teaspoons vanilla
3 cups flour
1 1/2 teaspoons baking
  soda
1 teaspoon salt
4 large ripe bananas,
  mashed
1 cup toffee bars
  (Heath bars), crushed

Preheat the oven to 350 degrees. Cream together the margarine and sugar. Add the eggs and vanilla and continue beating until creamy. In a separate bowl, combine the flour, baking soda and salt. Blend into the creamed mixture. Fold in the mashed bananas and Heath bars. Pour into 2 greased and lightly floured loaf pans. Bake for 1 hour or until it tests done.

*"Once again, I want to thank you for a great week! It's always like returning to my second home! I hope to return again next year, and etc, etc!"*

*Lois H.*
*Pittsburgh, Pennsylvania*

# Blueberry Muffins

Preheat the oven to 375 degrees. Combine the flour, sugar, baking powder and salt. In a separate bowl, beat the eggs. Blend in the milk, margarine, nutmeg and vanilla. Pour into the dry ingredients and mix until moistened. Fold in the blueberries. Spray muffin cups with cooking spray and fill 2/3 full. Bake for 20 to 25 minutes. Remove from the oven and brush tops with melted margarine; sprinkle with a sugar/cinnamon mixture. Serve warm.

*"…I wanted to let you know that we enjoyed our week with you and wanted to compliment you on how well organized your business is run. Everything is thoughtfully planned from the delicious menus to the varied activities…"*

*Susan, Harry, Rachel & Grayson B.*
*Waukesha, Wisconsin*

Cooking time: 20 to 25 minutes
Yield: 16 muffins
Temperature: 375 degrees

2 cups flour
2/3 cup sugar
1 tablespoon baking powder
1/2 teaspoon salt
2 eggs
1 cup milk
1/3 cup margarine, melted
1 teaspoon nutmeg
1 teaspoon vanilla
1 cup blueberries*
Melted margarine
Sugar-cinnamon mixture

*If using frozen blueberries, rinse and toss in a small amount of flour before adding to the batter.

# Crustless Cheesecake

Cooking time: 1 hour
Yield: 10 servings
Temperature: 325 degrees
Can be stored for 3 days
  in the refrigerator.

16 ounces cream cheese
2/3 cup sugar
3 eggs
1/2 teaspoon vanilla
1 teaspoon lemon juice

Topping:
2 cups sour cream
3 tablespoons sugar
1 teaspoon vanilla
1 teaspoon lemon juice

Preheat the oven to 325 degrees. Soften the cream cheese and beat well with sugar. Add the eggs, one at a time, beating well. Add the vanilla and lemon juice, mixing well. Pour into a buttered glass pie plate and bake 50 minutes or until light brown. Remove from oven and cool for 12 minutes.

Mix the topping ingredients and spread over the top of the pie. Bake for an additional 10 minutes. Chill for at least 4 hours before serving.

*"...thank you for a wonderful vacation. We all had a marvelous time. Your ranch is everything it claims to be and a lot more. We all loved the family atmosphere, the quiet, the relaxed pace. The delicious home cooking..."*

*Rhoda M.*
*Huxley, Iowa*

# Pumpkin Cheesecake

Combine 1 cup of cookie crumbs with 3 tablespoons melted margarine and the brown sugar. Brush the side of an 8-inch spring form pan with 1 tablespoon melted margarine. Sprinkle 3 tablespoons cookie crumbs over margarine, rotating pan to coat the sides. Pour the prepared crumb mixture evenly over the bottom of the pan, pressing firmly to make bottom crust. Refrigerate to set.

To make filling, sprinkle gelatin over 1/3 cup cool water in small glass bowl or cup. Let stand 5 minutes to soften. Place 1 cup of softened gelatin in a small saucepan with one inch of water. Cook on medium heat until the gelatin is dissolved, about 1 minute. Remove cup from water and set aside to cool slightly. Beat the heavy cream in a medium-size bowl until stiff; set aside. Beat the softened cream cheese with the sugar in a large bowl until smooth. Add the pumpkin, ginger, cinnamon and cloves, beating until well mixed. Stir in the gelatin. Gently fold in the whipped cream. Pour the mixture into the prepared crust. Refrigerate 4 hours to overnight.

*"I really enjoyed my vacation. I had fun riding Chocolate. Take care of her for me. I will look forward to seeing you next year."*

*Alexander S. (age 8)*
*Houston, Texas*

**Yield: 12 servings**

1 cup plus 3 tablespoons gingersnap cookie crumbs (about 24 cookies)
4 tablespoons margarine, melted
1 tablespoon light brown sugar
2 envelopes unflavored gelatin
1/3 cup cool water
1 cup heavy cream
16 ounces cream cheese, softened
2/3 cup sugar
1 can pumpkin
1/2 teaspoon ground ginger
1/2 teaspoon cinnamon
1/8 teaspoon ground cloves

# Apple Fritters

Cooking time: 5 minutes
Yield: 30 fritters
Temperature: 375 degrees

2 cups apples, grated
2 tablespoons milk
2 eggs, beaten
1 tablespoon margarine,
   melted
1 cup flour
3 tablespoons sugar
1 teaspoon baking
   powder
1/2 teaspoon salt
1/4 teaspoon cinnamon
1/8 teaspoon nutmeg
1 cup powdered sugar
Vegetable Oil

Mix all the ingredients, except the powdered sugar and vegetable oil, in a bowl. Pour oil into a deep kettle to about 2 inches deep. Heat to about 375 degrees or until a small amount of batter quickly pops to the surface. Drop batter by rounded teaspoonfuls into the hot oil. When browned on one side, turn with a ladle, cooking until golden brown on both sides. Drain on a paper towel. Place powdered sugar in paper or plastic bag. Shake the fritters in the bag a few at a time.

If the batter is not all used immediately, you may need to add extra flour.

We cook and serve Apple Fritters at our lunch cookout.

*"I had a great summer vacation. I had a lot of fun riding to breakfast, lunch and dinner. I also had a great time riding and rafting. I will see you next year…"*

*Alicia S. (age 8)*
*Houston, Texas*

# Cream Puffs

Boil the water and margarine. Add the flour all at once and stir until it comes away from the sides of the pan. Pour into a large mixing bowl and add the eggs, 3 at a time, beating well after each addition. Drop by rounded $1/4$-cupful onto a greased cookie sheet. Bake in a preheated oven at 425 degrees for 15 minutes, then at 350 degrees until very golden brown; cool. Slice off the tops of the puffs about $1/3$ down and gently scoop out the insides. Prepare the pudding according to the package directions. Combine the pudding with the whipped topping. Fill the hollowed out insides of the puffs with this mixture and replace the tops. Drizzle with chocolate syrup, if desired.

Cooking time: 20 to 25 minutes
Yield: 28 puffs
Temperature: 425 then 350 degrees

3 cups water
1 cup margarine
3 cups flour
12 eggs

Filling:
1 - 6 ounce package instant vanilla pudding
2 packages whipped topping (or large container frozen whipped topping, thawed)

*"Thank you so much for the wonderful week we spent with you at Waunita. After a vote, we all agree that it's the best family vacation we've ever had. We can't think of a thing we could add or change about Waunita, your service, food, staff, activities, etc..."*

*Charles & LaSandra A.*
*New Port Richey, Florida*

# Hawaiian Drop Cookies

Cooking time: 20 minutes
Yield: 4 1/2 dozen
Temperature: 325 degrees

1 3/4 cups flour
2 teaspoons baking
  powder
1/2 teaspoon salt
2/3 cup shortening
1 cup sugar
1/2 teaspoon vanilla
1/2 teaspoon almond
  flavoring
1 egg
3/4 cup crushed
  pineapple, drained
1/2 cup shredded
  coconut, chopped

Preheat the oven to 325 degrees. Mix the flour, baking powder and salt together in a bowl. In a separate bowl, cream the shortening, sugar and flavorings together. Beat in the egg until mixture is fluffy. Blend in the pineapple and dry ingredients. Drop the batter by teaspoonfuls 3 inches apart onto an ungreased cookie sheet. Sprinkle with coconut. Bake for about 20 minutes.

*"We just wanted to say thanks again for the best vacation we've ever had! And thank you for making us feel right at home..."*

*Michelle R.*
*Auburn, Massachusetts*

# Honey Crunch Mix

Combine the cereal, oats and nuts in a large mixing bowl. Mix the butter, honey, brown sugar and cinnamon in a saucepan. Cook until the sugar dissolves. Pour over the cereal and toss to coat. Spray two jelly roll pans with cooking spray. Spread mixture evenly in pans. Bake 30 minutes in an oven preheated to 325 degrees, stirring occasionally. Stir in the raisins and/or coconut. Spread onto waxed paper and cool. Store in a tightly covered container.

Cooking time: 30 minutes
Yield: 6 quarts
Temperature: 325 degrees
Can be stored for 2 weeks.

6 cups crisp corn/rice cereal
2 cups old-fashioned oats
2 cups pecan halves
2 cups sliced almonds
1 cup butter or margarine
2/3 cup honey
1/3 cup brown sugar
1 tablespoon cinnamon
1 cup raisins (optional)
1 cup coconut, coarsely flaked

*"…if we ever come back to a ranch in the U.S., be sure that it would be at your place. We have such great memories of the week we spent with all of you…"*

*Elie & Chantal B.*
*Montfavet, France*

# Whistling Acres Guest Ranch

**Whistling Acres Guest Ranch**
**PO Box 88CD**
**Paonia, CO 81428**
**(800) 346-1420**
**(970) 527-4560**
**www.whistlingacres.com**
**WRanch050@AOL.com**
**Bill and Bev Madison**
**Elevation 6,200 feet**

Less than twenty years ago Whistling Acres Ranch was a combination cattle ranch and haying operation. Ed Allen purchased the ranch with an eye toward getting into the guest ranch business. As a result the ranch still raises a couple hundred head of cattle, raises all of its own hay and has the privilege of playing host to some terrific guests.

Located just outside of Paonia, Cherry Capital of Colorado, Whistling Acres enjoys easy access to Gunnison National Forest. Being at an altitude of 6,200 feet in the scenic southwest section of the state, the ranch provides the perfect setting for a vacation get-away.

During the summers, the town of Paonia plays host to Cherry Days, filling City Park with artisan and food booths, as well as live entertainment. Guests can also visit nearby Black Canyon of the Gunnison National Monument, a spectacular natural gorge carved by the river in its tumultuous rush to join the Colorado River. Also close by is Grand Mesa, the largest flat-topped mountain in the world. In addition to the natural wonders surrounding Whistling Acres Guest Ranch there is Fort Uncompahgre, a living history museum run by two mountain men, who come to the ranch to entertain the guests each week.

There has never been a guest who left Whistling Acres Guest Ranch hungry. Guests often wake up to the smell of fresh-baked cinnamon rolls, eggs, bacon, pancakes and fresh brewed coffee. Thick roast beef sandwiches make an appearance for lunch, followed by a dinner of either steak or roast chicken. Meals are served in a pleasant, inviting atmosphere where the conversation is as good as the food. Guests have the chance to sit down to dinner with the ranch hands and get to know what life on a working ranch is really like. Other meals might be served in the picnic area, at barbecues, on hayrides, on the trail or just about any time the guests get hungry.

Whatever the season, Whistling Acres Guest Ranch is the ideal Colorado vacation spot for the whole family. Enjoy the food, the fun and an unforgettable vacation experience.

# Chicken Teriyaki

In a saucepan, stir together the brown sugar, soy sauce, sherry, onion and garlic. Cook and stir over low heat, until the sugar dissolves. Cook uncovered, until it looks like syrup, about 5 minutes. Allow to cool. Pour the soy mixture over the breast halves. Cover and keep refrigerated for 4 to 6 hours or overnight.

Remove the chicken and reserve the marinade to baste with while cooking. Grill the chicken over medium to hot coals for 10 minutes. Turn the meat and cook for another 10 to 15 minutes. Brush frequently with the marinade.

Leftovers make great salad mixings.

Cooking time: 30 to 40 minutes
Yield: 8 servings
Temperature: medium to hot coals

1/2 cup packed brown sugar
1/2 cup soy sauce
2 tablespoons cooking sherry or vinegar
1 tablespoon onion, minced
1 garlic clove, minced
8 to 10 boneless chicken breast halves

# Chile Relleno Casserole

Cooking time: 1 hour
Yield: 6 servings
Temperature: 350 degrees

5 eggs
1 1/4 cups milk
1/4 cup flour
1/2 teaspoon salt
1/2 teaspoon Tabasco
  sauce
1/2 teaspoon paprika
Pepper to taste
1 large can of whole
  green chiles
2 pounds Monterey Jack
  cheese
1/2 to 1 pound shredded
  Cheddar cheese

Preheat the oven to 350 degrees. Mix the eggs, milk, flour and spices together, until frothy. Stuff the chiles with sticks of Jack cheese. Layer the chiles into a 7 x 13-inch baking pan. Pour the egg mixture over the top of the chiles. Sprinkle with the Cheddar cheese and bake for 1 hour.

# Chinese Salad

Mix the dressing ingredients, blending well. Refrigerate in an airtight container.

Mix together the ingredients for the topping with the exception of the oil and margarine. Place in a shallow skillet and brown using the sesame oil and margarine. Once browned, let the mixture cool on a cookie sheet.

Just prior to serving, mix the cabbage, topping and dressing together. For variety you can add chopped green onions.

**Goes well with Chicken Teriyaki**

*"We had a great time, and we've had Karen's awesome Chinese Salad...thanks for the recipe!"*

*Mission Hills, Kansas*

Yield: 10 to 12 servings
The dressing can be
  stored for up to 2 weeks

Dressing:
1 cup oil
1 cup sugar
1/2 cup cider vinegar
1 package Ramen
  noodle seasoning
2 tablespoons soy sauce
1 teaspoon salt
1 teaspoon pepper
1 teaspoon garlic
  powder

Topping:
2 packages of Ramen
  noodles (chicken), bro-
  ken up
1/2 cup sesame seeds
1/2 cup slivered almonds
1/4 cup sesame oil
1/4 cup margarine

1 to 2 heads cabbage,
  chopped

# Cucumber Salad

Yield: 12 servings
The dressing can be
  stored for 8 to 10 days
  before mixing with the
  cucumbers. Keeps for 4
  or 5 days after mixing.

Dressing:
2 to 3 tablespoons sugar
3 tablespoons vinegar
  (cider vinegar is best)
2 tablespoons oil
1 teaspoon salt

6 or 7 cucumbers, peeled
  and sliced
1 large or 2 small red
  onions, sliced thin

Slice the cucumbers and onions and place in a large bowl with an air tight seal. Mix or shake together the dressing ingredients until dissolved. Pour over the cucumbers and onions; mix well. Refrigerate for at least 2 hours before serving. This is better if you let it sit in the refrigerator overnight.

This is a great summer salad for picnics or hayrides!

*"My favorite thing was riding Zipper. P.S. Thanks for the great food!"*

*An 8 year old*
*Denver, Colorado*

# Angel Biscuits

Dissolve the yeast in the warm water and set aside. Mix the dry ingredients in the order given, then cut in the shortening. Stir in the buttermilk and the yeast mixture, blending well. Knead the dough until it's the desired consistency. You can refrigerate the dough at this point, pulling off what you want to use at later times.

Roll the dough out on a floured board. Cut the dough with a biscuit cutter and place on a greased cookie sheet about 1/2 inch apart. You can either let the dough rise for approximately 30 minutes or bake immediately in an oven preheated to 400 degrees for 12 to 15 minutes.

This is always a popular item at our cowboy suppers.

Cooking time: 12 to 15 minutes
Yield: 18 biscuits
Temperature: 400 degrees
Can be stored for 3 to 4 days in a cooler before or after baking

1 package dry yeast
1/4 cup warm water (80 degrees)
2 1/2 cups flour
1/2 teaspoon baking soda
1 teaspoon baking powder
1 teaspoon salt
1/8 cup sugar
1/2 cup shortening
1 cup buttermilk

# Melt In Your Mouth Muffins

Cooking time: 25 to 30
  minutes
Yield: 12 muffins
Temperature: 400 degrees
Can be stored for several
  days or can be frozen

2 cups flour
1/4 cup sugar
3 teaspoons baking
  powder
1/2 teaspoon salt
1/4 cup oil
1 egg
1 cup milk

Topping:
1 cube of butter or
  margarine, melted
2 tablespoons cinnamon
2 teaspoons sugar

Preheat oven to 400 degrees. Mix all the muffin ingredients together, until just moist. The batter should be lumpy. Pour into muffin pans, filling each cup about 1/2 full. Bake for 25 to 30 minutes.

Mix the cinnamon and sugar together in a shallow bowl. When the muffins come out of the oven, dip each into the melted butter and roll in the cinnamon/sugar mix. Serve immediately.

# Crème de Menthe Cake

Prepare the cake mix as per the package directions, adding 3 tablespoons of the Crème de Menthe into the batter. Bake according to mix directions and let cool for 45 minutes. Spread the fudge on top of the cake. Let cool completely.

Mix the non-dairy topping and remaining Crème de Menthe together. Spread over the top of the fudge. Refrigerate the cake.

You can also garnish the cake with shaved chocolate curls in addition to the topping above.

Cooking time: follow
  package directions
Yield: 15 servings
Temperature: follow
  package directions
Can be stored for 2 to 4
  days

1 White cake mix
3 tablespoons Crème de
  Menthe liqueur
1 jar of Hershey's
  Chocolate Shoppe
  Fudge

Topping:
8 ounces non-dairy
  topping
3 tablespoons Crème de
  Menthe liqueur

# Peanut Crunch Ice Cream Pie

Yield: 8 servings
Can be stored for 2 to 3
  weeks in the freezer

1/2 cup peanut butter
1/2 cup white corn syrup
2 cups Rice Krispies
1 quart vanilla ice
  cream, softened

Mix the peanut butter and syrup until smooth. Add the Rice Krispies, mixing well. Press the mixture evenly and firmly around the sides and bottom of a 9-inch pie pan to form the pie crust. Spread the softened ice cream over the crust. Freeze until ready to serve.

Top with the fresh, canned or frozen fruit of your choice.

*"Still talking about the wonderful & delicious meals we had. If possible, could I get the recipe for that peanut ice cream pie?"*

*Corpus Christi, Texas*

# Buttermilk Brownies

Preheat the oven to 350 degrees. Mix the flour, sugar, salt and baking soda together on waxed paper and set aside. In a large bowl, heat the shortening, water and cocoa in a microwave to boiling, mixing thoroughly. Add the flour mixture, eggs, buttermilk and vanilla. Stir until well mixed. Pour into a greased 13 x 9-inch pan and bake.

To make the frosting, bring the milk and butter to a boil in the microwave. Add the chocolate chips and stir until melted. Add the powdered sugar until the desired consistency is achieved. Spread on the hot brownies.

Substitute mint chocolate chips or raspberry chips for the regular chocolate chips.

Cooking time: 25 to 30 minutes
Yield: 15 to 20 servings
Temperature: 350 degrees

Brownies:
2 cups flour
2 cups sugar
$1/2$ teaspoon salt
1 teaspoon baking soda
1 cup shortening
1 cup water
3 tablespoons cocoa
2 eggs, well beaten
$1/2$ cup buttermilk
1 teaspoon vanilla

Frosting:
6 tablespoons milk
6 tablespoons margarine, melted
1 $1/2$ cups powdered sugar
$1/2$ cup chocolate chips

# Sugar Cookies

Cooking time: 12 to 15
minutes
Yield: varies depending
on the size of the cookie
cutters
Temperature: 375 degrees
Can be stored in an air-
tight container for up to
2 weeks.

1 cup shortening
2 cups sugar
2 eggs
1 tablespoon vanilla
1 teaspoon salt
2 teaspoons baking soda
4 teaspoons baking
powder
1 cup buttermilk or sour
milk
6 cups flour

Preheat the oven to 375 degrees. Mix the shortening, sugar, eggs, vanilla and salt together in a bowl. Combine the baking soda and powder and stir into the milk. Add the milk mixture to the other ingredients, mixing well. Add the flour until the desired consistency for rolling dough is attained. Roll out and cut with cookie cutters. Sprinkle with sugar or leave them plain. Bake for 12 to 15 minutes. Decorate with colored sugar or frosting.

*"Thanks for everything...the food was terrific. I think we all gained about 5 lbs!"*

*Minneapolis, Minnesota*

# Women of the West

## Ann Bassett
## 1878 - 1956

Known in her lifetime as the Queen of Brown's Park, Ann Bassett was a mystery even to those who knew her best. Her life was a series of contradictions, starting with her birth in 1878. The third child of a family of ranching pioneers, she was nursed by a Ute woman from a nearby Indian village. She grew up on one of the most important ranches in Northwest Colorado's Brown's Park. Her father's place sprawled across the only route in or out of the vast high plain, thus insuring that the ranch house was always full of travelers, some of whom were on the run from the law. Here she learned to ride and rope as well as any of the cowboys working on the ranch.

Her father insisted on educating young Ann in more than just the ways of ranch life, so it was off to school, first in Salt Lake City, then on to Boston. Upon her parents' death, Ann returned to take up the reins of running the family ranch, determined to defend what her family had built. This quickly put her in conflict with the large-scale cattle operations that ran Brown's Park through economic terrorism and the use of hired thugs. Ann soon showed herself fully capable of striking back at the larger ranches by driving their trespassing cattle over cliffs and leading raids with her cowboys. She even went so far as to shelter rustlers, including the notorious Hole-in-the-Wall gang. The principle target of Ann's wrath was Ora Haley of the Two Bar Ranch.

Her battle with this Cattle King was the stuff of legends. To strike back at his adversary, Haley hired Tom Horn to assassinate Matthew Rash, Ann's fiancé. In retaliation, Ann married Haley's foreman, Hi Bernard, simply in the hope of luring him away from the Two Bar Ranch and causing considerable disruption to operations. Events finally culminated with Ann's arrest and later acquittal for rustling.

Ann's marriage to Bernard ended in divorce sometime after the trial. In 1923 Ann married a cattleman by the name of Frank Willis. They established a ranch near Leeds, Utah, where eventually Ann set out on a career as a writer and journalist. She remained in Utah until her death in 1956, bringing to a close the life of Ann Bassett, a Woman of the West.

## Susan Anderson, M.D. "Doc Susie"
## 1870 - 1960

Susan Anderson was born in Nevada Mills, Indiana in 1870. As a child, she moved to Wichita, Kansas with her father after her parents split up. With her mother no longer in the picture, her grandmother raised her. After she graduated from high school at the age of 21, her father moved the family again, this time to Cripple Creek, Colorado.

Her father, after becoming a successful stock trader with the mining companies, became wealthy enough to send Susan to Michigan to attend medical school. She earned her degree from the University of Michigan, but had to borrow the money from a friend to complete her classes, after her father was coerced by her step-mother to stop paying for her education. During this period, she developed tuberculosis and was unable to accept the offer of an internship at the Women's Hospital of Philadelphia.

She returned to Cripple Creek in 1897 and set up her medical practice in a small building. Business slowly increased for Dr. Anderson and within two years she was able to repay the college loan to her friend, Mary Lapham. Several years passed and things continued to improve for her, including her health. Then, around the turn of the century, she lost her brother to pneumonia and her fiancé, having a case of nerves, left her at the altar. The relationship with her father worsened as did her health. She lived in Greeley for a time and then moved her practice to a small shack in Frasier, Colorado, where her first patient was a horse.

Her patients called her both Dr. Anderson and Doc Susie and she struggled to save many of them from some of the terrible epidemics that swept through the area. Finally moving from her little shack into a larger log cabin, she was appointed Coroner of Grand County. Her first case as Coroner was that of a suicide, but she continued on and worked in the medical profession for many years. She died at the age of 90 and is buried in Mt. Pisgah Graveyard in Cripple Creek. She was a hero in a time when women doctors were scorned and up against staggering odds. She persevered in her profession, helped to promote women in the medical field, and was the real "Medicine Woman" of her era.

# Southern Mountains

# Colorado Trails Ranch

**Colorado Trails Ranch**
**12161 County Road 240-W**
**Durango, CO 81301**
**(800) 323-3833**
**(970) 247-5055**
**Elevation 7,500 feet**

Nestled in a valley high in the majestic Rocky Mountains, Colorado Trails Ranch is one of the few ranches designed to be a dude ranch. Prior to 1960 the ranch consisted only of a small barn and log house set on 500 acres of mountain wilderness adjoining the San Juan National Forest. Guests now find an impressive mountain lodge, surrounded by a replica of an old west town, complete with opera house, assay office and trading post. Thirteen cozy cabins offer the guests all the comforts after a busy day of ranch activities. All facilities on the ranch underwent further renovation in 1997.

Colorado Trails Ranch offers a wide range of activities for all age groups. Probably best known for its exceptional horse program, the ranch caters to riders of all levels of experience. Under the guidance of their certified riding instructors, the guests' riding ability and temperament are taken into account when pairing with horses. Following a lesson on how to communicate with their horses, riders are quickly out on the trail enjoying the spectacular mountain scenery that surrounds the ranch.

Another favorite activity is the newly expanded fishing program. With an on-staff fishing guide and four miles of private water, anglers are quickly lured to the ranch's ponds, streams and nearby rivers. For the avid fly fisherman, a float/wade trip to the renowned San Juan River can be arranged.

Colorado Trails Ranch has all types of supervised activities geared to the interests and abilities of children and young adults. Every day is a new adventure filled with riding, fishing, riflery, archery, water skiing or tubing, swimming, overnight campouts, hayrides and much more.

Colorado Trails Ranch is located twelve miles northeast of Durango, Colorado, in the southwest corner of the state. Durango is an old west mining town, established in 1881 and served as the terminus for the railroad connecting to the mining towns to the north. Today the Durango and Silverton Narrow Gauge Railroad operates as a tourist line along the same tracks as it did a century ago, taking visitors through the spectacular scenery of the Animas River Valley to the old mining town of Silverton.

In addition to some of the most beautiful mountain scenery to be found anywhere in North America, the area is home to Mesa Verde National Park. Mesa Verde was once the home of the Anasazi people and encompasses the finest examples of cliff dwellings to be found anywhere on Earth. The region also offers many smaller ruins built by this long vanished tribe, as well as the Anasazi Heritage Center in nearby Delores.

Besides the natural beauty of the Four Corners region, there is also any number of activities for the visitor to enjoy. Many come to enjoy the white water rafting, mountain biking, kayaking and mountain climbing. There is also tremendous opportunities for the shopper, as Durango hosts many factory outlet and novelty stores. Because there is so much to see and do, many travelers add Durango to their 'must come back' list.

# Game Hens a l'Orange

Preheat the oven to 325 degrees. Cut the hens in half and brown in butter in a large skillet. Remove the birds from the skillet and set aside; keep warm. Add the orange juice concentrate, water, steak sauce, honey, salt and rosemary to the skillet and stir with the browning juices. Bring the sauce to a boil, scraping the pan to loosen the cooked bits. Place the hens in a casserole dish and pour the sauce over them. Cover and bake for 75 minutes or until the hens are tender. Remember to baste several times during the baking.

This dish is good served with wild rice.

Cooking time: 75 minutes
Yield: 2 to 4 servings
Temperature: 325 degrees

- 2 - 1 pound game hens, thawed
- 2 tablespoons butter
- 3 ounces frozen orange juice concentrate
- 6 tablespoons water
- 1 tablespoon bottled steak sauce
- 1 tablespoon honey
- 1/2 teaspoon salt
- 1/2 teaspoon rosemary leaf, crumbled

*"Two of the pictures on my desk...one of our youngest grandson (who was two and a half at the time) and of his great grandmother (who was eighty-two and a half at the time). Both are sitting on horses with the biggest smiles...representing 80 years of difference yet both enjoying the same opportunity to be at your ranch and ride your horses."*

*Sharon*
*Phillips, Wisconsin*

# Colorado Trails Casserole

Cooking time: 30 minutes
Yield: 4 to 8 servings
Temperature: 375 degrees

$1/4$ cup butter
1 cup onion, chopped
4 cups cooked rice
2 cups sour cream
1 cup cottage cheese
1 large bay leaf,
   crumbled
1 tablespoon parsley
$1/2$ teaspoon salt
$1/8$ teaspoon pepper
1 $1/2$ cups whole chiles
   split open (Diced may
   be substituted)
2 cups shredded
   Cheddar cheese

Preheat the oven to 375 degrees. Sauté the onions in butter until tender. Remove from the heat, then stir in the rice, sour cream, cottage cheese, bay leaf, parsley, salt and pepper, mixing well. Grease a 9-inch square pan. Layer in $1/2$ the rice mixture, followed by $1/2$ of the chiles and $1/2$ of the Cheddar cheese. Repeat with the remaining ingredients to form a second layer. Cover and bake for 30 minutes or until it is hot and bubbly. Uncover during the last 10 minutes to allow the cheese to brown.

# Gazpacho

Place the tomato juice, sauce, dehydrated onions, coriander, Tabasco and a pinch of sugar in a saucepan. Bring to a boil over medium heat, turn down and simmer for 15 minutes. Mix the shrimp, green onions, celery, jicama, cucumber and tomato together and toss lightly with garlic powder. Pour the sauce over the vegetables and mix. Allow to chill. A little more tomato juice can be added if it appears to be too thick.

Yield: 6 cups

2 cups tomato juice
1 - 8 ounce can tomato sauce
1 tablespoon dehydrated minced onion
1 teaspoon ground coriander
1 teaspoon Tabasco
Sugar
3/4 cup small canned or frozen cooked shrimp
1/4 cup diced green onions
1/2 cup finely diced celery, including leaves
1/2 cup diced jicama
1/2 cup diced cucumber, peeled
1 medium tomato, diced
Garlic powder

# Caesar Salad Dressing

**Yield: 50 servings**

1/2 (15 ounces) can
  anchovy fillets
1/3 cup garlic cloves
1 1/2 cups pasteurized
  egg substitute
1 3/4 cups lemon juice
  (about 7 lemons)
1 tablespoon plus 1/2
  teaspoon dry mustard
1 3/4 cups plain non-fat
  yogurt
7 tablespoons
  Worcestershire sauce
7 tablespoons wine
  vinegar
1 1/3 cups olive oil
1 teaspoon Tabasco
  sauce
1 1/4 cups grated
  Parmesan cheese

Mix the anchovy fillets, Worcestershire sauce, garlic, wine vinegar, egg substitute, olive oil, lemon juice, dry mustard and Tabasco sauce in a blender until nearly smooth. Stir in the grated Parmesan cheese and yogurt.

Serve over Romaine lettuce with additional Parmesan cheese and garlic.

*"Thank you so much for the wonderful week we spent at Colorado Trails Ranch. Our family, all 13 of us, agreed that it was the best vacation ever and we would like to do it again."*

*Betty*
*Wichita, Kansas*

# Dill Bread

Mix the yeast with the water and set aside. Preheat the oven to 350 degrees. Cream the sugar and butter together. Add the cottage cheese and egg, mixing well. Mix in the dill seed, salt, baking soda, onions and yeast mixture. Add 1 cup of flour and mix well. Gradually add the rest of the flour and mix. Knead the dough until it's soft, but not sticky.

Place the dough in an oiled bowl and let it rise until it doubles in size. Punch it down and form into a ball. Place in a greased 3-quart casserole or bread pan. Let rise for 30 to 40 minutes or until doubled in size.

Bake the bread for about 35 to 45 minutes or until the crust is brown and the bread sounds hollow when tapped. Turn out of the pan and brush immediately with butter. Sprinkle with salt and let cool on a rack.

This recipe will work in a bread machine, although it is best to increase the flour to 3 cups.

Cooking time: 35 to 45 minutes
Yield: 1 loaf
Temperature: 350 degrees

1/4 cup water
2 tablespoons sugar
1 tablespoon butter
1 egg
1 cup creamed cottage cheese, heated to lukewarm
2 teaspoons dill seed (not weed)
1 teaspoon salt
1/4 teaspoon baking soda
1 tablespoon minced dehydrated onion
1 tablespoon yeast
2 1/4 to 2 3/4 cups flour

# Indian Fry Bread

Yield: 8 to 12 servings
Temperature: 365 degrees

2 cups flour
1/3 cup powdered milk
2 teaspoons baking
   powder
1 teaspoon salt
2 tablespoons shortening
3/4 to 1 cup warm water
Oil for frying

Mix the dry ingredients together in a bowl. Cut in the shortening until crumbly. Add the water and mix until a soft dough forms. Knead until the dough is smooth and springy in texture. Make into 24 small balls. Cover and set aside for 30 to 45 minutes.

Using both hands, stretch the balls out into thin rounds. Fry in 365 degree oil until lightly browned, turning once. The oil should be about 1 1/2 inches deep in the pan. It is important to keep the oil hot. When the bread is dropped into the oil it should be very bubbly and take only about 30 seconds to brown the bread.

Serve the bread with butter, honey, powdered sugar or cinnamon-sugar. You can also make 12 larger bread rounds and use in a buffet with chili, grated cheese, diced tomatoes, chopped onions and sour cream. This variation is called a Navajo Taco.

# Old Fashioned Rolls

Warm the milk over low heat, then add the butter and melt. Let cool slightly. Mix the sugar and salt by hand. Place the dry mixture in a large mixer and slowly add the cooled milk mixture, eggs and yeast.

If using a dough hook, add the flour by $1/2$ cupfuls, until the batter pulls away from the sides and creates a large ball. If not using a dough hook, when the dough becomes too much for the mixer, remove it from the bowl and knead in the rest of the flour on a floured board. The dough should turn out soft, not sticky.

Place the dough in a large, lightly greased bowl. Cover and place in a warm spot for 1 hour or until it doubles in size. Punch down and turn, then form into rolls. Place about an inch apart in a greased cake pan. Cover and place in a warm spot until the dough doubles in size.

Preheat the oven to 400 degrees. Bake the rolls for approximately 10 minutes or until golden brown. Brush the tops with melted butter immediately upon removing them from the oven.

These are a lot of fun served big and hot.

Cooking time: 10 minutes
Yield: 12 rolls
Temperature: 400 degrees

$1/3$ cup sugar
1 $1/2$ teaspoon salt
2 tablespoons yeast
   (2 packages)
4 $1/2$ to 5 $1/2$ cups flour
1 cup milk
$1/4$ cup butter
2 eggs

# Southern Biscuits

Cooking time: 10 to 12 minutes
Yield: 8 to 10 biscuits
Temperature: 475 degrees

2 cups all-purpose flour
1 teaspoon salt
1 tablespoon sugar
4 teaspoons baking powder
1/3 cup shortening
3/4 cup milk

Preheat the oven to 475 degrees. Mix together the flour, salt, sugar and baking powder. Cut in the shortening with a pastry blender or fork, until you have clumps the size of small peas. Stir in the milk until evenly combined, making sure not to over mix. The dough will be quite moist, but should be able to retain its shape. Adjust the liquid accordingly. It is a good idea to start with a little less milk and add more as needed.

Roll the dough to about 3/4-inch thickness on a well-floured surface. Cut out and place the biscuits on a greased baking sheet (parchment lined if possible). You can re-roll the scraps once, but any dough left after that should be thrown away. Bake at 475 degrees for 10 to 12 minutes or until golden brown.

Serve hot with butter and honey.

*"For 7 days I was living moments that I knew would become some of the best memories of my life."*

*Michelle*
*Indianapolis, Indiana*

# Southern Apple Cream Pie

Preheat the oven to 400 degrees. Mix the apples, sugar and flour together thoroughly. Add the buttermilk (or sour cream), egg and vanilla. Pour into the pie shell. Bake for 30 minutes.

Mix the topping ingredients. After the pie has baked for 30 minutes, remove it from the oven and sprinkle the topping over it. Replace in oven and bake for an additional 10 minutes. Allow to cool.

Cooking time: 40 minutes
Yield: 8 servings
Temperature: 400 degrees

1 unbaked pie shell
2 cups chopped apples
3/4 cup sugar
2 tablespoons flour
1 cup buttermilk or sour
   cream
1 egg, beaten
1/2 teaspoon vanilla

Topping:
1/2 cup sugar
1 teaspoon cinnamon
2 ounces butter
5 teaspoons flour

# Whoopee Pies

Cooking time: 8 to 10
  minutes
Yield: 2 dozen
Temperature: 375 degrees

Cookies:
1 cup butter, softened
2 cups sugar
2 eggs
1 tablespoon vanilla
2 cups water
$2/3$ cup non-fat dry milk
4 cups flour
1 teaspoon baking
  powder
1 tablespoon baking
  soda
1 teaspoon salt
1 cup sifted cocoa

Marshmallow Filling:
1 cup shortening
4 cups powdered sugar
2 cups marshmallow
  whip
2 teaspoons vanilla
2 to 3 tablespoons milk

Preheat the oven to 375 degrees. Mix all of the cookie ingredients together in a bowl, adding them in the order given. Beat until smooth. Drop by rounded tablespoonfuls onto a cookie sheet lined with parchment paper and lightly sprayed with vegetable oil. Bake for 8 to 10 minutes. Cool before making sandwiches with the marshmallow filling.

Start the filling by creaming the shortening and powdered sugar together. Beat in the remaining ingredients. Spread between cookies.

# Apple - Jalapeño Salsa

Combine all the ingredients, mixing well. Refrigerate.

Delicious served with pork roast or pork chops.

*"We loved letting the kids do whatever they wanted and not worrying about where they were (even the 5 year old!) It was a true vacation for me—no cooking, no driving kids all over town, no worries."*

*Debbie*
*Marietta, Georgia*

Yield: 9 cups

2 1/4 cups diced onion
1/3 cup minced Jalapeño peppers
1/4 cup minced garlic
9 cups apples, peeled, cored and small diced (use a combination of Granny Smith, Golden Delicious and Macintosh)
1 cup plus 2 tablespoons lemon juice
1/2 cup soy sauce
1 1/2 tablespoons curry powder
1 1/2 tablespoons ground allspice
1 cup honey

# The Historic Pines Ranch

**The Historic Pines Ranch**
**PO Box 311**
**Westcliffe, CO 81252**
**(800) 446-WHOA**
**(719) 783-9261**
**Dean and Casey Rusk, Christy Attebery**
**Elevation 8,700 feet**

The ranch was founded in the early 1880's by Irish-born brothers Reginald and Frank Cusack, who emigrated to the United States from their mother's home in England. In 1889 Reginald married Gertrude Urquhart and together they operated The Pines for almost half a century. The Pines' English heritage has created a unique blend of the Old West and European traditions.

The Colorado State Legislature officially gave The Pines its name in 1911. This is why you will find it on almost every state topographic or driving map. Located high in the magnificent Sangre de Cristo Mountains of South Central Colorado, The Pines overlooks the beautiful Wet Mountain Valley. Pristine forest with many high mountain lakes, streams, and spectacular vast views of the countryside below are everyday scenery at this location. Hiking trails and horseback trails wind through the Sangre de Cristo Wilderness Area and afford anyone with that special, quiet, back-to-nature time that our guests crave.

Amenities include comfortable cabins, hot tub and saunas, game rooms, dance hall (for our weekly square dance), comfortable dining room, with excellent views and an attached patio dining, several barns and corrals along with riding arenas, an indoor swimming pool, the newly added Mippy's Tea Room and the Historic Lodge.

The Lodge is the heart of The Pines. Ordered in the 1890's from a Montgomery Ward catalog, the "kit" for the Lodge was shipped by train from Chicago and then 30 miles by wagon train from nearby Texas Creek.

The Lodge is a dollhouse-type structure looking strangely out of place in the mountains. The inside walls and ceilings are tongue and groove pine and oak paneling while the floors are covered with planks of Douglas fir. This beautiful building is furnished in turn-of-the-century Victorian style.

Mippy's Tea Room has become a very popular spot at The Pines. Gertrude Cusack was given the nickname, Mippy, by her family and her descendants have graciously requested that we use the name for our Tea Room. The small tea room is furnished with a cozy Victorian charm. There are 16 seats and guests wander in and out during the appointed hours. Tea is served weekly, along with special sweets prepared in the kitchen. Guests and staff enjoy the casual conversation and magical atmosphere surrounding them during afternoon "tea-time" at Mippy's.

There is plenty to keep everyone busy at The Historic Pines Ranch. Horseback activities include trail rides, instruction, arena work-outs, team penning (with calves), and a guest rodeo each week. Evenings offer square dancing, fishing competitions, singing and marshmallow toasting around the fire, and a special staff show where staff and guests, alike, show off any talent they might have!

Just as the Cusack family did 100 years ago, the current owners have opened their home to the weary traveler wishing to escape the intensity of everyday living and return to a quieter, simpler time.

# Hamburger Wellington

Pre-cook the ground beef patties until almost done. Sauté the green onions and mushrooms in butter. Place the cheese slices, mushroom and onion mixture, along with a hamburger patty, on each pastry sheet. Moisten the edges of the pastry with water and wrap around all. Press edges securely together. Cut vents in the pastry and brush with egg wash. (1 egg beaten with 1 tablespoon water). Bake in a preheated 350 degree oven for 30 minutes or until heated through. Serve with green peppercorn sauce.

To begin the green peppercorn sauce, melt 3 tablespoons of butter in a small saucepan. Add the shallots and sauté until golden brown. Stir in the brandy and reduce over high heat by half. Add the remaining ingredients, except the softened butter and cook until thickened, stirring constantly. Swirl in the remaining butter.

The sauce is a bit hot and peppery for the kids so it is good to have a mild white or cheese sauce as well.

*"It was such a respite from the hurly-burly workaday world we live in. The pristine wilderness, the quiet, the wind in the pines stilled the noise within."*

*Mandy and Ken*
*Colorado*

Cooking time: 30 minutes
Yield: 6 servings
Temperature: 350 degrees
Can be stored for 1 week

6 - 4 to 6 ounce
  ground beef patties
6 to 8 green onions,
  finely diced
4 ounces mushrooms,
  sliced
6 - 1 ounce slices Swiss
  cheese
1 large sheet puff pastry
  cut into 6 squares

Green Peppercorn
Sauce:
3 tablespoons butter
3 tablespoons shallots,
  minced
3 tablespoons brandy
2 teaspoons Dijon
  mustard
1 cup heavy cream
1 bouillon cube, crushed
1 tablespoon green
  peppercorns, chopped
  or mashed
1 tablespoon butter,
  softened

# Jalapeño Pork Roast

Cooking time: 2 ¹/₂ to 3
hours
Yield: 13 to 16 servings
Temperature: 350 degrees
Can be stored for 4 days.

1 pork tenderloin, 5 to 6
  pounds
5 to 6 scallions, sliced
  thin
3 to 4 Jalapeño peppers,
  sliced thin
1 can frozen orange
  juice concentrate, (12
  ounces)
16 ounces Italian salad
  dressing

Butterfly the pork roast. Add the scallions and Jalapeños in the middle. Tie the roast back together. Mix the thawed orange juice concentrate and Italian salad dressing together. Marinate the roast in juice and dressing mixture overnight or for at least 5 to 6 hours, turning occasionally. Remove the roast from the marinade and reserve the liquid. Put the roast on a rack in a roasting pan. Bake in preheated 350 degree oven, basting with marinade occasionally, for 2 ¹/₂ to 3 hours or until a meat thermometer reads 160 to 170 degrees.

# Enchilada Casserole

Cut the tortillas into bite-sized pieces. Spread a little enchilada sauce on the bottom of a 9 x 13-inch pan. Layer with tortilla pieces, cheese, meat, and onion. Repeat the layers and top with cheese, Jalapeños, and olives. Bake in a preheated 350 degree oven for 30 to 45 minutes.

*"Absolutely the best vacation ever—loved the horses, great food, the best staff! Thanks."*

*The Olson Family*
*Minnesota*

Cooking time: 30 to 45 minutes
Yield: 12 servings
Temperature: 350 degrees
Can be stored for 1 week

1 1/2 pounds cooked shredded beef or chicken
3 cups shredded Colby Jack cheese
1 medium onion, diced
4 cups enchilada sauce
1 dozen corn tortillas
Sliced Jalapeño peppers and black olives, to taste

# Mexican Corn and Cheese Casserole

Cooking time: 30 to 45
  minutes
Yield: 8 servings
Temperature: 400 degrees
Can be stored for 1 week

4 cups fresh sweet corn
  or 20 ounces frozen
  thawed corn
2 cups sour cream or
  plain yogurt
1 - 8 ounce can whole
  green chiles, rinsed,
  seeded and chopped
2 eggs, lightly beaten
1 1/2 cups shredded
  sharp Cheddar cheese
  (about 6 ounces)
1 teaspoon salt
4 tablespoons melted
  butter or margarine

Preheat oven to 400 degrees. In a bowl, combine the corn, chiles, cheese, sour cream, eggs, salt and butter. Pour the mixture into a buttered 9 x 13-inch baking dish. Bake uncovered for 30 to 45 minutes or until a knife inserted in the center comes out clean.

Great side dish. Also good served at room temperature or cold.

*"Yeee-Haw! What a kick of a good time! What a great adventure! We've loved every minute."*

*The Anderson Family*
*Michigan*

# Cowboy Caviar

Rinse and drain the beans. Place in a food processor with the remaining ingredients. Process with pulse motion until finely ground. Let sit overnight to blend flavors.

Garnish with parsley sprigs. Serve with chips, crackers, or toast.

Yield: 3 cups
Can be stored for 2 weeks

2 - 15 ounce cans black beans or black-eyed peas
2 cloves garlic, chopped
1 onion, chopped
$1/2$ teaspoon salt
1 teaspoon pepper
$1/3$ cup parsley
$1/3$ cup olive oil
3 to 4 tablespoons red wine vinegar
Parsley sprigs for garnish

*"Fan-Bloody-Tastic!"*

*John and Joan*
*South Australia*

# Waldorf Salad

Yield: 6 servings
Can be stored for 1 week

6 cups apples, peeled
  and cored
8 to 10 maraschino
  cherries
1/2 cup walnuts or
  pecans, chopped
1 cup small
  marshmallows
1/2 cup pineapple
  chunks
2 cups sour cream
Extra strawberries and
  nuts
2 to 3 tablespoons
  strawberry jam

Mix the fruit together in a large bowl with the nuts. Mix the sour cream and strawberry jam until it is a light pink color; be careful not to make it too sweet! Combine the sour cream mixture with the fruit mixture and refrigerate. Garnish with additional strawberries and nuts.

*"Great staff, horses, views, food, and unforgettable experiences. We've been away too long. Look for us in the future!!"*

*The R. Family*
*Illinois*

# Herb Bread

In a mixing bowl dissolve the yeast in warm water. Add 2 tablespoons of the butter, the sugar, salt, all herbs and $1/2$ the flour. We also add small pepperoni pieces and $1/2$ cup shredded mozzarella cheese; sun dried tomatoes would substitute nicely for the pepperoni. Beat with a mixer for 2 minutes at medium speed. Scrape the sides of bowl frequently. Add the remaining flour and stir until smooth. Scrape the batter from the sides of the bowl. Cover with a damp towel and let rise in warm place until doubled.

Stir the batter 25 strokes, then spread evenly in a greased 9 x 5 x 3-inch bread pan. Lightly flour the top of the dough and let rise again until batter is 1 inch from the top. Bake in a preheated 350 degree oven for 45 to 60 minutes or until golden brown. Remove immediately from pan and place on cooling rack. Melt remaining butter and brush onto the top. Cool before cutting.

Wrap the cut bread in foil and freeze. Reheat before serving. Excellent with any dinner or also good as a sandwich bread. We really never got the bread wrapped and frozen; it smells and tastes too good not to be gobbled up right away!

Cooking time: 45 to 60 minutes
Yield: 8 servings
Temperature: 350 degrees
Can be stored for 1 week or longer in refrigerator or freezer

1 package dry yeast
1 $1/4$ cups warm water
3 tablespoons butter, softened
2 tablespoons sugar
2 teaspoons salt
1 teaspoon dry basil
1 teaspoon granulated garlic
3 cups flour, sifted
$1/2$ cup pepperoni pieces (optional)
$1/2$ cup shredded mozzarella cheese (optional)

# Milk And Honey Bread

Cooking time: 65 to 70
   minutes
Yield: 12 slices
Temperature: 350 degrees
Can be stored for 5 days
   or frozen for 1 month

1 cup milk
$1/2$ cup honey
3 tablespoons butter,
   melted
2 $1/2$ cups all-purpose
   flour
$1/2$ cup sugar
1 tablespoon baking
   powder
1 teaspoon salt
$3/4$ cup pecans, chopped
1 egg

Preheat the oven to 375 degrees. Butter a 9 x 5 x 3-inch loaf pan. In a medium saucepan, combine the milk and honey. Stir over medium heat until the honey dissolves. Stir in the melted butter. Set aside to cool. In a large bowl, sift together the flour, sugar, baking powder, and salt. Add the pecans and toss to mix. Set the mixture aside. Pour the cooled milk mixture into the large bowl of an electric mixer and beat in the egg. When it is well blended, add the flour mixture. With the mixer at medium speed, beat just until the ingredients are blended. Spread the batter evenly in the prepared pan. Turn down the oven to 350 degrees and bake the bread for 65 to 70 minutes, or until a toothpick inserted in the center of the loaf comes out clean. Cool the bread in the pan on a wire rack for 10 minutes. Remove it from the pan and let it cool completely on the rack.

We serve this during "tea-time" at Mippy's Tea Room, however it makes a good dessert for lunch too.

# Scones

Mix the sugar into the beaten egg. Add the egg-sugar mixture, butter, and milk to the flour. Mix well by hand. On a floured board, pat into a round about 1 inch thick. Cut into 2-inch rounds. Place close together on a lightly greased baking sheet. Brush the tops with a small amount of butter mixed with milk. Bake at 425 degrees, until lightly browned, about 15 minutes.

Scones are served in our Tea Room. Joan Henderson of Australia gave this recipe to me. They have tea everyday and these scones are served with any jam or spread and then topped with whipped (unsweetened) cream. This, Joan tells me, is called Devonshire Tea and is quite popular in her country.

*"What a view! Good grub and lots of great people."*

*Jayette*
*Georgia*

Cooking time: 15 minutes
Yield: 8 to 10 servings
Temperature: 425 degrees
Can be stored for 4 days

3 cups self rising flour
1 tablespoon butter, melted
1 egg, beaten
1 rounded tablespoon sugar
1 cup milk

# Pumpkin Dutch Apple Pie

Cooking time: 50 minutes
Yield: 8 servings
Temperature: 375 degrees
Can be stored for 1 week

2 cups green apples,
  peeled, thinly sliced
1/4 cup sugar
2 teaspoons flour
1 teaspoon lemon juice
1/4 teaspoon cinnamon
  (optional)
9-inch unbaked pie shell
3/4 teaspoon cinnamon
2 eggs, slightly beaten
1 1/2 cups pumpkin
1 cup evaporated milk
1/2 cup sugar
1 tablespoon margarine,
  melted
1/8 teaspoon nutmeg
1/4 teaspoon salt

Crumble Topping:
1/2 cup flour
5 tablespoons sugar
3 tablespoons softened
  butter
1/3 cup walnuts or
  pecans, chopped

Combine the topping ingredients in bowl and mix with a pastry blender until crumbly.

Toss the apples with the 1/4 cup sugar, flour, lemon juice, and 1/4 teaspoon cinnamon in a bowl. Place the mixture in the pie shell. Combine the eggs, pumpkin, evaporated milk, 1/2 cup sugar, butter, 3/4 teaspoon cinnamon, nutmeg, and salt in a bowl. Mix thoroughly. Pour over the apples. Bake in a preheated 375 degree oven for 30 minutes. Remove from the oven. Sprinkle with Crumble Topping. Return to the oven for 20 minutes or until custard is set. Cool on wire rack.

*"We can't imagine a more perfect vacation. Everything was great! The staff, food, and horses are incomparable! "*

*Jim and Donna*
*West Virginia*

# Snickers Cake

Mix the cake according to package directions. Pour $1/2$ the batter into a greased and floured 9 x 13-inch pan and bake for 20 minutes at 350 degrees. Meanwhile, melt the caramel, margarine and milk together. Pour over the baked batter. Sprinkle with nuts and chocolate chips. Add the remaining batter and bake at 250 degrees for 20 minutes and then at 350 degrees for 10 minutes.

Our guests go crazy for this one and it is so easy!

Cooking time: 50 minutes
Yield: 15 servings
Temperature: 350 and
  250 degrees
Can be stored for 1 week

1 German chocolate
  cake mix
1 package caramel
1 stick butter or
  margarine
$1/3$ cup milk
1 cup nuts, chopped
$2/3$ cup chocolate chips

*"We love The Pines! The staff is just wonderful. We've had so much FUN! The horses and trails are great! We love the food!"*

*Randy, Jeremy, Erin, and Lauren*
*Ohio*

# Lake Mancos Ranch

**Lake Mancos Ranch
42688 C.R.N.
Mancos, CO 81328
(800) 325-9462
(970) 533-1190
ranchlml@fone.net
The Sehnert Family
Elevation 8,000 feet**

Lake Mancos Ranch is nestled in the San Juan Mountains on the western slope of the Rockies. This area, often referred to as the 'Four Corners', is where the desert meets the mountains and was home to ancient Indian tribes. Archaeological sites dot the region and the unique ruins at Mesa Verde National Park are only twelve miles from the ranch.

After the Anasazi Indians abandoned these magnificent cliff dwellings the Ute and Navajo Indians settled the area. Mormon pioneers and ranchers arrived in the late 1870's. While the country has lush vegetation and large stands of Ponderosa pine, Spruce and Aspen, these settlers soon found that irrigation was required to grow crops. An irrigation project in the 1940's gave rise to the founding of Lake Mancos Ranch.

The ranch has drawn guests from all over the world, including a few celebrities. They come to ride the scenic trails of the San Juan National Forest and relax in the air of genuine western hospitality. Many come away with family memories that span the generations.

Saddle up for a memorable ride on a trail savvy mountain horse; it's a rejuvenating experience, since the folks on the ranch guarantee that you can't pack your worries in a saddle bag. If you choose not to ride, that's just fine with them. As they say at Lake Mancos Ranch, "we have gentle horses for gentle people, spirited horses for spirited people and for folks that don't like to ride we have horses that don't like to be ridden."

Mancos, Colorado is a sleepy little cowboy town that is not far from Durango. Horses on the main street are not unusual and its one of a kind western shops outnumber both grocery stores and banks combined. Lake Mancos Ranch reflects a wholesome, homey atmosphere, with its friendly folks, home style cooking and unhurried feeling. The coffeepot is always on and the cookie jar is bottomless. As the verse printed on an elk hide in the dining room proclaims, "...set deep, come often, you're one of the folks."

# Amber Onions

Preheat the oven to 300 degrees. Cut the onions in half crosswise. Place in a large, shallow greased casserole dish. Combine the remaining ingredients. Pour the sauce over the onions and cover the casserole. Bake for 1 hour or until the onions are tender.

Serve with roasts or steaks.

Cooking time: 1 hour
Yield: 8 to 9 servings
Temperature: 300 degrees

9 medium white or
  yellow onions
1 teaspoon salt
$1/4$ teaspoon paprika
2 tablespoons butter or
  margarine, melted
$1/4$ cup tomato juice
3 tablespoons honey

*"The enthusiastic staff at Lake Mancos Ranch pampered us. They made us feel part of the ranch family. The kids wrote to many of them after we left."*

*Bade & Carolyn*
*San Antonio, Texas*

# Barbecued Ham Balls

Cooking time: 90 minutes
Yield: 12 servings
Temperature: 350 degrees

2 $1/2$ pounds ground ham
2 pounds lean ground pork
1 pound ground beef
3 eggs
2 cups milk
3 cups graham cracker crumbs

BBQ Glaze:
2 $1/2$ cups tomato soup
$3/4$ cup cider vinegar
2 $1/4$ cups brown sugar
2 teaspoons dry mustard

Preheat the oven to 350 degrees. In a bowl, mix the eggs and milk. Mix the meats and cracker crumbs together in a large bowl. Pour the egg and milk mixture over the meat mixture and combine thoroughly. Form into 24 meatballs (or press flat into the pan) and place into a pair of 9 x 13-inch pans.

Mix all the glaze ingredients together. Pour over the pan of meatballs. Place in the oven and bake for 1 $1/2$ hours.

# Painted Chicken

Preheat the oven to 425 degrees. Mix the flour, salt and paprika, then stir into the melted butter. Brush each piece of chicken with the mixture, making sure they are well coated. Place the chicken on a foil lined baking sheet. Bake for 20 minutes at 425. Reduce the heat to 350 degrees and continue baking for an additional 1 hour or until chicken is done.

This is an excellent oven fried chicken that's great for taking on picnics.

Cooking time: 80 minutes
Yield: 4 servings
Temperature: 425 then
   350 degrees

3 tablespoons flour
1 teaspoon salt
1 teaspoon paprika
1/3 cup butter or
   margarine, melted
1 whole fryer, cut into
   pieces

# Miner's Pies
# (Cornish Pasties)

Cooking time: 45 to 60 minutes
Yield: 8 servings
Temperature: 350 degrees

3 cups cooked lean beef, cubed
3 cups boiled potatoes, cubed
1/4 cup chopped onion
3/4 teaspoon celery salt
1 1/2 cups beef gravy

Never Fail Pie Dough:
3 cups flour
1 teaspoon salt
1 1/4 cups shortening
1 egg
1 teaspoon vinegar
5 tablespoons ice water

Prepare the dough first, making a double recipe. In a bowl, mix the flour and salt. Cut in the shortening, until the dough is crumbly. Lightly beat the egg, vinegar and water. Add all at once to the flour mixture. Mix just until moist.

Cook the beef and potatoes well in advance of making this recipe. In a large bowl, mix the beef, potatoes, onion, salt and gravy.

For each pie, take a small handful of the pie dough and form it into a thick circle about the size of a large dessert plate. Moisten the edge of the dough with water. Place about 3/4 cup of the filling in the center of the pie dough. Fold the dough over and press down to form a half circle shape. Press the dough around the edges to seal the pie. Trim off any excess dough.

Preheat the oven to 350 degrees. Place the pies on an ungreased baking sheet. Brush the tops with a glaze made by mixing 1 egg to 1/3 cup milk. Bake for 45 to 60 minutes until light brown. Serve with more gravy if desired.

Cornish pasties were a typical lunch for miners. Their lunch pails had a lower compartment that would hold coffee, while the upper compartment usually contained a pastie. The whole lunch pail could be placed over a small fire, so that the coffee would be hot and the pastie warmed.

# Alaskan Fisherman's Baked Beans

Preheat oven to 350 degrees. Dice the bacon and brown in a large skillet. Drain off the fat. Add the sliced onions, vinegar and brown sugar. Cook until the onions are clear. Add the beans, along with their liquid. At this point you can simmer on the stove top for at least 1 hour or you can transfer the beans to a baking dish and bake for 1 hour.

Cooking time: 1 hour
Yield: 12 servings
Temperature: 350 degrees
This can be made ahead
  of time and stored in the
  refrigerator

1 pound bacon
4 large onions, sliced
  thin
1 1/2 cups vinegar
1 cup brown sugar
2 cans baked beans
1 can kidney beans
1 can lima beans

*"Our son learned a great lesson in independence fostered by the safe, family atmosphere at Lake Mancos."*

*Norman*
*Plantation, Florida*

# Snow Capped Beets

Yield: 8 servings

4 cups beets, sliced and
   cooked
$1/4$ cup sour cream
$3/4$ teaspoon sugar
1 tablespoon vinegar
$1/2$ teaspoon salt
1 teaspoon chopped
   onion
Cayenne pepper to taste

Stir the sour cream, sugar, vinegar, salt, onion and cayenne together to make a sauce. Slowly heat the sauce in a pan, just until hot, making sure not to let it boil. Pour over the hot, cooked beets. Do not stir. Serve immediately.

# Sweet and Sour Brussels Sprouts

Cook the Brussels sprouts just until tender, then drain well. Mix the cornstarch with cold water. Melt the margarine in a saucepan. Add the cornstarch mixture, vinegar, sugar, mustard and onion. Cook and stir until thickened. Pour over the Brussels sprouts. Stir to coat and serve hot.

Yield: 8 servings

1 pound fresh or 2 - 10 ounce packages of frozen Brussels sprouts
1 cup water
$1/2$ cup brown sugar, packed
$1/4$ cup white vinegar
$1/4$ teaspoon dry mustard
1 tablespoon margarine
1 tablespoon cornstarch
1 teaspoon grated onion

# Family Favorite Tossed Salad

Yield: 8 to 10 servings

1/2 cup sliced almonds
3 tablespoons sugar
1/2 head iceberg lettuce,
  torn
1/2 head romaine
  lettuce, torn
1 cup chopped celery
1/2 large red onion,
  sliced thin
1 - 11 ounce can
  mandarin oranges,
  drained

Sweet Oil Dressing:
1/4 cup vegetable oil
1/2 teaspoon salt
Black pepper to taste
2 tablespoons sugar
2 tablespoons vinegar
Tabasco sauce
1 tablespoon fresh or
  dried parsley

Place the almonds in a heavy skillet and mix with the sugar. Roast over medium heat, stirring constantly until the almonds are coated and all the sugar is dissolved. Watch carefully as they can burn easily. Cool.

To make the dressing, start by placing the oil in a blender. Blend at medium speed, adding the remaining ingredients one at a time, with the exception of the parsley. Blend well. Add the parsley and blend just until mixed.

Mix together the lettuce, celery and onion. Just before serving add the almonds and oranges, then toss with the dressing.

# Chocolate Peanut Butter Pie

Prepare the crust first. Melt the peanut butter and margarine together. Blend the sugar with the cracker crumbs. Stir the butter mixture into the crumb mixture. Pat evenly into a 9-inch pie tin. Chill to set.

Prepare the chocolate pie filling according to the package directions. Pour the filling into the pie crust and chill.

Pile on the whipped topping to suit your taste. Sprinkle with mini chocolate chips or shaved chocolate. Serve well chilled.

Yield: 8 servings

Crumb Nutty Crust:
1 1/2 cups graham
   cracker crumbs
6 tablespoons white
   sugar
3/4 cup peanut butter,
   chunky or smooth
2 tablespoons margarine

Filling:
1 large box chocolate pie
   filling

Whipped topping
1/2 cup mini chocolate
   chips

# No Bake Chocolate Cookies

Yield: 2 to 3 dozen
Keeps best in the refrigerator or a cool spot.

2 cups white sugar
1/2 cup milk
1/2 cup margarine
2 tablespoons baking
   cocoa
3 cups quick cooking
   oatmeal
1 teaspoon vanilla
1/2 cup peanut butter

Mix the sugar, milk, margarine and cocoa in a saucepan. Cook until the mixture is well blended and boils for 1 minute. Remove from the heat. Mix in the peanut butter and stir until completely melted. Add the oatmeal and vanilla. Drop by spoonfuls onto waxed paper. Let set until firm.

*"Homemade cowboy cookies—I love 'em!"*

*Barbara*
*Philadelphia, Pennsylvania*

# Old Fashioned Ginger Cookies

Preheat the oven to 350 degrees. Cream the shortening and sugar together. Add the egg, beat well, then add the molasses. Stir in the flour, baking soda, salt, ginger and cinnamon. Roll the dough into small balls or scoop with a small ice cream scoop. Place the balls on a cookie sheet.

Dip the bottom of a drinking glass in white sugar and slightly press the top of each dough ball with it. Place the cookies in the oven and bake until lightly browned, but still soft in the center.

The cookies will store well, if covered. To prevent drying out when storing the cookies in a cookie jar, place a piece of bread in the jar.

*"We did so much at just the right pace. We left feeling invigorated and rested."*

*Fran & Cos*
*Hillsdale, New Jersey*

Cooking time: 10 to 12 minutes
Yield: 4 dozen
Temperature: 350 degrees

3/4 cup shortening
1 cup white sugar
1 egg
4 tablespoons molasses
2 1/4 cups flour
1 1/2 teaspoons baking soda
1/2 teaspoon salt
1 teaspoon ginger
1 teaspoon cinnamon

# Robin's Praline Pecans

Yield: 3 cups
Can be stored in a cov-
ered container for up to
3 weeks

1/4 cup evaporated milk
1 cup sugar
1/4 teaspoon cinnamon
2 tablespoons water
1/4 teaspoon vanilla
3 cups pecan halves

Combine all the ingredients, with the exception of the pecans, in a heavy skillet. Cook until the sugar dissolves. Add the pecans and cook, stirring, until no syrup is left. The nuts will start to look sugary. Spread on waxed paper to cool.

*"Our children request to return to Lake Mancos, even as teenagers. Despite our different interests and ages, there are activities for everyone in our family."*

*Judy & Marshall*
*Pasadena, California*

# Walsenburg Green Chili

Cook the pork, chiles, tomatoes, garlic salt and oregano in a large pot over medium heat for approximately 1 1/2 hours, until the pork is well cooked. Stir frequently and add water as necessary to prevent sticking. Make a flour and water paste with a thick consistency. Add the paste to the chili slowly, stirring in with a whisk. Add the soup and broth. Cook an additional 1 hour on low heat.

Serve with beans, chopped onions, shredded cheese and tortillas as desired.

*"I liked being near everything. The grandkids could easily go to the lodge on their own or join their new friends on the playground while I caught a quick nap before dinner."*

*Fran*
*El Paso, Texas*

Cooking time: 2 1/2 hours
Yield: 8 servings

2 1/2 pounds diced or
   ground pork
27 ounces diced green
   chiles
1 small can diced
   Jalapeño peppers
1 - 16 ounce can stewed
   tomatoes
1 tablespoon garlic salt
1 tablespoon oregano
1 - 10 1/2 ounce can
   cream of chicken soup
3 - 10 1/2 ounce cans
   chicken broth
1 cup flour
Water

# Rainbow Trout Ranch

**Rainbow Trout Ranch**
**PO Box 458**
**Antonito, CO 81120**
**(800) 633-3397**
**(719) 376-5659**
**rainbow2@amigo.net**
**The Van Berkum Family**
**Elevation 9,000 feet**

The Spanish moved into the area around the Rainbow Trout Ranch in the 1600's and their legacy still exists. Preceding and interwoven with the local history of the Spanish is that of the Indians, including the Ute, Cheyenne, Arapaho and Kiowa. Early cliff dwellers made their homes to the south and west of the ranch, followed by the Pueblo Indians. In fact, the remarkable Taos Pueblo is just an hour and a half from the ranch.

In the 1870's the relative tranquillity in the area was shattered by the discovery of gold and silver. Miners flocked to the region and numerous small towns sprang up in the mountains around the ranch. Just to the north are the remains of Platoro, Jasper and Stunner. Most such towns were abandoned by the early 1900's.

Rainbow Trout Ranch is a very special place for a unique summer vacation. It combines the best of the Colorado Rockies and the enchantment of northern New Mexico. Located in the beautiful secluded Conejos (Co-nay-hos) River valley, the ranch features vast amounts of unspoiled country in which to ride, hike, fish and ponder. It is perfect for both adults and children, with great horses, exceptional fishing, swimming, children's programs, day trips to Taos, white water rafting and the chance to ride America's longest and highest narrow-gauge steam train. Enjoy the atmosphere of their rustic log cabins and feast on wonderful home cooked meals.

At an elevation of 9,000 feet the summer temperatures are near perfect, with warm, sunny days and cool evenings. Ponderosa pine and Aspen are in abundance, and a countless variety of wildflowers populate the meadows. From over 10,000 feet at the north end, the ranch drops down into the river valley, providing a view from the lodge area that is breathtaking. Over a mile and a half of the river winds through the ranch, providing guests with abundant opportunities to fish. Within a short walk or horseback ride are numerous small lakes and streams as well as some impressive waterfalls—all in the seclusion of the National Forest.

The southern portion of the ranch is less than a dozen miles from the New Mexico border. A historic ranch surrounded by Rio Grande National Forest, it is within easy access from Albuquerque, Denver, Colorado Springs or Alamosa.

The grand lodge was constructed in the 1920's, utilizing not a single nail in the entire 18,000 square foot structure. It remains the focal point of the ranch with its splendid porches, enormous living area, expansive dining room, library, office and kitchen. It also houses some of the staff as well as the laundry facilities. Nearby is the heated swimming pool with deck area for lounging, and the volleyball/basketball court.

The guest cabins are grouped amongst the picturesque Aspen and Ponderosa pine a short distance above the lodge. There are fifteen separate guest cabins, each with a wonderful porch. These vary in configuration, with half of the cabins having a living room with fireplace, two to three bedrooms and either one or two bathrooms. The other half consist of a suite of two rooms with a single bath. All are very comfortably furnished. Daily maid service is provided for all cabins.

While visiting the Rainbow Trout Ranch guests can enjoy such varied activities as horseback riding, river rafting, fishing and hiking. For those who would like to ride the train, there is the nearby historic Chama and Antonito Railway, the highest and longest narrow gauge line in the country.

Each meal is a special occasion at the ranch. They take great care in the preparation and serving of every dish. This is home cooking in the traditional sense. Almost everything is prepared from scratch and baking is a specialty. In addition to the wonderful entrés (such as steak, ribs, fresh trout, turkey, etc.), they always have an abundance of vegetables, fruits and salads. All meals are served family style with all you care to eat. Barbecues form the highlight of any week at the ranch. Special dietary needs can be accommodated and children's menus are available.

# Flank Steak in Marinade

Combine all the ingredients for the marinade. Marinate the steak for at least 3 hours or overnight, if you like highly seasoned meat.

Grill or broil the meat to the desired temperature.

We use this marinade for chicken as well. It also makes great beef and chicken fajitas. This makes just enough marinade for 5 pounds of meat.

Yield: 5 to 7 servings
Can be stored for up to 1
  week in the refrigerator

5 pounds flank steak
  that has been trimmed

Marinade:
3 cups vegetable oil
1 cup lemon juice
1 cup soy sauce
1 cup green onions,
  chopped
2 tablespoons garlic
  powder
$1/4$ cup pepper
$1/4$ cup celery salt

# Shrimp Dijon

**Yield: 5 servings**

1 ¹/₂ pounds shrimp
7 tablespoons butter
2 teaspoons fresh
  parsley
1 small can pimento
1 teaspoon
  Worcestershire sauce
1 tablespoon lemon
  juice
1 tablespoon flour
1 cup milk
¹/₄ teaspoon pepper
1 teaspoon dry mustard
¹/₂ pound shredded
  Cheddar cheese

Preparation should begin 15 minutes before serving time. Shell and de-vein the shrimp. Melt ¹/₄ cup (4 tablespoons) of the butter in a skillet. Add the shrimp, parsley, pimento, Worcestershire sauce and lemon juice. Sauté for 5 to 10 minutes Melt the remaining butter in a saucepan or skillet; add the flour and stir until smooth. Gradually stir in the milk. Add the pepper, dry mustard, and shredded cheese. Cook over low heat until the sauce thickens. Add the shrimp mixture to the cheese sauce and serve over rice.

# Cauliflower Salad

Brown the bacon until crisp, then crumble. Break the cauliflower and broccoli into small flowerets. Chop the onion. Mix the vegetables and bacon in large bowl. Mix the mayonnaise, sugar, vinegar and Parmesan cheese in a small bowl. Add the dressing to the vegetables. Add mozzarella cheese and refrigerate.

Yield: 8 to 10 servings

1 small head cauliflower
1 bunch broccoli
1 small onion
$1/2$ pound bacon
2 cups mayonnaise (or salad dressing)
$1/4$ cup sugar
2 tablespoons vinegar
$1/4$ cup Parmesan cheese
8 ounces shredded mozzarella cheese

# It's The Berries Salad

Yield: 8 servings
Can be stored for 1 week
  in the refrigerator

4 bunches fresh spinach
  leaves, torn into
  bite-sized pieces
2 pints quartered
  strawberries

Dressing:
1/2 cup sugar
1 tablespoon poppy
  seeds
2 tablespoons sesame
  seeds
1 1/2 teaspoons minced
  onion
1/4 teaspoon
  Worcestershire sauce
1/4 tablespoon paprika
1/2 cup cider vinegar
1/2 cup salad oil

In a blender, blend all ingredients, except for the spinach, strawberries and salad oil. Add the oil. Pour over the spinach leaves. You may not use all of the dressing, so be sure not to over dress the salad. Top with quartered strawberries.

# Walnut Apple Salad

Wash, tear, and drain the lettuce. Combine all the dressing ingredients and mix well. Just before serving mix the lettuce and dressing with the apples. Top with walnuts and bleu cheese.

Yield: 15 to 20 servings

3 heads of red leaf or
   any preferred lettuce
2/3 cup walnuts, chopped
2/3 cup bleu cheese,
   crumbled
1 green and 1 red apple,
   diced

Dressing:
2 tablespoons minced
   green onion
2 tablespoons apple
   cider vinegar
2 tablespoons lemon
   juice
3/4 teaspoon pepper
1/2 teaspoon salt
1/2 cup honey
2/3 cup vegetable oil

# Honey Oatmeal Bread

Cooking time: 25 to 30
  minutes
Yield: 2 loaves
Temperature: 350 degrees

Cold water and ice (to
  make $1/2$ cup total)
1 cup cooked oatmeal
$1/2$ cup honey
2 tablespoons yeast
$1/3$ cup margarine,
  melted
1 tablespoon salt
2 eggs, beaten
1 cup whole wheat flour
2 cups white flour

Combine the cooked oatmeal with the ice water, until the temperature is between 105 and 115 degrees. Add the honey and yeast. Set aside for a while to give the yeast time to work.

Add margarine, salt and eggs; beat well. Stir in the whole-wheat flour and mix well. Stir in the white flour and mix well. A mixer that has a dough hook can be used, until dough has formed a soft ball. turn the dough out onto a floured table and knead until it has an elastic feel, but is not sticky. Place in a greased bowl; grease the top of the dough, set in a warm place and let rise until doubled. Punch the dough down, shape into loaves, and let rise again. Place dough into 2 loaf pans. Bake in a preheated oven for 25 to 30 minutes.

# Peaches and Cream Muffins

Mix the eggs, sugar, oil, milk, salt, baking powder, and flour together in a bowl. Beat 2 minutes and stir in the peaches.

Preheat the oven to 350 degrees. Mix together all the filling ingredients, until smooth. Drop 1 tablespoon of filling in the middle of each muffin. Sprinkle the muffin tops with cinnamon and sugar mixture. Bake for 20 to 25 minutes.

For variety, this also makes a great coffeecake. After pouring the filling over the batter, take a knife and draw through the filling, making swirls. Add the topping and bake at 350 degrees for 35 minutes.

Cooking time: 20 to 25
  minutes
Yield: 15 to 20 servings
Temperature: 350 degrees

Batter:
3 eggs
2 cups sugar
$3/4$ cup oil
2 cups milk
$1/2$ teaspoon salt
2 teaspoons baking
  powder
4 cups flour-plus 3 tablespoons for every cup
2 cups peaches, diced
  and drained

Filling:
1 cup cream cheese,
  softened
$1/3$ teaspoon almond
  extract
2 tablespoons peach
  juice
$3/4$ cup sugar

Topping:
$1/3$ cup cinnamon/sugar
  mixture

# San Juan Guest Ranch

**San Juan Guest Ranch**
**2882 Highway 23**
**Ridgway, CO 81432**
**(800) 331-3015**
**(970) 626-5360**
**Pat and Scott MacTiernan**
**Elevation 7,100 feet**

The San Juan Mountains were sacred ground to the Ute Indians, who lived and hunted here until the phrase "Go West, young man" encouraged explorers and homesteaders. Miners made inroads into the Uncompaghre Valley before the Civil War, and despite several treaties between federal government and tribes, the lure of gold and silver made its mark. After the Civil War, ranching and tourism flourished, as word of the beauty and richness of the Valley spread. Mining has since declined, but not much else has changed since the turn of the century. The cowboy way of life—hard work in unpredictable elements—is still strong. You will find the real spirit of Southwest Colorado in the people who live here. The people who believe that this place and this way of life somehow makes them stronger and more honest, because success is just around the corner for almost any one willing to give it a try.

Scott's father, a history teacher, instilled in Scott a love for learning that is contagious. When you come to visit San Juan Guest Ranch, you learn the lingo, the history, the ecology and the philosophy of the Southwest Colorado region. To survey the beauty of the San Juan Mountains is a pleasure. To truly understand this place is a joy.

Listen to the wind blowing through valleys and canyons; it's the same wilderness melody that played to the Indians and the ranchers and the miners.This same song will play to your sense of adventure.

# Sticky Buns

Cooking time: 35 minutes
Yield: 8 servings
Temperature: 350 degrees

1/2 cup melted
   margarine
1/4 cup brown sugar
1/4 cup honey
1/2 to 1 teaspoon
   cinnamon
1/3 package instant
   butterscotch pudding
   mix
1/2 cup chopped nuts
20 balls of frozen dinner
   roll dough

In a medium-sized bundt pan, place 20 balls of frozen dinner roll dough. Combine the cooled melted margarine, brown sugar, honey, cinnamon and pudding mix. Pour over the frozen dough. Sprinkle with chopped nuts. Cover and allow to rise 6 to 8 hours (overnight). Bake 35 minutes in a preheated 350 degree oven, until brown. Turn out upside down on serving platter and enjoy.

# Cauliflower with Water Chestnuts and Mushrooms

Trim and wash cauliflower; break into flowerets. If they're too large, slice the flowerets into smaller pieces. Heat the oil in a pan; sauté the cauliflower and mushrooms for about 30 seconds. Add the broth, water chestnuts, soy sauce, and salt. Bring to a boil and cover. Simmer until the cauliflower is tender, but still crunchy. Mix the cornstarch with enough cold water to make a smooth paste. Slowly add to the cauliflower mixture, stirring constantly until thickened.

Cooking time: 20 minutes
Yield: 4 servings

1 small cauliflower
2 tablespoons oil
8 mushrooms, sliced
1 cup hot chicken broth
1/4 cup water chestnuts, sliced
2 tablespoons soy sauce
Salt to taste

# Cheese Potatoes

Cooking time: 45 minutes
  to 1 hour
Yield: 4 to 6 servings
Temperature: 375 to 400
  degrees

4 or 5 large baking
  potatoes, peeled and
  cut into thick French
  fries
$^3/_4$ cup Parmesan cheese
$^3/_4$ cup flour
1 teaspoon salt
1 tablespoon paprika
$^1/_2$ cup margarine

Preheat the oven to 375 degrees. Mix the flour, Parmesan cheese, paprika and salt in a plastic bag. Add the potatoes and shake to coat. Place the coated potatoes on a baking sheet in a single layer with the melted margarine and bake until golden brown. Turn the potatoes halfway through cooking time.

# Snap Beans Italian Style

Heat the oil and garlic in a saucepan. Add the onion and green pepper and cook 2 to 3 minutes. Stir in the beans, water, salt, and basil. Cover and cook 15 minutes or until tender. Stir in 1/4 cup cheese. Turn into a serving dish and sprinkle with remaining cheese.

Garnish with green pepper rings.

Cooking time: 20 minutes
Yield: 6 to 8 servings

1/2 pound Italian green beans, washed and snapped to 1-inch lengths
1/4 cup olive oil
1 clove garlic, crushed
1 teaspoon onion, chopped
3/4 cup green pepper, diced
1/4 cup boiling water
1 teaspoon salt
1 teaspoon basil
1/2 cup Parmesan cheese, grated
Green pepper rings

# Sweet Potato Crunch

Cooking time: 30 minutes
Yield: 8 to 10 servings
Temperature: 350 degrees
Can be stored frozen for
   up to 6 months


**Sweet Potato Custard:**
3 cups sweet potatoes
   cooked, mashed
1 cup sugar
$1/2$ cup butter, melted
2 eggs, beaten
1 teaspoon vanilla
$1/3$ cup milk

**Crunch Topping:**
$1/2$ cup packed brown
   sugar
$1/4$ cup flour
3 tablespoons
   margarine, melted
$1/2$ cup chopped nuts

Preheat the oven to 350 degrees. Combine all the custard ingredients and mix well. Turn into a greased 2-quart shallow baking dish. Sprinkle with the crunch topping. Bake for 30 minutes or until bubbly.

Word has it from a past guest that $1/4$ cup of port makes this recipe a taste sensation.

# Italian Sausage Soup with Tortellini

Brown the sausage; drain. Mix with the rest of the ingredients, excepting the tortellini and peas, in a 4 or 5-quart soup pot. Bring to a slow boil and cook for 30 minutes or until the carrots are done. Add the tortellini according to cooking time on package, depending on whether they are frozen or dry. Add the frozen peas 5 minutes before the soup is done, allowing just long enough for them to thaw. Serve with crusty bread and a sprinkle of Parmesan cheese on top.

Cooking time: 45 minutes
Yield: 8 to 10 servings

1 pound Italian sausage
2 cloves garlic, minced
3 leeks, diced
2 quarts water
2 carrots, diced
1 celery heart, diced
2 - 15 ounce cans
   crushed tomatoes
Pinch of oregano, basil,
   & pepper
2 tablespoons
   concentrated chicken
   soup base
1 - 12 ounce package
   frozen or dried
   tortellini
1 - 10 ounce box frozen
   peas

# Vegetable Soup

Cooking time: 45 minutes
Yield: 10 servings

1 cup onion, diced
1 tablespoon instant
  chicken broth mix
3 cloves garlic, minced
1 cup carrots, sliced
$1/2$ cup celery, sliced
1 cup tomatoes, chopped
  and seeded or 1 - 15
  ounce can diced,
  canned tomatoes
2 cups zucchini, sliced
  $1/4$-inch thick
2 teaspoons parsley,
  chopped
1 teaspoon basil
$1/2$ teaspoon pepper
6 cups water
Diced potatoes, barley,
  rice or pasta (optional)

In a 5-quart saucepan combine the onion, broth mix and garlic; cook, stirring occasionally until the onion is translucent. Add the remaining ingredients, except the water, and stir to combine. Cover and cook over low heat for about 10 minutes. Add a small amount of water, if necessary to prevent mixture from burning. Add the remaining water and bring to a boil. Reduce heat to medium, cover and cook until the vegetables are soft.

# Banana Crumb Muffins

Preheat oven to 375 degrees. In a large bowl, combine the dry ingredients. In a separate bowl, combine the bananas, sugar, egg and margarine; mix well. Stir into the dry ingredients, just until moistened. Fill greased muffin tins 3/4 full. Combine the first 3 topping ingredients; cut in the margarine until crumbly. Sprinkle over muffins. Bake for 18 to 20 minutes or until the muffins test done. Cool in the pan for 10 minutes before moving to a wire rack.

Cooking time: 18 to 20 minutes
Yield: 1 dozen
Temperature: 375 degrees

1 1/2 cups flour
1 teaspoon baking soda
1 teaspoon baking powder
1/2 teaspoon salt
3 large ripe bananas, mashed
3/4 cup sugar
1 egg, lightly beaten
1/3 cup margarine

Topping:
1/3 cup brown sugar
1 tablespoon flour
1/8 teaspoon cinnamon
1 tablespoon margarine, melted

# Oatmeal Cake

Cooking time: 35 minutes
Yield: 20 servings
Temperature: 350 degrees

Cake:
1 3/4 cups quick oatmeal
1 cube butter or
    margarine
1 1/4 cups boiling water
1 cup brown sugar
1 cup sugar
2 eggs
1 1/3 cups flour
1 teaspoon baking soda
1 teaspoon cinnamon
1/2 teaspoon salt
1/2 teaspoon baking
    powder
1/2 cup nuts, chopped

Topping:
6 tablespoons butter,
    melted
1/2 teaspoon vanilla
1/2 cup sugar
1/4 cup milk
1 cup nuts, chopped
1 cup coconut
1 cup oatmeal

Place the oatmeal and butter in a bowl, then pour the boiling water over them; mix and let stand for 20 minutes. Add in the sugars and eggs; mix well. Sift together and add the flour, baking soda, cinnamon, salt, and baking powder. Stir in the nuts. Pour into a 9 x 13-inch cake pan and bake for 35 minutes.

While the cake is baking, mix together the topping ingredients and cook over low heat until the sugar is completely melted and mixture is slightly thick. Spread topping over the cake when both are cool.

# Wacky Cake

Preheat the oven to 350 degrees. Mix together the dry cake ingredients. Add the liquids and beat until smooth. Bake in a 9 x 13-inch greased cake pan until a toothpick inserted in the middle comes out clean or for approximately 35 minutes.

To make the frosting, in a small mixing bowl, beat together the cream cheese and margarine. Add the powdered sugar and vanilla. Adjust the thickness with milk or more powdered sugar.

Often a child will come and whisper in our ear that Mom or Dad or their sister or brother is having a birthday during their stay at the ranch. This is our signal to get ready for a whole lot of fun. We then enlist the aid of the child to make a birthday cake and decorate it.

This Chocolate Cake recipe is very simple and tasty. Top it with a basic Cream Cheese Frosting and with just a little guidance small children have little trouble executing their first ever cake-baking endeavor. Most of the time they enlist the aid of 2 or 3 of their new buddies and the afternoon is spent making a work of art. The little wrangler's excitement is almost tangible and dinner becomes an after thought for them; forget the barbecued ribs and let's get on to the important part. We occasionally find frosting in some very unlikely places even late into the winter. This evokes some very fond memories as we look forward to next summer.

Cooking time: 35 minutes
Yield: 20 servings
Temperature: 350 degrees

Cake:
3 cups flour
2 cups sugar
2 teaspoons salt
2 teaspoons baking soda
6 tablespoons cocoa
2 cups water
1 teaspoon vinegar
1 teaspoon vanilla
3/4 cup margarine, melted

Frosting:
8 ounces cream cheese
2 tablespoons margarine
1 cup powdered sugar
1 tablespoon milk
1 teaspoon vanilla

# Chocolate Chip Cookies

Cooking time: 8 to 10 minutes
Yield: 4 dozen
Temperature: 350 degrees

1 cup margarine, softened
3/4 cup sugar
3/4 cup brown sugar
1 egg
2 1/2 cups flour
1 teaspoon baking soda
1/2 teaspoon salt
18 ounces chocolate chips
1 cup coarsely chopped nuts (optional)

Heat oven to 350 degrees. Mix margarine, sugars and egg. Stir in the flour, baking soda and salt (dough will be stiff). Stir in the nuts and chocolate chips. Drop by rounded teaspoonfuls about 2 inches apart onto an ungreased cookie sheet. Bake until light brown or for 8 to 10 minutes. Cool slightly and remove from the cookie sheets.

Here at the SJR one of the most pleasant aspects of our summer is the opportunity to enjoy with our guests the many delights of watching the children experience the wonders of ranch life, inside and out. We routinely invite the children to come into the kitchen and give us a hand with "the grub". Of course this usually means that their choice will be Chocolate Chip Cookies. Just seeing a 25 pound box of chocolate chips puts them in the right frame of mind for some real serious cooking. While Mom and Dad roll up the rugs in the dining room and work up an appetite dancing Country Swing with the wranglers on Friday night, the kids whip up some mighty fine cookies. After the cookies are done and served to the dancers, the children join in the fun and dance as long as they can stay awake, usually as late as 9:30 after a full day of "horsing around".

# Fresh Salsa

Chop the tomatoes in a mixing bowl to the desired size and add the finely chopped chiles, peppers, green onions, and cilantro. Add the garlic, lemon juice, hot sauce, and cumin to taste.

Serve with tortilla chips, tacos, or any Mexican food

Yield: 6 servings

2 - 15 ounce cans diced
   or chopped tomatoes-
   Southwest style or
   regular
2 mild green chiles
2 green bell peppers
2 bunches green onions
1/2 bunch cilantro
2 to 3 cloves garlic,
   minced
2 teaspoons lemon juice
Hot sauce to taste-
   Tabasco or chopped
   Jalapeños
Powdered cumin

# Spaghetti Sauce

Cooking time: 2 hours
Yield: 10 to 12 servings

3 pounds Italian sausage
1 - #10 can tomato
  sauce
1 - 12 ounce can tomato
  paste
12 ounces water
2/3 cup red wine
1/4 cup sugar
2 teaspoons Italian
  seasoning
1 teaspoon oregano
1 teaspoon basil
1/2 teaspoon black
  pepper
2 cloves garlic, minced
1 medium onion, diced
3/4 large bell pepper,
  diced
Mushrooms if desired

Brown the sausage; drain. Add to the rest of the ingredients in a 4 or 5-quart heavy pot. Bring to a slow boil for 30 minutes. Reduce the heat to a slow simmer and cook for approximately 2 hours, stirring often until thick.

Serve over pasta with garlic bread.

# Skyline Guest Ranch

**Skyline Guest Ranch**
**PO Box 67**
**Telluride, CO  81435**
**(888) 754-1126**
**(970) 728-3757**
**skyline-ranch@toski.com**
**www.ranchweb.com/skyline/glance.htm**
**The Farny Family**
**Elevation 9,600 feet**

The folks at Skyline Guest Ranch are committed to sharing with their guests a special spirit they like to call "mountain joy". Guests begin to experience it when they wake to sunlit views of the snowcapped peaks surrounding the ranch, some of which soar to over 14,000 feet above sea level.

One of the special expressions of this spirit can also be felt on the breakfast rides the ranch offers. Guests are taken on horseback up into the back country, where they ride through flower filled meadows before sitting down to a scrumptious breakfast.

Another activity enjoyed by guests at the ranch is fly fishing. There are three lakes brimming with trout on the property, as well as many other nearby lakes and streams. So make sure you bring your tackle and try your luck with some of the finest fishing available in the Rockies.

While at the Skyline Guest Ranch be sure to plan on exploring the majestic San Juan Mountains, either by Jeep, horseback, mountain bike, or even on foot. A visit to the world famous Anasazi ruins at Mesa Verde National Park outside of Durango is also a must for any visitor to this area of Colorado. And of course there is the simple pleasure of kicking back in a chair and relaxing.

# Chili Verde Stew

Cooking time: 2 ¹/₂ hours
Yield: 6 servings
Temperature: simmer on
  stove top

1 ¹/₂ pounds pork
  shoulder or beef, cubed
4 cups whole tomatoes
¹/₂ cup beef consommé
1 medium garlic clove,
  crushed
¹/₄ teaspoon sugar
1 - 7 ounce can whole
  green chiles, cut into
  thin strips
1 teaspoon cumin
¹/₄ teaspoon ground
  cloves
2 tablespoons lemon
  juice
¹/₃ cup chopped parsley
Salt to taste

Brown the pork or beef. Add all the other ingredients. Simmer, covered 2 ¹/₂ hours.

# Carrot Ginger Soup

Sauté the onion, garlic and ginger in unsalted butter. Add the curry, stock, wine and carrots. Let simmer for 30 to 45 minutes, covered. When slightly cooled, puree the soup. Add lemon juice; season with salt and pepper. Garnish with chopped parsley.

Yield: 8 servings
Temperature: simmer on stove top

6 tablespoons unsalted butter
1 large yellow onion
$1/4$ cup ginger, minced
3 cloves garlic, minced
Pinch of curry
Parsley for garnish
7 cups chicken stock
1 cup dry, white wine
1 $1/2$ pounds carrots
2 tablespoons lemon juice
Salt and pepper to taste

# Dill Cottage Cheese Rolls

Cooking time: 10 to 15
  minutes
Yield: 8 servings
Temperature: 350 degrees

1 package dry yeast
1/4 cup warm water
1/2 cup cottage cheese
1/2 cup sour cream or
  yogurt
1/4 cup butter
2 tablespoons sugar
1 tablespoon onion,
  minced
1 1/2 teaspoons dill seed
1/4 teaspoon baking
  soda
1 teaspoon salt
1 egg
2 1/4 cups white flour

Dissolve yeast in warm water. Heat the cottage cheese and sour cream to warm. Stir in the butter, onion, sugar, dill, salt and egg. When the mixture reaches the same temperature as the yeast, combine the two together. Add the flour and knead for 5 minutes. Let rise for 1 hour. Shape into rolls. Let rise a second time. Bake at 350 degrees. Brush with butter and dill seed before serving.

# Cheese Wine Bread

In a large bowl, combine 1 $\frac{1}{2}$ cups flour and the yeast. Heat together the wine, butter, sugar and salt until warm, stirring constantly until the butter is melted. Add to the dry ingredients. Add the eggs and beat at low mixer speed for 30 seconds. Beat at high speed for 3 minutes. By hand, stir in the cheese and enough remaining flour to make a soft dough. Knead until smooth and elastic. Let rise until double in size, about 1 $\frac{1}{2}$ hours. Punch down and let the dough rest for 10 minutes. Shape into an 8-inch round loaf. Place in a greased 9-inch pie plate, cover and let rise for 40 minutes. Bake at 375 degrees for about 40 minutes. Cover with foil the last 20 minutes of baking.

Cooking time: 40 minutes
Yield: 1 loaf
Temperature: 375 degrees

1 package dry yeast
$\frac{1}{2}$ cup dry, white wine
$\frac{1}{2}$ cup butter
3 cups white flour
2 teaspoons sugar
1 teaspoon salt
3 eggs
1 cup Monterey Jack
  cheese, cubed

# Cheese Cake

Cooking time: 72 minutes
Yield: 12 servings
Temperature: 550 then
  200 degrees

Crust:
1 cup flour
$1/4$ cup sugar
1 egg yolk
$1/4$ teaspoon lemon rind
$1/4$ teaspoon vanilla
$1/2$ cup butter

Cheese Filling:
4 $1/2$ packages (8 ounce)
  cream cheese, room
  temperature
$1/2$ cup butter
$1/4$ teaspoon vanilla
1 $3/4$ cups sugar
3 tablespoons flour
1 teaspoon grated lemon
  and orange peel
5 whole eggs
2 egg yolks
$1/4$ cup heavy cream

Mix the crust ingredients until a stiff dough forms. Use $1/2$ of the dough to press into the bottom of a 9-inch spring form pan. Bake at 400 degrees for 15 minutes. Let cool. Place the remaining dough on the sides and seal into the bottom.

Beat the cream cheese and butter together, until light and creamy. Slowly add the sugar, flour, peels and vanilla. Beat the whole eggs in 1 at a time, then the yolks. Lastly, beat in the heavy cream until the filling is really smooth. Pour into the spring form pan and bake for 12 minutes in a hot oven at 550 degrees. Reduce the heat to 200 degrees and bake for 1 more hour. Cool in opened oven. If the top begins to brown too much, place foil over pan.

# Rhubarb Cake

Cream the butter and just 1 cup of brown sugar together. Add the egg and vanilla. Add the dry ingredients in thirds with the buttermilk, beating until smooth. Fold in the rhubarb. Turn into a 9 by 12-inch well greased baking pan. Sprinkle the remaining brown sugar on top. Bake at 350 degrees for 45 minutes.

Cooking time: 45 minutes
Yield: 12 servings
Temperature: 350 degrees

$1/2$ cup butter
2 cups brown sugar, packed
1 egg
1 teaspoon vanilla
1 cup pecans, chopped
2 cups flour
1 teaspoon baking soda
$1/2$ teaspoon salt
1 cup buttermilk
2 cups rhubarb, sliced

# Dreamy Cheese Nut Roll

Yield: 12 servings

1 - 8 ounce package
    cream cheese
$1/2$ cup bleu cheese,
    crumbled
1 teaspoon lemon juice
$1/2$ teaspoon salt
Salted peanuts, chopped
Dash of Worcestershire
    sauce
3 tablespoons green
    onion, finely chopped
$1/4$ teaspoon garlic salt
A little cream, if needed

Mix all ingredients, except for the peanuts. Form into the shape or shapes of your choice. Roll it in the chopped and salted peanuts. Chill in the refrigerator. Decorate with parsley or flowers just prior to serving.

# Skyline Salsa

Mince the shallots and garlic. Add the chopped tomatoes and other ingredients; mix well.

Yield: 1 quart

2 pints cherry tomatoes, chopped
1 large shallot
1 large clove of garlic
1 1/4 teaspoon salt
1 tablespoon wine vinegar
2 Serrano chiles, seeded and minced
1 tablespoon lime juice
2 tablespoons cilantro, chopped

# Wilderness Trails Ranch

**Wilderness Trails Ranch**
**Winter: 1766 County Road 302R**
**Durango, CO 81301**
**Summer: 23486R County Road 501**
**Bayfield, CO 81122**
**(800) 52-RANCH**
**(970) 247-0722**
**FAX (970) 247-1006**
**www.wildernesstrails.com**
**wtrcb@wildernesstrails.com**
**The Roberts Family**
**Elevation 7,800 feet**

Bob Venuti, Sr. and his son, Bob Venuti, Jr. had a dream. They hoped to build a dude ranch with buildings constructed completely from logs taken from the land. This dream began in 1946. At that time, Bob, Sr. was the manager of Teelawuket Ranch, an operating dude ranch adjacent to the property which would become Wilderness Trails. At the same time Bob, Jr. was studying engineering at the University of Colorado.

The property consisted of 160 acres in the secluded Los Pinos Valley, 35 miles northeast of Durango. In earlier years exploratory mining had been done in the area and the Southern Ute Indian tribe at one time used the valley as their summer hunting camp. When the land became available for purchase, Bob, Sr. jumped at the opportunity.

Construction began in 1947 after a sawmill was set up on the ranch property. Logs were taken both from the ranch property and the National Forest. It took two years and over 2 million board feet of lumber to construct the first cabins and the lodge. On July 1, 1950 the ranch opened its doors for the first guests.

The ranch came under the ownership of Gene and Jan Roberts in March, 1970. Since that time there have been numerous improvements, including the addition of a swimming pool, hot tub, two barns, pipe corrals, four cabins, a second stocked trout pond, plus many positive changes in the activities and horse programs.

The ranch herd consists of 80 head of horses, that are the heart of the operation. Part of the Roberts' philosophy is to convey an attitude of understanding, communicating, and caring about horses.

The ranch family and staff members are committed to providing an extraordinary vacation for their guests during the months of June, July and August. During each September they offer an adults only season.

This commitment to excellence has earned the ranch national recognition. They were featured in the February, 1995 edition of *Horse and Rider* magazine. They have also been featured on such programs as *Good Morning America* and the PBS travel special, *Going Places* during 1997.

Guests are invited to explore the wonders of the beautiful San Juan Mountains of Southwestern Colorado; rekindle a time when family and place were all that really mattered. Share the passion of the Roberts Family for the legacy of western living. Wilderness Trails Ranch—*a blend of the past and the present.*

# Brachiole

Arrange the ribeye on a cutting board. Place the prosciutto ham on each slice. Add the provolone and 1 teaspoon pesto brushed on top of the cheese. Roll up and dredge in the flour. Sauté the seam side first, then all sides. Cook enough to barely brown the meat. Finish cooking, covered in a 350 degree oven for 20 to 30 minutes.

Can be served with a Bordelaise or mushroom sauce.

Cooking time: 20 to 30 minutes
Yield: 6 servings
Temperature: 350 degrees

Boneless rib roast, sliced into 6 - 8 ounce pieces
1 slice prosciutto ham per piece of ribeye
1 slice Provolone cheese per ribeye
3 tablespoons pesto
Enough flour to cover meat pieces

*"I'm sure you could tell, but I'll mention it anyway— Lynne and I had a terrific time at Caballeros week. I can't decide which part was the best—the ranch, the riding or the people. All come to mind during our frequent thoughts about our vacation."*

*Lynn and Brad*
*San Juan Capistrano, California*

# Chicken Paprikosh

Yield: 4 servings

1 frying chicken, cut up
3 tablespoons paprika
1 onion, sliced
Salt
Pepper
Garlic powder

In a frying pan, place some oil and the cut up frying chicken. Brown nicely, turning the chicken. Add enough water to come up to about halfway on the chicken. Add the paprika, onion, a little salt and pepper, and garlic powder. Cover and simmer until the chicken is soft. Salt to taste.

Serve with any vegetable.

*"I wanted to thank all of you on behalf of my family for a great vacation. The beautiful mountains, lake and views were so peaceful. The horse trails and activities were so invigorating. But the friendships my sons developed were perhaps the best of all. Thanks to your hospitality a summer guest ranch ranks at the top of our list for future vacations."*

*The M. Family*
*North Carolina*

# Noodles Romanoff

Cook and drain the noodles. Sauté the onion, green pepper, and mushrooms. Place the noodles in a roasting pan. Add the sautéed vegetables and 1/2 pint sour cream, plus 1/4 pound melted butter. You may heat the sour cream and the butter at the same time and it will smooth out nicely. Mix in the Parmesan cheese and place in oven for about 25 minutes.

Cooking time: 25 minutes

2 cups dried medium-
  sized noodles
1 small onion
1 small green pepper
1/4 pound mushrooms,
  sliced
1/2 pint sour cream
1/4 pound butter
1/4 cup Parmesan cheese

*"I want to thank you one and all for the most memorable time this summer, not just speaking for me but the whole family. We all felt so well taken care of and relaxed."*

*Jackie*
*San Diego, California*

# Broccoli Italian

Cooking time: 10 minutes
Temperature: deep fried

Fresh or frozen broccoli
1 egg
Small amount of milk
Parmesan cheese

If using fresh broccoli, boil for about 5 minutes, separating the stalks. If frozen broccoli is used, just heat until thawed. Make the batter from 1 egg and a little milk, whipping it well. Dip the pieces of broccoli into this batter, and then place into a frying pan with a little olive oil. Sprinkle with Parmesan cheese. Serve when batter has set.

*"Our week with you was so much fun. We thoroughly enjoyed everything—being with you, enjoying the beautiful ranch, meeting your lovely children, the food and entertainment and meeting your delightful staff! We hope to repeat next year."*

*Annabelle*
*Aztec, New Mexico*

# To Hell With Texas Cornbread

Preheat oven to 325 degrees. Mix all the ingredients , except for the liquid shortening, for 15 seconds with a mixer. Add the liquid shortening. Pour into a 12 x 9-inch pan. Bake until a toothpick comes out clean or about 45 minutes.

Serve with honey. For variety, add Jalapeño peppers or green chiles to the batter.

Cooking time: 45 minutes
Yield: 1 loaf
Temperature: 325 degrees

2 1/2 cups cornmeal
2 1/2 cups all-purpose flour
2 cups sugar
4 eggs
2 tablespoons baking power
2 tablespoons salt
1 pint milk
1/2 cup liquid shortening

*"Wanted to thank you for the wonderful week we spent at Wilderness Trails Ranch. Our fun memories will last us a lifetime. The food was out of this world for a guest ranch and above our expectations. The cabins were perfect. Warm, clean and comfortable."*

*Linda and Shari*
*Dallas, Texas*

# Apple Cake

Cooking time: 30 minutes
Yield: 1 cake
Temperature: 350 degrees

2 cups apples, diced
1 cup sugar
1 egg
$1/2$ cup liquid
　shortening
$1/2$ cup cold water
1 teaspoon vanilla
1 teaspoon cinnamon
$1/2$ teaspoon baking
　soda
1 $1/2$ cups flour
$1/2$ cup brown sugar for
　topping

Preheat the oven to 350 degrees. Mix all the ingredients together, except for the brown sugar, until well incorporated. Spread in a 9-inch baking pan. Sprinkle with the brown sugar. Bake for 30 minutes.

*"My family and I truly enjoyed our vacation. We chose your ranch from a catalog of dude ranches and chose 5 or 6 to call for information. We called your ranch first and I remember Linda saying that she was ready to pick WTR after the first phone call. The friendliness and enthusiasm that we encountered in our initial phone call was still there when we arrived at the ranch; and it never wavered at all for the entire week."*

*Randy, Linda, Kyle and Stuart*
*Cincinnati, Ohio*

# Black Nasty

Use a mixer with a whip attachment to cream together the butter and sugar; add in the hot melted chocolate. Add the eggs 1 at a time, scraping down the sides of the bowl. Whip until thick enough to mound in the pie crust. Chill in the refrigerator.

Cooking time: 15 minutes
Yield: 1 pie

1 graham cracker pie
  crust
1 cup butter
2 cups sugar
2 teaspoon vanilla
12 ounces melted
  chocolate (hot)
8 eggs

*"We all had a wonderful time and even my mother and mother-in-law who were hesitant (to say the least) about beginning horseback riding at their age, were thrilled. The staff were all wonderful including those staff who took care of the kids. The twins cried to have to leave Taffy and Cisco and I'm sure if he could have, Michael would have stowed away in one of the cabins for another week. It was a vacation that we will remember and cherish those memories for a long time."*

*J. M.*
*Charleston, Illinois*

# Crème Brulee

Cooking time: 45 minutes
  or until set
Yield: 7 servings
Temperature: 400 degrees

1 quart heavy cream
Dash of vanilla
3/4 cup sugar
10 egg yolks

Preheat the oven to 400 degrees. Scald the cream and vanilla, then mix in the sugar and eggs. Mix well. Fill 7 ramekins (5 ounce size) and place on a sheet pan. Place the pan in the oven. Add water to fill the pan. Bake in water bath at 400 degrees for 45 minutes or until set.

Garnish with fresh fruit or fruit sauce.

*"What a wonderful time we enjoyed at your ranch. As grandparents, we highly recommend the adventure. Everyone working for you is gracious and hospitable. Truly, memories of the ranch will live with us forever. Unforgettable experience and one our little ones will always treasure".*

*Ginny and Doug*
*Orland Park, Illinois*

# Peanut Butter Bars

Use a mixer to blend together all of the ingredients, except for the chocolate chips. Spread the mixture in a 9-inch baking pan. Melt the chocolate, then spread on top of the batter and chill. Bring to room temperature for easier cutting.

Garnish with chopped walnuts or pecans, if desired.

*"Just a note to tell you how much the entire Leonard clan enjoyed our week with all of you at WTR. It couldn't have been more perfect—-for all of us!"*

*Peggy*
*Pasadena, California*

Yield: 12 squares

2 packages graham crackers
$3/4$ pound peanut butter
$1/2$ pound powdered sugar
$1/4$ pound butter, softened
1 pound chocolate chips

# Sopapillas

Cooking time: 7 minutes
Yield: 8 servings
Temperature: deep fried

1 tablespoon yeast
$1/8$ cup warm water
4 tablespoons sugar
$3/4$ cup milk
$1/2$ teaspoon salt
1 egg
3 $1/2$ cups high gluten
   flour
1 tablespoon oil

Mix the ingredients for 5 minutes on medium speed with a mixer. Roll out the dough to $1/4$-inch thickness. Cut into squares and deep fry. Flip once in oil.

Serve with powdered sugar and honey.

*"Just wanted to tell you that the girls and I had a wonderful stay at the ranch. Your food and hospitality are great, your staff was always a pleasure, and the horses amazingly well trained, which shows your devotion to the place, as it must be difficult with the range of guests you serve. Thanks again for all your courtesies."*

*Dick,*
*Bridgeton, New Jersey*

# Sheep Dip

Mix together all of the ingredients. Heat in a saucepan, stirring frequently.

Serve with warm Pita chips or bagels

*"Your ranch is a perfect place. Everything from the activities to the meals or just walking by the pasture on a quiet evening, listening to the sounds of the river and the horses was wonderful."*

*Peggy,*
*St. Petersburg, Florida*

Yield: 3 cups

12 artichoke bottoms, sliced
$3/4$ pound cream cheese
$1/2$ cup heavy whipping cream
1 tablespoon garlic, chopped
$1/4$ pound fresh spinach, chopped
$1/4$ pound sour cream
$1/8$ pound Parmesan cheese

# Bora Bora Sauce

Cooking time: 2 minutes
Yield: 3 cups

1 cup soy sauce
1 cup water
1/2 cup sherry
4 tablespoons honey
2 tablespoons brown
  sugar
1 teaspoon garlic
  powder
1/2 teaspoon ginger

Mix all the ingredients together in a saucepan. Bring to a boil and remove from heat. This is spread on the meat as it is being roasted or broiled.

Teriyaki sauce has beer or sake instead of the sherry and you marinate the meat in it overnight. Broil and baste it.

*"Thank you so much for a wonderful time and for the special attention you gave to me and my family! Even my son who didn't want to ride horses on vacation became quite attached to Lena. Your ranch is a beautiful haven—thank you for sharing it with us. You and your staff were very gracious."*

*Rachel*
*Orange Park, Florida*

# Crème Anglais

Scald the heavy cream with vanilla. Slowly mix with the egg yolk, sour cream, and sugar. Chill

Serve over crepes or under any dessert.

Cooking time: 4 minutes
Yield: $1/2$ cup

$1/2$ cup heavy cream
Dash of vanilla
1 egg yolk
$1/2$ tablespoon sour
    cream
1 tablespoon sugar

*"Thank you for a brilliant week at Wilderness Trails. We enjoyed ourselves even more than last time which we didn't believe was possible. Love to you all."*

*Barry and Jane*
*England*

# Pesto

Yield: 1 pint

1 pound fresh basil
  leaves
2 tablespoons fresh
  garlic
1 cup grated Parmesan
2 cups olive oil

Place all the ingredients, except for the olive oil, into a food processor and blend to a paste. Pour into a container and cover with the olive oil.

This is great for pizza, pasta, breads, meats or chicken.

*"I can't tell you enough how much Amy and I enjoyed our week at WTR in August. I came to the ranch with incredibly high expectations, yet everyone one of them was not only met, but surpassed. The generous hospitality of you both is deeply appreciated. My heartfelt thanks for a wonderful, unforgettable week at WTR.."*

*Anne*
*Austin, Texas*

# Vera Cruz Sauce

Sauté the scallions and garlic in the olive oil until translucent. Add the remaining ingredients. Bring to a boil. Thicken with roux or corn starch. Season to taste.

Yield: 1 quart

3 bunches scallions, chopped
1 tablespoon garlic, chopped
1/4 cup tomato paste
2 tablespoons olive oil
16 ounce can chopped tomatoes
16 ounces beef stock
1/2 cup dry sherry
1/2 tablespoon coriander
Salt and pepper to taste

*"I remember the bright blue summer sky of Colorado and those trail rides to luscious green meadows. Day after day getting on that spunky Bandito climbing higher and higher, surrounded by Ponderosas, Blue spruce and quiet. The beautiful quiet—no car horns, no commuter trains, no telephones. I recall sitting on the porch of my cabin in the rocking chair, my eyes closed, listening to the sound of the wind through the trees. Can they bottle that stuff? The other thing I remember so well was the smiles and courtesy of your staff. The city life sometimes makes one very cynical, especially about young people and their lack of manners, respect and courtesy. Your staff brought me back to realize that it only takes a few bad kids to make you forget about all the great kids that are around. I look at my vacation pictures often—the draft horses rolling in the front pasture, our peaceful little cabin, the two foals snuggling with mom, the evening get togethers, and I even videotaped the staff show.*

*Chesteen
Richmond, California*

# Women of the West

**Emily Griffith**
**1880 - 1947**

Emily Griffith came to Colorado in 1904 and took a teaching job at a school in Denver. She continued teaching, while at the same time working for the *Denver Post*. It was while working at the newspaper that she was interviewed about her dream of opening an Opportunity School that would be open to anyone wishing to learn. After the interview hit the newspaper, several people came forward to help her realize this dream and by 1916 her Opportunity School had opened in Denver.

Few people attended the first day of school, but within a short time the school grew and at times as many as 1,400 students attended. The first classes taught at the Opportunity School were in subjects such as writing, reading and math, business, typing, sign making, lip reading and auto mechanics.

Emily's days were long and many of the students grew quite hungry during the long hours in class. Emily and her sister solved the problem by bringing large pots of soup to school each day to assure that no one would be hungry during school hours.

She continued teaching "For All Who Wished to Learn", as the sign on the wall noted, until her retirement in 1933. Ever since arriving in Colorado, she lived in a small cabin with no phone, electric lights or running water. Unfortunately, in June of 1947, Emily and her sister were both found murdered in their cabin home. No one has ever been brought to trial for the crime.

Today, the Emily Griffith Opportunity School continues to thrive and has a large student body. It is located on Welton Street in Denver, Colorado and the sign still reads "For All Who Wish to Learn". Emily Griffith was a pioneer in the education of all and a true Woman of the West.

## Carrie Chapman Catt
## 1859 - 1947

Born in Ripon, Wisconsin, Carrie Chapman Catt grew up to be one of the most influential and active people in the fight for women's rights. Educated in Iowa, she became first a teacher and later a school principal in Mason City. In 1890 she put aside her teaching career and joined the Woman's Suffrage Movement. She worked hard and became a leader in the organization. She organized the 1894 referendum that resulted in making Colorado the first state in the Union to give women the right to vote in local and national elections. At the time she was described as the "noble woman, to whom more than any one other person we owe the glorious fact or our citizenship."

During her fight for women's suffrage, as well as after the right to vote was won, she often said, "Women have suffered an agony of the soul…that you and your daughters might inherit political freedom. That vote has been costly. Prize it!"

In 1900 she served as the president of the National American Woman Suffrage Association, which was modeled on the national Democratic and Republican parties. In 1904 she was elected president of the International Woman Suffrage Alliance. She held the post of president of the national association until her death.

The strategy of the national association was to fight for the women's vote in large cities and win state by state. By 1915, Carrie Chapman Catt and her group had helped to bring the women's vote to most of the larger states. During 1919 and 1920, she participated in the last push for suffrage in the United States, helping to make Tennessee the 36th and final state needed to ratify the constitutional amendment for women's right to vote.

Upon passage of the 19th Amendment to the Constitution, she proposed changing the name of the National American Suffrage Association. It continues today as the League of Women Voters.

Besides working for women's right to vote, she fought for a variety of other important issues. She continued to be active, working from 1925 to 1932 for international peace and serving as the head of the National Committee on the Cause and Cure of War. Carrie Chapman Catt was a tireless worker and an extraordinary Woman of the West.

## Pat Schroeder
## 1940 -

After her birth in Portland, Oregon, Pat Schroeder's family moved from place to place. She graduated from Harvard Law School in 1964, then settled in Colorado and became an activist in the First District Democratic Group. She was elected to Congress in 1973, winning the seat with 52% of the vote. At that time she was one of only thirteen congresswomen.

After being elected to Congress, she moved her family to Washington, D.C. She took her fight to the center of government and was instrumental in helping to bring an end to the Vietnam War. Later she became the first woman to have a seat on the Armed Forces Committee. She worked for and sponsored legislation giving divorced military, diplomatic and CIA spouses protection from losing their medical and other benefits.

In 1985 she introduced the Family Military Act setting standards for child-care in wartime and became a member of the House Select Committee on Children, Youth and Families. She also supported the "Deadbeat Dads Act" and sponsored the national Family and Medical Leave Act, which was passed and then signed into law by President Clinton in 1993. American families are and have been a top priority for Pat Schroeder. As she has said, "It is our country's future that is at stake."

In 1987, she considered running for President of the United States. During her campaign for the nomination the hard work and constant travel, as well as lack of funding, caused her to re-consider. She finally decided against continuing the campaign. She continued her work in Congress, though and finally retired in 1996. After retirement, she spent a year at Dartmouth as a professor before becoming President and Chief Executive Officer of the Association of American Publishers, the principal trade association of the book publishing industry.

Pat Schroeder represented Colorado in Congress for over twenty years and was active in many causes during her career, always fighting for what she believed in. During that time she helped to make major changes for the betterment of the men and women of the United States and she continues to do so today. Her work with the military and for the women and families of this country make her a true Coloradan and a great Woman of the West.

# Ranch Locator

1) Aspen Canyon Ranch
   Parshall, Colorado
2) Aspen Lodge Ranch Resort
   Estes Park, Colorado
3) Bar Lazy J Guest Ranch
   Parshall, Colorado
4) C Lazy U Ranch
   Granby, Colorado
5) Cherokee Park Ranch
   Livermore, Colorado
6) Colorado Trails Ranch
   Durango, Colorado
7) Coulter Lake Guest Ranch
   Rifle, Colorado
8) Deer Valley Ranch
   Nathrop, Colorado
9) Drowsy Water Ranch
   Granby, Colorado
10) Elk Mountain Ranch
    Buena Vista, Colorado
11) The Historic Pines Ranch
    Westcliffe, Colorado
12) Lake Mancos Ranch
    Mancos, Colorado
13) Latigo Ranch
    Kremmling, Colorado
14) Lazy H Guest Ranch
    Allenspark, Colorado
15) Lost Valley Ranch
    Sedalia, Colorado

16) North Fork Ranch
    Shawnee, Colorado
17) Old Glendevey Ranch
    Glendevey, Colorado
18) Powderhorn Guest Ranch
    Powderhorn, Colorado
19) Rainbow Trout Ranch
    Antonito, Colorado
20) Rawah Ranch
    Glendevey, Colorado
21) San Juan Guest Ranch
    Ridgway, Colorado
22) Sky Corral Ranch
    Bellvue, Colorado
23) Skyline Ranch
    Telluride, Colorado
24) Sylvan Dale Guest Ranch
    Loveland, Colorado
25) Tarryall River Ranch
    Lake George, Colorado
26) Waunita Hot Springs Ranch
    Gunnison, Colorado
27) Whistling Acres Guest Ranch
    Paonia, Colorado
28) Wilderness Trails Ranch
    Durango, Colorado
29) King Mountain Ranch
    Granby, Colorado
30) Laramie River Ranch
    Jelm, Wyoming

# Ranch Locator

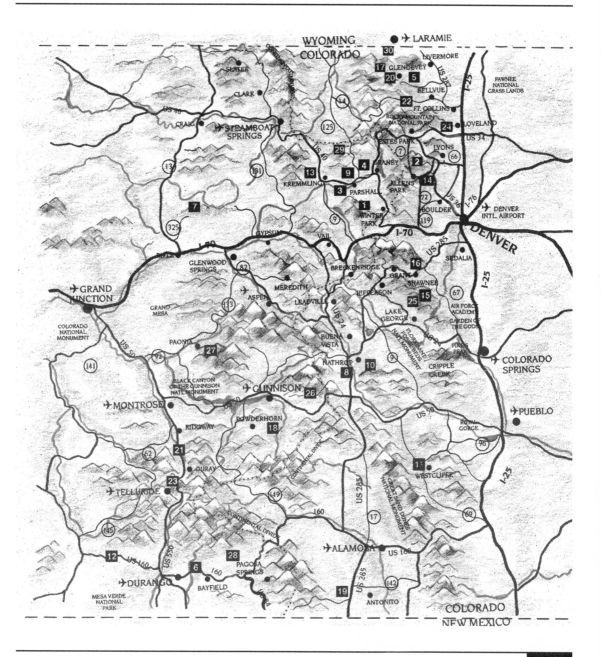

# Index

Adobe Chicken Casserole....................97
Alaskan Fisherman's Baked Beans....323
Almond Cheesecake ..........................143
Aloha Banana Bread ..........................262
Amber Onions....................................319
Angel Biscuits....................................279
**Appetizers**
   Amber Onions ................................319
   Cheese and Bacon In A Bread
      Boat....................................215
   Crab Spread Appetizer .....................37
   Dreamy Cheese Nut Roll ..............364
   Fried Tomatoes .................................25
Apple - Jalapeño Salsa.......................301
Apple Cake .........................................374
Apple Cider Syrup .............................181
Apple Crisp ..........................................52
Apple Fritters .....................................268
Aspen Canyon Ranch Cookies ...........86
Baja Seafood Taco with Purple Cabbage,
   Chayote and Nopali Cactus Slaw...139
Baked Chicken Breast Stuffed with
   Sautéed Spinach and Mushrooms ..136
Baked Spiced Pork Chops .................256
Banana Chocolate Chip Muffins .........30
Banana Crumb Muffins .....................351
Banana Nut Pancakes ........................237
Barbecue Beans..................................229
Barbecue Chicken Salad .....................24
Barbecue Pork Ribs ............................79
Barbecued Ham Balls ........................320

**Beef Entrés**
   Beef Stroganoff .............................216
   Beef Tenderloin with Maple Sage
      Sauce.................................111
   Beef Teriyaki .................................165
   Brachiole .......................................369
   Flank Steak in Marinade ...............335
   Grilled Ribeye with Tobacco
      Onions................................135
   Hamburger Wellington ...................305
   Prime Rib ......................................134
   Sherry's Barbecue Brisket.............217
   Sloppy Joes With A Twist .............192
   Swiss Cream Steak........................254
Beef Stew with Shitake Mushrooms
   and Baby Veggies .......................240
Beef Stroganoff..................................216
Beef Tenderloin with Maple Sage
   Sauce ...........................................111
Beef Teriyaki.....................................165
Beef Vegetable Casserole..................126
Best Dude Dip in the West .................60
**Beverages**
   Coffee Mocha................................212
   Glogg.............................................234
**Biscuits & Rolls**
   Angel Biscuits ...............................279
   Dill Cottage Cheese Rolls .............360
   Dill Rolls ......................................170
   Nancy's Cinnamon Buns.................22
   Old Fashioned Rolls......................297

# Index

**Biscuits & Rolls (cont'd)**
Overnight Potato Rolls....................154
Scones.............................................313
Southern Biscuits ..........................298
Sticky Buns ...................................344
Biscuits and Sausage Gravy ...............46
Black Bean Chili Chowder.................98
Black Nasty...................................375
Blackened Buffalo Quesadilla ..........138
Blueberry Filled Coffeecake.............221
Blueberry Muffins............................265
Blueberry Smoothie ........................175
Blueberry Streusel Cake ..................180
Blueberry Tart ...............................53
Bora Bora Sauce ............................380
Brachiole........................................369
Braided Onion and Chive Bread..........84

**Breads**
Aloha Banana Bread ......................262
Braided Onion and Chive Bread......84
Buttermilk Banana Bread...............205
Buttermilk Corn Bread....................29
Cheese Wine Bread .......................361
Cinnamon Bread.............................85
Corn Bread ...................................68
Dill Bread .....................................295
Emily's Pumpkin Bread ..................15
Herb Bread ...................................311
Honey Oatmeal Bread....................340
Indian Fry Bread ...........................296
Jeannine's Garlic Bread .................244

**Breads (cont'd)**
Lemon Nut Bread...........................220
Milk and Honey Bread...................312
Parmesan Mini Loaves...................153
Poppy Seed Bread .........................16
Super Easy Beer Bread .................196
Swiss Cheese Rolls or Bread ........206
To Hell With Texas Cornbread.......373
Toffee Banana Bread......................264
Broccoli - Cauliflower Salad ............194
Broccoli Italian ...............................372
Broccoli Pasta Soufflé ......................116
Broccoli Tomato Salad......................101
Buttermilk Banana Bread .................205
Buttermilk Brownies........................283
Buttermilk Corn Bread .....................29
Buttermilk Pie.................................207
Caciucco Alla Livornese...................241
Caesar Salad Dressing .....................294
Cajun Crevettes...............................90

**Cakes & Pies**
Almond Cheesecake.......................143
Apple Cake....................................374
Black Nasty ..................................375
Buttermilk Pie ..............................207
Carrot Cake ..................................129
Cheesecake....................................362
Chocolate Peanut Butter Pie ..........327
Chocolate Sheet Cake with Raspberry
Sauce..............................................31
Colorado's Cheesecake ..................245

# Index

## Cakes & Pies (cont'd)

Cream Cheese Pound Cake ..............39
Crème de Menthe Cake ..................281
Crustless Cheesecake ......................266
Fluffy Strawberry Pie ......................155
Fresh Apple Cake with Caramel
     Frosting ............................................69
Hot Fudge Cake ...............................104
Key Lime Pie ...................................208
Oatmeal Cake ...................................352
Oatmeal Pie .......................................40
Peanut Butter Pie .............................130
Peanut Crunch Ice Cream
     Pie .................................................282
Pumpkin Cake ...................................105
Pumpkin Cake Dessert ....................198
Pumpkin Cheesecake .......................267
Pumpkin Dutch Apple Pie ...............314
Pumpkin Ice Cream Pie ...................156
Rhubarb Cake .....................................41
Rhubarb Cake ...................................363
Scrumptious Chocolate Cake ...........246
Snickers Cake ...................................315
Southern Apple Cream Pie ...............299
Strawberry Cookie Pie .....................171
Wacky Cake ......................................353
Caramel Frosting ..................................69
Carrot - Mushroom Loaf .....................100
Carrot Cake ...........................................129
Carrot Ginger Soup .............................359
Carrot Soup ..........................................243

## Casseroles

Adobe Chicken Casserole ................97
Beef Vegetable Casserole ...............126
Chile Rellenos Casserole ...............276
Colorado Trails Casserole ..............292
Country Egg Casserole ....................259
Egg - Cheese Casserole ...................125
Enchilada Casserole ........................307
Hominy and Green Chile
     Casserole ......................................227
King Crab and Shrimp Noodles .....228
King Mountain Ranch Casserole ...142
Mexican Cheese ...............................203
Mexican Corn and Cheese
     Casserole ......................................308
Miner's Pies .....................................322
Scalloped Corn and Sausage ..........161
Spaghetti Pie ....................................127
Sylvan Dale Corn Casserole ...........65
Cauliflower Salad ................................337
Cauliflower with Water Chestnuts and
     Mushrooms ...................................345
Cheese and Bacon In A Bread Boat ..215
Cheesecake ...........................................362
Cheese Potatoes ...................................346
Cheese Wine Bread ..............................361
Cheesy Potato Soup .............................128
Cherokee Hot Fruit ...............................12

## Chicken Entrés

Baked Chicken Breast Stuffed with
     Sautéed Spinach & Mushrooms .136

# Index

**Chicken Entrés (cont'd)**
Chicken Alfredo with Vegetables...113
Chicken 'n Rice.............................193
Chicken Paprikosh .........................370
Chicken Pot Pie.............................137
Chicken Scaloppini with Linguini
    and Mushrooms ..........................239
Chicken Teriyaki .............................275
Cowboy Chicken.............................57
Devils Chicken and Wine Rice ........47
Farm House Chicken......................92
Mushroom Chicken Bake...............255
Oven Baked Chicken ......................64
Oven Fried Chicken ......................166
Painted Chicken .............................321
Paprika Chicken .............................160
Sesame Ginger Chicken .................114
Tarragon Chicken ..........................115
Chicken Alfredo with Vegetables ......113
Chicken and Wild Rice Salad ............169
Chicken 'n Rice .............................193
Chicken Paprikosh ..........................370
Chicken Pot Pie.............................137
Chicken Quesadillas .........................238
Chicken Scaloppini with Linguini and
    Mushrooms....................................239
Chicken Teriyaki.............................275
**Chili**
Black Bean Chili Chowder .............98
Green Chili ....................................119
Ranch Chili....................................80

**Chili (cont'd)**
Santa Fe Green Chili with Pork .......54
Walsenburg Green Chili ................331
Chile Egg Puff ...............................56
Chile Relleno Soufflé .......................167
Chile Rellenos Casserole ..................276
Chili Verde Stew ............................358
Chinese Chews................................232
Chinese Salad................................277
Chocolate Chip Cookies ...................354
Chocolate Peanut Butter Brownies....131
Chocolate Peanut Butter Pie.............327
Chocolate Sheet Cake with
    Raspberry Sauce ..........................31
Cinnamon Bread .............................85
Cinnamon Bun French Toast .............21
Citrus Encrusted Pork Tenderloin......112
Coconut Barbecue Sauce ...................33
Coffee Mocha .................................212
Cole Slaw.......................................51
Colorado Pine Nut Salad ..................179
Colorado Trails Casserole.................292
Colorado's Cheesecake......................245
**Cookies & Desserts**
Honey Pecan Butter ......................183
Apple Crisp ...................................52
Aspen Canyon Ranch Cookies.........86
Buttermilk Brownies .......................283
Chinese Chews................................232
Chocolate Chip Cookies..................354
Chocolate Peanut Butter Brownies 131

# Index

**Cookies & Desserts (cont'd)**
Cowboy Cookie Pie ........................209
Cowboy Cookies ............................210
Crème Brulee ................................376
Frosted Oatmeal Squares ..............106
Hawaiian Drop Cookies ................270
Homemade Oreo Ice Cream..........222
Ice Cream Dessert .........................107
Mother's Apple Pie Crisp..............199
No Bake Chocolate Cookies ..........328
Old Fashioned Ginger Cookies......329
Old Time Gingerbread ...................197
Peanut Butter Bars ........................377
Pumpkin Bars ...............................132
Rhubarb Crumble ..........................200
Smore Pudding Dessert..................233
Strawberry/Blueberry Fool............247
Sugar Cookies ...............................284
White Chocolate Macadamia
    Cookies .....................................248
White Chocolate Raspberry Bars.....87
Whoopee Pies................................300
Coq Au Vin ......................................242
Corn Bread.........................................68
Corn Chowder..................................260
Corn Meal Flapjacks...........................45
Country Egg Casserole .....................259
Cowboy Beans....................................82
Cowboy Caviar .................................309
Cowboy Chicken.................................57
Cowboy Cookie Pie ..........................209

Cowboy Cookies...............................210
Crab Spread Appetizer........................37
Cream Cheese Frosting.....................129
Cream Cheese Pound Cake.................39
Cream Puffs ......................................269
Creamy Potato Soup ...........................81
Creamy Tomato Soup .......................148
Crème Anglais..................................381
Crème Brulee ...................................376
Crème de Menthe Cake ....................281
Crunchy Cabbage Salad......................83
Crustless Cheesecake........................266
Cucumber Salad................................278
Devil's Chicken and Wine Rice..........47
Dill Bread.........................................295
Dill Cottage Cheese Rolls.................360
Dill Rolls..........................................170
**Dips & Salsas**
    Apple - Jalapeño Salsa ..................301
    Best Dude Dip in the West..............60
    Fresh Salsa ...................................355
    Pizza Dip .....................................223
    Sheep Dip .....................................379
    Skyline Salsa ................................365
Dirty Rice.........................................230
Dreamy Cheese Nut Roll...................364
**Eggs**
    Chile Egg Puff................................56
    Oven Baked Eggs............................63
Egg - Cheese Casserole ....................125
Egg Asparagus Breakfast Burritos.......23

# Index

Egg Rolls..............................................253
Elk Maison.............................................91
Emily's Pumpkin Bread.......................15
**Enchiladas**
  Out of the Saddle Enchiladas...........58
Enchilada Casserole............................307
Family Favorite Tossed Salad............326
Farm House Chicken .........................92
**Fish Entrés**
  Rainbow Trout Almondine...............93
  Salmon Patties.................................258
  Smoked Trout ..................................178
  Trout a'la Meuniere........................141
Flank Steak in Marinade....................335
Florentine Lasagna Rollups ...............218
Fluffy Strawberry Pie ........................155
**French Toast**
  Cinnamon Bun French Toast............21
  Grand Marnier French Toast..........174
Fresh Apple Cake with Caramel
  Frosting............................................69
Fresh Cranberry - Pineapple
  Salad ...............................................195
Fresh Salsa ..........................................355
Fried Tomatoes.....................................25
Frosted Oatmeal Squares ...................106
**Frosting & Topping**
  Caramel Frosting...............................69
  Cream Cheese Frosting ..................129
  Nancy's Frosting .............................22
  Powdered Sugar Frosting................70

**Fruit**
  Cherokee Hot Fruit...........................12
  Blueberry Smoothie .......................175
  Kiwi Crush .....................................176
**Game**
  Elk Maison ......................................91
  Game Hens a l'Orange...................291
  Grilled Raspberry Wheat Marinated
    Quail ...........................................140
Game Hens a l'Orange ......................291
Garlic Steak Marinade.........................17
Gazpacho.............................................293
Glogg..................................................234
Gonzales Sauce ..................................182
Grand Marnier French Toast.............174
**Granola & Nuts**
  Honey Crunch Mix.........................271
  Jennie's Granola .............................211
  Robins Praline Pecans....................330
Green Chili..........................................119
Grilled Raspberry Wheat Marinated
  Quail ...............................................140
Grilled Ribeye with Tobacco Onions 135
Hamburger Wellington.......................305
Harvest Winter Soup............................27
Hash Brown Casserole.........................13
Hawaiian Drop Cookies.....................270
Heart J Dressing...................................67
Herb Bread..........................................311
Homemade Oreo Ice Cream ..............222
Hominy and Green Chile Casserole ..227

# Index

Honey Baked Beans............................49
Honey Crunch Mix ...........................271
Honey Oatmeal Bread.......................340
Honey Pecan Butter ..........................183
Hot Fudge Cake ...............................104
Ice Cream Dessert.............................107
Incredible Latigo Dinner Muffins......157
Indian Fry Bread................................296
Italian Sausage Soup with Tortellini..349
It's The Berries Salad.........................338
Jalapeño Pork Roast...........................306
Jeannine's Garlic Bread .....................244
Jennie's Granola.................................211
Katy's Pasta Salad..............................102
Key Lime Pie .....................................208
King Crab and Shrimp Noodles ........228
King Mountain Ranch Casserole.......142
Kiwi Crush..........................................176
Korean Salad Dressing ......................150
Lasso Lasagna......................................59
Lemon Nut Bread ..............................220
Maka's Sweet Yams .............................14
Mandarin Orange Salad .....................162
Melt In Your Mouth Muffins .............280
Mexican Cheese..................................203
Mexican Corn and Cheese Casserole 308
Milk and Honey Bread ......................312
Miner's Pies .......................................322
Mother's Apple Pie Crisp ..................199

**Muffins**
Banana Chocolate Chip Muffins......30

**Muffins (cont'd)**
Banana Crumb Muffins.................351
Blueberry Muffins .........................265
Incredible Latigo Dinner
Muffins .......................................157
Melt In Your Mouth Muffins ........280
Peaches and Cream Muffins .........341
Mushroom Chicken Bake ..................255
Mustard Sauce.....................................42
Nancy's Cinnamon Buns ....................22
Nancy's Frosting ................................22
No Bake Chocolate Cookies..............328
Noodles Romanoff .............................371
Oatmeal Cake.....................................352
Oatmeal Pie.........................................40
Old Fashioned Ginger Cookies..........329
Old Fashioned Rolls ..........................297
Old Time Gingerbread .......................197
Orzo with Thyme and Lemon Zest.....48
Out of the Saddle Enchiladas .............58
Oven Baked Chicken ...........................64
Oven Baked Eggs ................................63
Oven Fried Chicken...........................166
Overnight Potato Rolls ......................154
Painted Chicken .................................321

**Pancakes**
Banana Nut Pancakes....................237
Corn Meal Flapjacks ......................45
Yummy Oatmeal Pancakes............191
Paprika Chicken ................................160
Parmesan Mini Loaves .....................153

# Index

**Pasta**

Florentine Lasagna Rollups ...........218
Lasso Lasagna ..................................59
Noodles Romanoff .........................371
Orzo with Thyme and Lemon Zest ..48

**Pastry**

Apple Fritters .................................268
Blueberry Filled Coffeecake ..........221
Blueberry Streusel Cake.................180
Blueberry Tart ..................................53
Cream Puffs....................................269
Sopapillas .......................................378
Sour Cream Pecan Tea Ring ............70
Swedish Kringlor .............................71

Pea and Cauliflower Salad..............231
Peaches and Cream Muffins .............341
Peanut Butter Bars ..........................377
Peanut Butter Pie .............................130
Peanut Crunch Ice Cream Pie............282
Pesto.................................................382
Pink Beans with Herbs ......................50
Pizza Dip..........................................223
Poppy Seed Bread..............................16

**Pork Entrés**

Baked Spiced Pork Chops...............256
Barbecue Pork Ribs...........................79
Barbecued Ham Balls.......................320
Citrus Encrusted Pork Tenderloin .112
Jalapeño Pork Roast .......................306
Ranch Ribs .......................................26
Sausage Balls .................................226

**Pork Entrés (cont'd)**

Teriyaki Pork Loin .........................177
Powdered Sugar Frosting....................70
Prime Rib ........................................134
Pumpkin Bars..................................132
Pumpkin Cake..................................105
Pumpkin Cake Dessert......................198
Pumpkin Cheesecake .......................267
Pumpkin Dutch Apple Pie .................314
Pumpkin Ice Cream Pie ....................156

**Quesadillas**

Blackened Buffalo Quesadilla........138
Chicken Quesadillas.........................238

Rainbow Trout Almondine .................93
Ranch Baked Beans ...........................204
Ranch Chili .......................................80
Ranch Ribs .........................................26
Raspberry Dijon Salad Dressing........152
Raspberry Sauce .................................32
Rhubarb Cake ....................................41
Rhubarb Cake ..................................363
Rhubarb Crumble..............................200

**Rice**

Dirty Rice .......................................230
Southwestern Couscous .................149
Tabouli............................................168

Roasted Garlic Maple Sauce..............120
Robin's Praline Pecans .....................330

**Salads & Dressings**

Broccoli - Cauliflower Salad..........194
Broccoli Tomato Salad....................101

# Index

**Salads & Dressings (cont'd)**

Caesar Salad Dressing....................294

Cauliflower Salad............................337

Chicken and Wild Rice Salad ........169

Chinese Salad.................................277

Cole Slaw .......................................51

Colorado Pine Nut Salad................179

Crunchy Cabbage Salad ..................83

Cucumber Salad .............................278

Family Favorite Tossed Salad ........326

Fresh Cranberry - Pineapple
    Salad ...........................................195

Heart J Dressing ..............................67

It's The Berries Salad.....................338

Katy's Pasta Salad..........................102

Korean Salad Dressing....................150

Mandarin Orange Salad .................162

Pea and Cauliflower Salad.............231

Raspberry Dijon Salad Dressing ....152

Spicy Chicken Salad with
    Raspberry Balsamic Vinaigrette ...28

Spinach Salad and Dressing............66

Strawberry Pretzel Jell-O Salad .....151

Taco Salad ......................................38

Waldorf Salad.................................310

Walnut Apple Salad........................339

Wild Rice Salad..............................103

Salmon or Swordfish Marinade.........108

Salmon Patties................................258

**Sandwiches**

Barbecue Chicken Salad .................24

Santa Fe Green Chili with Pork..........54

**Sauces & Marinades**

Apple Cider Syrup .........................181

Biscuits and Sausage Gravy............46

Bora Bora Sauce.............................380

Coconut Barbecue Sauce ................33

Crème Anglais ...............................381

Garlic Steak Marinade ....................17

Gonzales Sauce .............................182

Mustard Sauce................................42

Pesto ..............................................382

Raspberry Sauce.............................32

Roasted Garlic Maple Sauce ..........120

Salmon or Swordfish Marinade .....108

Spaghetti Sauce..............................356

Spicy Apple Cider Sauce ...............224

Tarryall Ham Glaze.........................249

Vera Cruz Sauce.............................383

White Sauce For Lasagna ...............219

Wild Mushroom Sauce...................121

Sausage Balls.................................226

Scalloped Corn and Sausage...........161

Scones ...........................................313

Scrumptious Chocolate Cake...........246

**Seafood Entrés**

Cajun Crevettes .............................90

Shrimp Dijon .................................336

Shrimp and Angel Hair Pasta..........99

Sesame Ginger Chicken...................114

Sheep Dip......................................379

Sherry's Barbecue Brisket ...............217

# Index

Shrimp Dijon.....................................336
Shrimp and Angel Hair Pasta ..............99
Skyline Salsa.....................................365
Sloppy Joes With A Twist.................192
Smoked Trout.....................................178
Smore Pudding Dessert.....................233
Snap Beans Italian Style ...................347
Snickers Cake ...................................315
Snow Capped Beets ..........................324
Sopapillas..........................................378
**Soufflés**
   Broccoli Pasta Soufflé....................116
   Chile Relleno Soufflé.....................167
**Soups**
   Carrot Ginger Soup .......................359
   Carrot Soup ...................................243
   Cheesy Potato Soup .......................128
   Creamy Potato Soup........................81
   Creamy Tomato Soup.....................148
   Gazpacho........................................293
   Harvest Winter Soup .......................27
   Italian Sausage Soup with
      Tortellini ....................................349
   Tomato Chowder............................117
   Tortellini Soup...............................118
   Vegetable Soup...............................350
Sour Cream Pecan Tea Ring................70
Southern Apple Cream Pie ................299
Southern Biscuits..............................298
Southwestern Couscous.....................149
Spaghetti Pie ....................................127

Spaghetti Sauce.................................356
Spicy Apple Cider Sauce ..................224
Spicy Chicken Salad with Raspberry
   Balsamic Vinaigrette .......................28
Spinach Balls ....................................146
Spinach Salad and Dressing ...............66
**Stews**
   Beef Stew with Shitake Mushrooms
      and Baby Veggies .......................240
   Caciucco Alla Livornese ...............241
   Chili Verde Stew ...........................358
   Coq Au Vin....................................242
Sticky Buns.......................................344
Strawberry Cookie Pie......................171
Strawberry Pretzel Jell-O Salad.........151
Strawberry/Blueberry Fool ...............247
Sugar Cookies...................................284
Super Easy Beer Bread......................196
Swedish Kringlor ...............................71
Sweet and Sour Brussels Sprouts .....325
Sweet Potato Crisp............................261
Sweet Potato Crunch.........................348
Swiss Cheese Rolls or Bread.............206
Swiss Cream Steak ...........................254
Sylvan Dale Corn Casserole ...............65
Tabouli .............................................168
**Tacos & Burritos**
   Tacoritas ........................................257
   Baja Seafood Taco with Purple
      Cabbage, Chayote and Nopali
      Cactus Slaw ...............................139

# Index

**Tacos & Burritos (cont'd)**
Egg Asparagus Breakfast Burritos ...23
Taco Salad................................................38
Tacoritas.................................................257
Tarragon Chicken..................................115
Tarryall Ham Glaze...............................249
Teriyaki Pork Loin................................177
To Hell with Texas Cornbread...........373
Toffee Banana Bread ...........................264
Tomato Chowder...................................117
Tortellini Soup .....................................118
Trout a'la Meuniere ..............................141

**Vegetables**
Alaskan Fisherman's Baked
    Beans................................................323
Barbecue Beans.....................................229
Broccoli Italian.....................................372
Carrot - Mushroom Loaf......................100
Cauliflower with Water Chestnuts
    and Mushrooms ..............................345
Cheese Potatoes....................................346
Corn Chowder ......................................260
Cowboy Beans .......................................82
Cowboy Caviar......................................309
Hash Brown Casserole ...........................13
Honey Baked Beans ...............................49
Maka's Sweet Yams ...............................14
Pink Beans with Herbs...........................50
Ranch Baked Beans ..............................204
Snap Beans Italian Style ......................347
Snow Capped Beets ..............................324

Spinach Balls........................................146
Sweet and Sour Brussels Sprouts...325
Sweet Potato Crisp ...............................261
Sweet Potato Crunch.............................348
Zippy Carrots .......................................147
Vegetable Soup .....................................350
Vera Cruz Sauce....................................383
Wacky Cake ..........................................353
Waldorf Salad........................................310
Walnut Apple Salad ..............................339
Walsenburg Green Chili........................331
White Chocolate Macadamia
    Cookies............................................248
White Chocolate Raspberry Bars ........87
White Sauce for Lasagna.......................219
Whoopee Pies .......................................300
Wild Mushroom Sauce .........................121
Wild Rice Salad ....................................103
Yummy Oatmeal Pancakes ...............191
Zippy Carrots .......................................147

# Cooking Tips

## Metric Conversions

1 teaspoon = 5 milliliters
1 tablespoon = 15 milliliters
1 cup =≈ $^1/4$ liter
1 pint = .4732 liter
1 quart = .9463 liter
1 gallon = 3.785 liters
1 ounce =≈ 30 grams
1 pound =≈ 454 grams
1 teaspoon =≈ 3 grams
1 centimeter = .394 inch
1 meter = 39.37 inches
1 inch = 2.54 centimeters

## Equivalents

8 ounces = 1 cup
2 cups = 1 pint
2 pints = 1 quart
4 quarts = 1 gallon
60 drops = $^1/3$ teaspoon
1 teaspoon = $^1/3$ tablespoon
3 teaspoons = 1 tablespoon
2 tablespoons = 1 fl. ounce
4 tablespoons = $^1/4$ cup
$5^1/3$ tablespoons = $^1/3$ cup
8 tablespoons = $^1/2$ cup
16 tablespoons = 1 cup
$^1/4$ cup = 2 ounces
1 cup = 8 ounces =
16 tablespoons =
48 teaspoons

## Temperatures

Water freezes at 32°

**At Sea Level:**
Water simmers at 115°
Water scalds at 130°
Water boils at 212°
Soft boil at 234-238°
Firm boil at 240-242°
Hard boil at 248-250°
Slow oven 268°
Moderate oven 350°
Deep fat 375-400°
Hot oven 450-500°
Broil 550°

**At 5,000 Feet:**
Water boils at 203°

**At 10,000 Feet:**
Water boils at 194°

## Low Altitude Adjustments

Since all of the ranches contributing recipes for this cookbook are located at high altitude, the recipes have already been adjusted for this factor. In order to have the dishes turn out the way they were intended, cooks at altitudes below 3,000 feet above sea level should make some adjustments.

When preparing these dishes at a lower altitude, please note that the time to boil foods will be decreased. Also, there will need to be a change in the proportions of ingredients used in leavened foods such as cakes; increasing the amount of leavening and/or sugar, for example. In some cases it will be necessary to adjust the baking temperature as well. Should this become necessary the general rule is to decrease the oven temperature 25 degrees when baking batters and dough. Repeated experimentation is sometimes necessary before the correct procedure is arrived at for low altitude baking.

General guidelines to follow are:

Increase baking powder ¹/8 to ¹/4 teaspoon for each teaspoon

Increase sugar 1 to 3 tablespoons for each cup

Decrease liquid 1 to 4 tablespoons for each cup

# Spices and Herbs

## Allspice

Used whole in soups, stews, pot roasts, sauces and marinades, boiled, steamed or poached seafood. Used ground in cakes, cookies, candy, spaghetti and barbecue sauces, sweet potatoes or squash, chili, tomato sauces.

## Basil

Used whole or ground with lamb, fish, roasts, stews, ground beef, vegetables, dressing and omelets.

## Bay Leaves

Whole leaf is used, but must be removed before serving. Good in vegetable dishes, fish and seafood, stews and pickles.

## Caraway

Its spicy smell and aromatic taste goes well with cakes, breads, soups, cheese and sauer-kraut.

## Chives

An herb with a sweet mild onion flavor that is excellent in salads, fish, soups and potatoes.

## Cinnamon

Used whole in pickling and preserving, hot chocolate, mulled wine, stewed fruit and compotes. Ground it can be used in cookies, cakes, French toast, dessert sauces, sweet potatoes and squash, lamb roast, stews, ham glaze, apple sauce and butter, puddings and custard.

## Cloves

Used whole as a garnish for ham, fruit peels, onions, glazed pork or beef, beverages, pot roast, marinades and sauces. Ground it goes well in cakes, gingerbread, plum pudding, cookies, breads, fruit salad, chili sauce, green vegetables, meringue, glazes and mincemeat.

## Dill

Both seeds and leaves are flavorful when used as either a garnish or cooked in fish, soup, dressings, potatoes and beans.

## Fennel

Seeds and leaves are used. Sweet hot flavor that can be used sparingly in pies, baked goods or boiled with fish.

## Garlic

Used primarily in tomato dishes, soups and sauces, dips, butter, gravy, meat, poultry and fish. Also used in salad dressings and cheese dishes.

# Spices and Herbs

## Ginger

A pungent root that can be used either fresh, dried or ground. Used in pickling and preserving, cakes, cookies, soups and meat dishes.

## Marjoram

Can be used fresh or dried. Flavors fish, poultry, omelets, lamb stew, stuffing and tomato juice.

## Mint

Excellent in beverages, fish, cheese, lamb, soup, peas, carrots and fruit desserts.

## Nutmeg

Used in sweet foods such as cakes, cookies, pies or pastries. Enhances the flavor of meats, vegetables, poultry, seafood, eggnog, fruit, puddings and soups.

## Oregano

Used whole or ground to spice tomato juice, fish, eggs, pizza, omelets, chili, stew, gravy, poultry and vegetables.

## Paprika

Used in meat, vegetables and soups. Can be used as a garnish for potatoes, salads or eggs.

## Parsley

Best fresh, but can be used dry in fish, omelets, soup, meat, stuffing and mixed greens.

## Rosemary

Used to season fish, stuffing, beef, lamb, poultry, onions, eggs and bread.

## Saffron

Used as flavoring or to color foods. Used in soup, chicken, rice and fancy breads.

## Sage

May be used in tomato juice, fish, fondue, omelets, beef, poultry, stuffing, cheese spreads, cornbread and biscuits.

## Tarragon

Flavor sauces, salads, meat, poultry, tomatoes and dressings.

## Thyme

Used in meat, poultry and fish. Combines well with butter over vegetables or broiled seafood. Good in stuffing for fish and meats, cheese and tomato dishes or clam chowder.

# Cooking Terms

## Au gratin

Topped with crumbs and/or cheese and browned in the oven or under the broiler.

## Au jus

Served in its own juices.

## Baste

To moisten foods during cooking with pan drippings or special sauce to add flavor and prevent drying.

## Bisque

A thick cream soup.

## Blanch

To immerse in rapidly boiling water and allow to cook slightly.

## Cream

To soften a fat, especially butter, by beating it at room temperature.

## Crimp

To seal the edges of a two-crust pie either by pinching them at intervals with the fingers or by pressing them together with the tines of a fork.

## Degrease

Removal of fat from the surface of stews, soups or stock.

## Dredge

Lightly coat with flour, cornmeal, crumbs, etc.

## Entré

The main course.

## Fold

Incorporating a delicate substance, such as whipped cream or beaten egg whites, into another substance without releasing air bubbles.

## Glaze

To cover with a glossy coating, such as a melted and somewhat diluted jelly for fruit desserts.

## Julienne

Cutting vegetables, fruits or cheeses into match-sized slivers.

## Marinate

To leave food soaking in a liquid in order to tenderize or add flavor.

# Cooking Terms

**Meuniere**

Dredged with flour and sautéed in butter.

**Mince**

Chopping or cutting food into very small pieces.

**Parboil**

To boil until partially cooked.

**Pare**

Removal of the outermost skin of a fruit or vegetable.

**Poach**

Cooking very gently in a liquid that is kept just below the boiling point.

**Puree**

To mash foods until perfectly smooth by hand, rubbing through a sieve or food mill, or by whirling in a blender or food processor.

**Sauté**

Cooking or browning food in a small quantity of oil or butter.

**Scald**

Heating just below the boiling point.

**Simmer**

Cook in liquid just below the boiling point.

**Steep**

To let food stand in hot liquid to extract or the enhance flavor.

**Toss**

Combining ingredients with a lifting motion.

**Whip**

To beat rapidly to incorporate air and produce expansion.

# *Pantry Press*

8547 E. Arapahoe Road, #J224
Greenwood Village, Colorado  80112
(303) 694-1664 or FAX (303) 694-4098
www.starsend.com

Please ship _____ copies of *Mountain Magic Cuisine.* (for shipments to destinations outside of the United States, please call prior to ordering)

$23.95 per copy                              _____

$ 3.00 shipping per copy (USA only)          _____

Colorado residents please add 3.8% sales tax _____

     TOTAL             _____

Make check payable to: **StarsEnd Creations**

Ship To: Name  _____

   Address _____

   City  _____ State ___ Zip _____

Please allow three weeks for delivery

---

# *Pantry Press*

8547 E. Arapahoe Road, #J224
Greenwood Village, Colorado  80112
(303) 694-1664 or FAX (303) 694-4098
www.starsend.com

Please ship _____ copies of *Mountain Magic Cuisine.* (for shipments to destinations outside of the United States, please call prior to ordering)

$23.95 per copy                              _____

$ 3.00 shipping per copy (USA only)          _____

Colorado residents please add 3.8% sales tax _____

     TOTAL             _____

Make check payable to: **StarsEnd Creations**

Ship To: Name  _____

   Address _____

   City  _____ State ___ Zip _____

Please allow three weeks for delivery

I would like to have the following
stores and shops in my area carry

## Mountain Magic Cuisine
### Secret Recipes of the Dude & Guest
### Ranches of Colorado

Store Name _____

Address _____

City _____ State _____ Zip _____

Store Name _____

Address _____

City _____ State _____ Zip _____

---

I would like to have the following
stores and shops in my area carry

## Mountain Magic Cuisine
### Secret Recipes of the Dude & Guest
### Ranches of Colorado

Store Name _____

Address _____

City _____ State _____ Zip _____

Store Name _____

Address _____

City _____ State _____ Zip _____